1941

THE REFERENCE SHELF

Volume XII

No.
1. Anglo-American Agreement. H. B. Summers. $1.25.
2. Discussion Methods Explained and Illustrated. J. V. Garland and C. F. Phillips. (rev. ed. 1940) $1.25.
3. The State Sales Tax. E. R. Nichols and others. $1.25.
4. Dictatorships vs. Democracies. 1938 (Supplement to Anglo-American Agreements) H. B. Summers and R. E. Summers. 75c.

No.
5. Pump-priming Theory of Government Spending. E. R. Nichols and William E. Roskam. $1.25.
6. United States Foreign Policy: Isolation or Alliance. J. E. Johnsen. $1.25.
7. Chain Stores and Legislation. Daniel Bloomfield. $1.25.
8. The United States and War. J. E. Johnsen.
9. Debate Index. E. M. Phelps. 75c.
10. Radio Censorship. H. B. Summers. $1.25.

Volume XI. $6

No.
1. Unicameral Legislatures. H. B. Summers.
2. Consumers' Cooperatives. J. E. Johnsen, J. V. Garland, C. F. Phillips.
3. Industrial versus Craft Unionism. J. E. Johnsen.
4. Reorganization of the Supreme Court. J. E. Johnsen.
5. Unicameralism in Practice: The Nebraska Legislative System. H. B. Summers.

No.
6. Modern Group Discussion. L. and E. Judson.
7. Arbitration and the National Labor Relations Board. E. R. Nichols and J. W. Logan.
8. Peace and Rearmament. J. E. Johnsen.
9. Chinese-Japanese War, 1937-. J. E. Johnsen.
10. Representative American Speeches: 1937-1938. A. C. Baird. $1.25.

Volume X. $4.20

No.
1. Collective Bargaining. J. E. Johnsen.
2. Lotteries. H. M. Muller.
3. Old Age Pensions. J. E. Johnsen.
5. Socialization of Medicine. J. E. Johnsen.

No.
6. Limitation of Power of Supreme Court to Declare Acts of Congress Unconstitutional. J. E. Johnsen.
9. Government Ownership of Electric Utilities. J. E. Johnsen.
10. The Crisis in the Electric Utilities. Garland and Phillips.

it may be kept

THE REFERENCE SHELF

Vol. 15   No. 1

REPRESENTATIVE AMERICAN
SPEECHES: 1940-1941

Selected by

A. CRAIG BAIRD

Department of Speech, State University of Iowa

NEW YORK
THE H. W. WILSON COMPANY
1941

PREFATORY NOTE

Representative American Speeches: 1940-1941 is the fourth in the annual series. Largely through the development of the radio, speech-making in the United States in the past score of years has no doubt increased in amount. We Americans more and more have taken to public address, either as contributors or as listeners. This annual collection attempts to provide a record, year-by-year, of the character of that oral output so far as it is created by and for the people of the United States.

The present volume, like its predecessors, includes addresses chosen not only because they offer significant examples of oral discourse, but because they furnish illustrations of representative speaking occasions, such as those of the legislature, courtroom, conference table, committee chamber, pulpit, political stump, lecture platform, public forum, dinner gathering, or broadcasting studio. Obviously in any single volume comparatively few examples in a given category of speech types can be inserted. The combined group, comprising more than one hundred addresses in the four volumes, sets forth a fairly complete listing of each special type, and a fairly inclusive anthology of the leading political, industrial, educational, religious, business and professional speakers in the United States since 1937. The "Cumulative Author Index" accompanying this Volume aims to help the reader in his systematic survey of these recent orations, debates, and more informal talks.

These speakers and speeches, in addition to their intrinsic importance and their exemplification of a specific speaking situation, furnish a revealing picture of American thought and motive during the period. The classification of the speeches, as given in the Table of Contents of the present volume, suggests the relationship of the addresses to the immediate and recurrent problems facing the American nation,—problems of war, peace, national defense, education, labor, industry, religion, science, and social living. Literary artists may sometimes in solitary brooding create great literature. Not so the effective speaker. He weaves his material only in the market place and in the midst of an audience. His ideas articulate at every point with the sentiments and mood of his listeners, both the visible auditors and the larger group who by radio, press, or hearsay report attend his discourse. Hence the student of speaking who reads these current addresses will probably understand better the thought and culture of contemporary America. To facilitate this insight into a given speech the editor has prefixed short introductory notes. The reader is thus encouraged to reconstruct something of the circumstances attending the speech, to turn to similar speeches on the same theme, and to evaluate more accurately the address as a possible contribution to the course of our national history.

The Introduction, immediately following, should be read in conjunction with the similar, brief introductions of the preceding editions. These editorial statements outline the present editor's philosophy of speech, his approach to the criticism of speeches, and his estimate of the quality and trend of American speaking of the past five years.

CONTENTS

AMERICAN AID TO GREAT BRITAIN

AMERICAN NATIONAL DEFENSE

THE PRESIDENTIAL CAMPAIGN OF 1940

ATMOSPHERE OF THE SECOND WAR OF THE NATIONS

AMERICA'S WAR AIMS AND PEACE AIMS

NATIONAL ATTITUDES

AMERICAN EDUCATION

REPRESENTATIVE AMERICAN SPEECHES

INTRODUCTION

This fourth volume of recent American speeches has at least a two-fold purpose: (1) to furnish a collection of ideas that reflect the thinking and speaking of these immediate days; (2) to provide a group of interesting examples of oral discourse usable for students of public speaking.

A Textbook of American Ideals

What of this book as a collection of contemporary ideas? This brief assembly of important addresses turns out to be more than a compilation of "representative speeches." It is a textbook of American ideals. The theme and tenor of its combined utterances are the voicing of American democracy and the vigorous restatement of the principles of American political and cultural civilization. The student who absorbs the ideas and spirit of the speeches here recorded will gain, it is believed, a clearer understanding of the traditions and motives behind our recent national deliberations and decisions. The book, interpreted in relation to events of these months, is a primer of our governmental system and of the educational, social, economic, moral, and religious life related to that system. In spite of dissident voices among the talkers in this book, it enunciates directly or indirectly well-defined American principles. These principles declare that (1) the American system of democratic government is worthy of our supreme loyalty; (2) the personalities of our citizens, whatever their race, color, religion, or economic status, are worthy of our highest allegiance; (3) we Americans belong together, and every agency that creates division or undermines that solidarity is to be resisted as foreign to our philosophy and program of toleration and equality; (4) the more fortunate members of our national family are more and more to demonstrate the art of ameliorating the lot of the underprivileged; (5) industry, labor, public and private education, art, recreation, religion and every other phase of our common life should be directed toward the progressive realization of these ideals; (6) through coöperative thinking and speaking, through freedom of assembly, press, speech, and worship, we shall continually interpret our needs and solve our problems; (7) we wish for other nations only stability and permanent opportunity to protect their own national character and destiny, free from foreign oppression; (8) if necessary, we shall enlist our combined civil, military, and moral might, even to the extent of the sacrifice of millions of lives and billions of wealth, to defend this heritage of organized freedom. Practically all of these speakers, in this and in the earlier volumes of this series, proceed on these premises in their detailed and partial exposition of a single topic.

Can the student of affairs, however, read into these lines such sentiments? Helpful will it be to the investigator to recall the circumstances of presentation of each example. If these speeches, when committed to paper, lose the glow that once stirred audience and speaker, a reconstruction of the speaking situation, of the speaker's tones and personality, of the impulses, attitudes, and immediate concerns of the audiences, may enable the reader to enter more fully into the mental and emotional movement of the speech. Roosevelt on the "National Emergency," Willkie in his "Acceptance Speech," Hutchins on "Opposition to Aid for Britain," Green on "Labor, Freedom, and Democracy," should be examined not as talks on "dated" and no longer living issues, but as significant statements, the broader relations of which and the causes and results of which are not to be lightly dismissed.

The assumption of the editor of this volume, then, is that one way to strengthen national morale and to educate young men and women for effective participation in national life is to encourage the study of outstanding contemporary speeches. Oral addresses, perhaps, no less than written literature, are a key to the experiences and ideals of a given generation. Hence, in the interest of cosmopolitan education, high school and college students should know and interpret these and similar speeches.

Because of the limited size of the book, it has been impracticable for the editor to include in each division more than a few speeches. The chief regret has been that a wealth of excellent material has had to be omitted. In the "campaign" section, for example, the stirring addresses by Thomas Dewey and Norman Thomas, other stump speeches by Willkie (for example, that one delivered at San Francisco), the more measured but none the less acceptable appeals by Wallace, by Hoover, should have a place. I have thus conceived of two books, the one you are now reading, and a vastly larger one which would fully set forth the recent discussions related to American art, education, religion, industry, and the other categories. The classifications, it should be added, are merely for convenience. A speech under one division may be logically shifted to another.

In the light of the discussion above, teachers will readily recognize that this book belongs with that considerable number of similar volumes which directors of English composition, extempore speaking, and similar courses have found highly serviceable as "thought-provoking" materials.

Examples of Types of Speech-Making

A second purpose of this book is to offer examples of addresses that may guide students in their study of speech composition and delivery. To this end this volume, like its predecessors, continues to represent a diversity of speaking types and occasions. Senator Pepper, for example, is effective in vigorous Senate address. The "fireside chat," radio news commentary, town hall or Senate debate, committee hearing, formal lecture, oration, business talk, sermon, and the other types appear. In your review of the previous four volumes, you will note that demonstrative, forensic, deliberative, sermonic speeches, with their sub-classifications, are all included. Special speaking situations, like the America's Town Meeting of the Air, are inserted to give the student a complete example of such popular types of debate-discussion.

THE CRITICISM OF A SPEECH

How shall we test the speech and the speaker? In the Introductory Note to each of the three previous annual volumes, I have attempted briefly to suggest criteria for evaluation. Standards of good speaking require that (1) the thought or ideas should be important, should be logically put together and carefully analyzed, and that analysis or division should be made clear to an audience; (2) these ideas should be organized for maximum clearness, coherence, and emphasis; (3) each phase of the thinking should be buttressed by concrete details, designed for proof, clarification, or illumination; (4) this thinking and these details should be couched in oral language, accurate and interesting; (5) the speech in its structure and modes of appeal should be adapted to the audience, with ample motivative materials to accompany the facts and logic; (6) the speaker's delivery should exhibit satisfactory voice quality, proper rate, pitch, intensity, articulation and pronunciation, and bodily movements (including gestures) that aid in interpreting the ideas; (7) the speaker's "personality" should reveal sincerity, tact, humor, and other traits that mark him as a "good man" and one who knows and adjusts himself to his group.

By such criteria are the speakers in this volume selected. No assumption is here made that this particular list of items is a final one. We do, however, need standards of judgment; with their aid we can appraise speakers and speeches. We need, nevertheless, to muster supporting data about the speaker's previous speeches and other training, his experiences and modes of thinking; we need data about the specific audience—its attitudes, interests, and other characteristics; and we need knowledge about the immediate occasion. Such facts concerning speaker, audience, and occasion will enable us to make a more adequate estimate of the speaker as we test him from the seven-fold approach listed above. A satisfactory critic of speeches, in short, should have a norm by which to judge; and he should be a careful listener to the speech (or reader of it). Furthermore, he should be a student of English composition (structure and style), of psychology (audience adaptation), of logic (argument and evidence), and of history (background of speaker, occasion, and audience).

I wish again, as in previous volumes, to disavow any pretense that these speeches are "the best" or "superior to all others" of the period. They happen to be merely those addresses selected by one person (who has, however, consulted several scores of colleagues and has examined hundreds of speeches) for the two-fold purpose of this book. Why should I include a given speech? Because it (a) happens to be a "good" speech; (b) it illustrates a certain type of speaking; (c) it happens to be not too long or too short; (d) the book, even though short, has room for it; (e) publishers and author have graciously allowed me to reprint it; (f) it illustrates a certain aspect of American character or problem of the hour. I have deliberately tried to avoid partisanship in the selection. If Roosevelt looms large in this book, it is not because I am a New Dealer, but because when the President speaks, millions listen.

ACCURACY OF TEXTS

Critics of public speaking need to be sure that the text they examine is genuine. Rhetorical critics have made progress during the past fifteen years in their maturity of technique both in higher criticism (the problem of answering the question, Did the speaker compose the speech he delivered, or did he take it from ghost writers?) and in lower criticism (the problem of answering the question, Is the text as recorded accurate? Does it duplicate exactly what was spoken?). In the present volume, to illustrate, I have had to take one by one the Willkie, Roosevelt, and all other speeches and attempt to gauge the extent to which the speaker actually determined the material and style of the document. If speeches that are here included turn out to be exclusively "ghost writer" performances, then this critic has used questionable judgment.

My second problem has been to check the accuracy of the text itself. Does it represent what was said? Limitations in settling that problem of fact are that (1) in Congress, and in many court rooms electrical or other mechanical recording of the speech is not made; (2) shorthand reports, the best of them, are not accurate; (3) speakers in Congress and elsewhere have the right and privilege of correcting their remarks in minor and even major items; (4) an accurate reproduction of certain speeches (for example, conversational, panel discussions), would be unfair to the authors and uninteresting to all readers (because of the broken sentences) except students of textual criticism. Although I have taken ediphone transcriptions of radio talks, it would probably be a betrayal on my part for me to reproduce exactly what was said unless the speaker himself approved my version. In view of practical considerations, we who deal with texts do the best we can. At least we are alive to these problems that have always confronted historians and literary students.

CHARACTER AND TREND OF SPEAKING IN 1940-41

Events since June, 1940, have forced Americans to immediate decisions of vast consequence. Moreover we have found ourselves compelled to reexamine the political and other philosophies underlying our civilization. In the first volume of this series I intimated that the speaking of 1937 was not especially distinguished, partly because "we Americans have had no international, economic, or religious crisis cataclysmic enough to give our prophets tongues of eloquence." Four years later it is clear that "cataclysmic" crises have descended upon us of sufficient severity to release fully the energy and expression of our important speakers. The speaking of 1940-41 offers, by contrast to that of four years ago, a long list of comparatively superior addresses for consideration. Possibly we are now entering upon a stage where talk will be eclipsed by action (except as an occasional American Churchill interprets to the world our national mind). During the months prior to July 1, 1941, in Congress, over the radio, in every church, in every professional and business gathering, the speakers faced and answered with much speaking ability the issue: In view of the upheavals of the Second War of the Nations, what policies, internal and international, shall the United States follow?

Debaters and discussional speakers in Congress and in the committee chambers partly answered the question by arguing and settling the program of military conscription of Americans between 21 and 36 years of age; by appropriating billions upon billions for national defense; by setting up the machinery by which our entire economic system has been completely upset and reorganized for the military emergency; by debating and settling the problem of lend-lease legislation; and by arguing about and enacting other measures designed to lead us into more active support of England and her cause.

Paralleling these legislative addresses, President Roosevelt gave his frequent and potent talks to the people, as did his cabinet, especially Wallace, Knox, Stimson, and Hull; the radio commentators and their broadcasting fellows continued to expound with increasing skill; sermonizers, dinner speakers, educational lecturers, business executives, labor officials, and legal leaders all treated from their several angles with insight and speaking force the same insistent themes.

In one division only of our speaking activity did the speaking fail to rise above mediocrity—the political campaign speaking of 1940. If we exclude Roosevelt, Willkie (when the latter possessed his public speaking voice), Thomas Dewey, Stassen, and a few others, the political oratory was dull and inconsequential. In the national conventions ineptitude was especially marked. Many political speakers still talk as they did in 1910 and as some of them do in Congress.

The truth is that radio is transforming the character and quality of speech making in America. Radio is restoring speaking to that proper key of conversational directness, close speaker-listener contact, semantic simplicity, that teachers of public speaking have long advocated. Because people are much better informed about issues through the radio, because microphone listeners are instructed about many things, including the false ways of propaganda, because over the radio come superior voices and excellent articulation and pronunciation, the average listener is no doubt more critical and more appreciative of good speaking than was his father or grandfather. Speech makers are adjusting themselves to these new standards of effectiveness in speech composition and delivery. Roosevelt is a symbol of present day speaking because he has adjusted himself (if adjustment he needed) to the contemporary audiences. Many political speakers have failed to do so, as the campaign oratory of 1940 revealed. But present lag in political speaking will disappear. Four or eight years from now fewer stump speakers will harangue us. Public speaking of tomorrow in America will no doubt produce another Franklin Roosevelt.

To the authors of the addresses who so generously permitted the reprinting and in a number of cases provided the texts, the author expresses his deep appreciation. The editor is also grateful to his colleagues in speech and to the graduate students in his courses and seminar in the History and Criticism of American Public Speaking, who contributed their critical judgment.   He is especially indebted to Elaine Pagel, of Ohio University, for her valuable editorial assistance and to Dean Zenor who also assisted in the preparation of this book.

                                        A. CRAIG BAIRD

July 10, 1941

AMERICAN AID TO GREAT BRITAIN

THE PRESERVATION OF AMERICAN INDEPENDENCE [1]

FRANKLIN DELANO ROOSEVELT [2]

President Roosevelt gave the following address on Sunday evening, December 29, 1940, at 9:30, Eastern Standard Time. It was delivered as the fifteenth fireside chat, in the Diplomatic Reception Room of the White House, where representatives of the warring nations have repeatedly gathered. Cordell Hull, Secretary of State, other cabinet members, and a considerable number of the President's other friends were in the room.

More than 500 radio stations in the United States were tuned to this outlet. Short-wave stations carried the message throughout the world. And there were rebroadcasts in various languages.

Washington, and apparently the President himself, considered the talk as more important than any delivered by him since those in the days immediately after the beginning of his first administration. The significance of the address lay in its expression of official philosophy concerning Roosevelt's foreign policy and its "pattern of action," to be unfolded during the following twelve months.

The address has all the rhetorical elements that make the Rooseveltian speeches effective. It is well constructed. It has a high degree of audience adaptation (note the opening paragraphs). It has concreteness of illustration and of language. It is extremely blunt, as when the speaker denounces the Nazis. It has simplicity of language. Comparatively few words are used that would not be readily apprehended by the average listener. It uses dialogue for vividness. It has much ethical proof (note the speaker's references to himself). It removes inhibitions as it proceeds (answers objections). It uses the rhetorical question, parallel structure, appeals to fear, indignation, sense of fair play, patriotism, courage, and hope. It omits those arguments that might arouse opposition among those undecided citizens. In short,

[1] By permission of President Roosevelt. Text secured by ediphone transcription and checked by the White House official version.

[2] For biographical note see Appendix.

it is a speech calculated to get maximum response. Moreover, the speaker had his usual excellent voice, his sense of deliberation and pause, his strong emphasis on the all-important word, his conversational intimacy.

The President grappled in turn with such issues and sub-issues as, How great is the danger? Are European wars of concern to Americans? Exactly who is the enemy (Germany, Italy, Japan)? What is the Nazi program? Can we have a negotiated peace? Can the word of Hitler be trusted? If Great Britain falls will America not also fall? Should we not attempt to appease the Axis? What is our program to be?

In spite of the informality of the occasion, the address was generally regarded as marking a historic landmark in American foreign policy. The consensus of opinion regarding the speech was summarized editorially by *The New York Times* of December 31, 1941: "The President's address on Sunday night will take its place among the historic state papers of this nation, not because it proposed a sudden departure from a previously established policy, but because with extraordinary eloquence and deep sincerity it affirmed a doctrine intrinsically as old as the Republic."

The American press was unanimous in its support of the address. Said the *New York Herald Tribune*, "It was one of the greatest efforts of his career." The Philadelphia *Evening Bulletin* called it "a great state paper." The Baltimore *Sun* referred to the President's "remarkable powers of persuasion." The Baltimore *Evening Sun* concluded that "President Roosevelt has never made a better speech."

Rome minimized the speech. London was elated. Roosevelt became a hero to Athenian crowds. Tokyo believed the speech would mean more aid to China. Berlin was extremely cautious in its comment. Canadians regarded it as epochal. Latin America, including Mexico, endorsed it warmly.

The various polls taken later indicated that public sentiment endorsed this Presidential policy. Senator Wheeler, speaking twenty-four hours after Roosevelt, took issue with the premises of the address and called for a "just, reasonable, and generous peace." Senator Vandenberg and other isolationists warned that "all out aid" would mean war. Verne Marshall, head of the No Foreign Wars Committee, also raised his voice against the Administration's position.

On Monday, January 6th, the President delivered his message to Congress, in which he more specifically outlined his plans for "all out aid" to Britain. This message contained his statement of aims, including the "four freedoms." [3]

[3] See the address on "Four Human Freedoms," p. 185.

German criticism of this message to Congress was caustic and bitter. The German press called it a sample of "bad logic," and filled with "untruths," "personal hatred," and "misrepresentation of facts." Hitler himself replied in an extended oration to his own soldiers: "It is a dumb and infamous lie that the German Reich or Italy intends to conquer the world, while in reality existing world conquerors require wars in order to realize higher interest on their capital."

The address to Congress was followed by a budget message, recommending a three-year defense program involving about $28,000,000,000. And on January 20th, the President delivered his third inaugural address.[4]

The President's recommendations were embodied in House Report 1776, and in a corresponding Senate bill, through which Congress would attempt to translate into deeds the splendid counsel contained in these various pronouncements by the White House.[5]

My Friends: This is not a fireside chat on war. It is a talk on national security; because the nub of the whole purpose of your President is to keep you now, and your children later, and your grandchildren much later, out of a last-ditch war for the preservation of American independence and all of the things that American independence means to you and to me and to ours.

Tonight, in the presence of a world crisis, my mind goes back eight years ago to a night in the midst of a domestic crisis. It was a time when the wheels of American industry were grinding to a full stop, when the whole banking system of our country had ceased to function.

I well remember that while I sat in my study in the White House, preparing to talk with the people of the United States, I had before my eyes the picture of all those Americans with whom I was talking. I saw the workmen in the mills, the mines, the factories; the girl behind the counter, the small shopkeeper; the farmer doing his spring plowing; the widows and the old men wondering about their life's savings.

I tried to convey to the great mass of American people what the banking crisis meant to them in their daily lives. Tonight,

[4] The editor of this volume regrets that space does not permit him to reprint this address.

[5] See Lindbergh's statement before the House Committee, p. 75.

I want to do the same thing, with the same people, in this new crisis which faces America. We met the issue of 1933 with courage and realism. We face this new crisis—this new threat to the security of our nation—with the same courage and realism.

Never before since Jamestown and Plymouth Rock has our American civilization been in such danger as now. For, on September 27, 1940, by an agreement signed in Berlin, three powerful nations, two in Europe and one in Asia, joined themselves together in the threat that if the United States interfered with or blocked the expansion program of these three nations—a program aimed at world control—they would unite in ultimate action against the United States

The Nazi masters of Germany have made it clear that they intend not only to dominate all life and thought in their own country, but also to enslave the whole of Europe, and then to use the resources of Europe to dominate the rest of the world.

Three weeks ago their leader stated "There are two worlds that stand opposed to each other." Then in defiant reply to his opponents, he said this: "Others are correct when they say: With this world we cannot ever reconcile ourselves. . . . I can beat any other power in the world." So said the leader of the Nazis. In other words the Axis not merely admits but proclaims that there can be no ultimate peace between their philosophy of government and our philosophy of government.

In view of the nature of this undeniable threat, it can be asserted, properly and categorically, that the United States has no right or reason to encourage talk of peace, until the day shall come when there is a clear intention on the part of the aggressor nations to abandon all thought of dominating or conquering the world.

At this moment, the forces of the states that are leagued against all peoples who live in freedom, are being held away from our shores. The Germans and Italians are being blocked on the other side of the Atlantic by the British, and by the Greeks, and by thousands of soldiers and sailors who were able to escape from subjugated countries. The Japanese are being engaged in Asia by the Chinese in another great defense. In the Pacific is our fleet.

Some of our people like to believe that wars in Europe and in Asia are of no concern to us. But it is a matter of most vital concern to us that European and Asiatic war-makers should not gain control of the oceans which lead to this hemisphere.

One hundred and seventeen years ago the Monroe Doctrine was conceived by our Government as a measure of defense in the face of a threat against this hemisphere by an alliance in Continental Europe. Thereafter, we stood on guard in the Atlantic, with the British as neighbors. There was no treaty. There was no "unwritten agreement." Yet, there was the feeling, proven correct by history, that we as neighbors could settle any disputes in peaceful fashion. The fact is that during the whole of this time the Western Hemisphere has remained free from aggression from Europe or from Asia.

Does anyone seriously believe that we need to fear attack anywhere in the Americas while a free Britain remains our most powerful naval neighbor in the Atlantic? And does anyone seriously believe, on the other hand, that we could rest easy if the Axis powers were our neighbor there? If Great Britain goes down, the Axis powers will control the continents of Europe, Asia, Africa, Australasia, and the high seas—and they will be in a position to bring enormous military and naval resources against this hemisphere. It is no exaggeration to say that all of us in the Americas would be living at the point of a gun—a gun loaded with explosive bullets, economic as well as military. We should enter upon a new and terrible era in which the whole world, our hemisphere included, would be run by threats of brute force, and to survive in such a world, we would have to convert ourselves permanently into a militaristic power on the basis of war economy.

Some of us like to believe that even if Britain falls, we are still safe, because of the broad expanse of the Atlantic and of the Pacific. But the width of these oceans is not what it was in the days of clipper ships. At one point between Africa and Brazil the distance is less than from Washington to Denver, Colorado—five hours for the latest type of bomber. And at the north of the Pacific Ocean America and Asia almost touch each other. Why, even today we have planes which could fly from the British Isles to New England and back without refueling. And remember the range of the modern bomber is ever being increased.

During the past week many people in all parts of the nation have told me what they wanted me to say tonight. Almost all of them expressed a courageous desire to hear the plain truth about the gravity of the situation. One telegram, however, expressed the attitude of the small minority who want to see no evil and hear no evil, even though they know in their hearts that evil exists. That telegram begged me not to tell again of the ease with which our American cities could be bombed by any hostile power which had gained bases in this Western Hemisphere. The gist of that telegram was: "Please, Mr. President, don't frighten us by telling us the facts." Frankly and definitely there is danger ahead—danger against which we must prepare. But we well know that we cannot escape danger, or the fear of danger, by crawling into bed and pulling the covers over our heads.

Some nations of Europe were bound by solemn non-intervention pacts with Germany. Other nations were assured by Germany that they need never fear invasion. Non-intervention pact or not, the fact remains that they were attacked, overrun and thrown into the modern form of slavery at an hour's notice or even without any notice at all. As an exiled leader of one of these nations said to me the other day—"The notice was a minus quantity. It was given to my Government two hours after German troops had poured into my country in a hundred places." The fate of these nations tells us what it means to live at the point of a Nazi gun.

The Nazis have justified such actions by various pious frauds. One of these frauds is the claim that they are occupying a nation for the purpose of "restoring order." Another is that they are occupying or controlling a nation on the excuse that they are "protecting it" against the aggression of somebody else. For example, Germany has said that she was occupying Belgium to save the Belgians from the British. Would she hesitate to say to any South American country, "We are occupying you to protect you from aggression by the United States"? Belgium today is being used as an invasion base against Britain, now fighting for its life. And any South American country, in Nazi hands, would always constitute a jumping off place for German attack on any one of the other Republics of this hemisphere.

Analyze for yourselves the future of two other places even near to Germany if the Nazis won. Could Ireland hold out? Would Irish freedom be permitted as an amazing exception in an unfree world? Or the Islands of the Azores which still fly the flag of Portugal after five centuries? You and I think of Hawaii as an outpost of defense in the Pacific, and yet, the Azores are closer to our shores in the Atlantic than Hawaii is on the other side.

There are those who say that the Axis powers would never have any desire to attack the Western Hemisphere. This is the same dangerous form of wishful thinking which has destroyed the powers of resistance of so many conquered peoples. The plain facts are that the Nazis have proclaimed, time and again, that all other races are their inferiors and therefore subject to their orders. And most important of all, the vast resources and wealth of this hemisphere constitute the most tempting loot in all the world.

Let us no longer blind ourselves to the undeniable fact that the evil forces which have crushed and undermined and corrupted so many others are already within our own gates. Your Government knows much about them and every day is ferreting them out. Their secret emissaries are active in our own and neighboring countries. They seek to stir up suspicion and dissension to cause internal strife. They try to turn capital against labor, and vice-versa. They try to reawaken long slumbering racial and religious enmities which should have no place in this country. They are active in every group that promotes intolerance. They exploit for their own ends our natural abhorrence of war. These trouble-breeders have but one purpose. It is to divide our people into hostile groups and to destroy our unity and shatter our will to defend ourselves.

There are also American citizens, many of them in high places, who, unwittingly in most cases, are aiding and abetting the work of these agents. I do not charge these American citizens with being foreign agents. But I do charge them with doing exactly the kind of work that the dictators want done in the United States.

These people not only believe that we can save our own skins by shutting our eyes to the fate of other nations. Some of them go much further than that. They say that we can and should become the friends and even the partners of the Axis powers. Some of them even suggest that we should imitate the methods of the dictatorships. Americans never can and never will do that.

The experience of the past two years has proven beyond doubt that no nation can appease the Nazis. No man can tame a tiger into a kitten by stroking it. There can be no appeasement with ruthlessness. There can be no reasoning with an incendiary bomb. We know now that a nation can have peace with the Nazis only at the price of total surrender. Even the people of Italy have been forced to become accomplices of the Nazis; but at this moment they do not know how soon they will be embraced to death by their allies.

The American appeasers ignore the warning to be found in the fate of Austria, Czechoslovakia, Poland, Norway, Belgium, the Netherlands, Denmark, and France. They tell you that the Axis powers are going to win anyway; that all of this bloodshed in the world could be saved, and that the United States might just as well throw its influence into the scale of a dictated peace, and get the best out of it that we can. They call it a "negotiated peace." Nonsense! Is it a negotiated peace if a gang of outlaws surrounds your community and on threat of extermination makes you pay tribute to save your own skins? Such a dictated peace would be no peace at all. It would be only another armistice, leading to the most gigantic armament race and the most devastating trade wars in all history. And in these contests the Americas would offer the only real resistance to the Axis powers.

With all their vaunted efficiency, with all their parade of pious purpose in this war, there are still in their background the concentration camp and the servants of God in chains. The history of recent years proves that shootings and chains and concentration camps are not simply the transient tools but the very altars of modern dictatorships. They may talk of a "new order" in the world, but what they have in mind is but a revival of the oldest and the worst tyranny. In that there is no liberty, no religion, no hope.

The proposed "new order" is the very opposite of a United States of Europe or a United States of Asia. It is not a government based upon the consent of the governed. It is not a union of ordinary, self-respecting men and women to protect themselves and their freedom and their dignity from oppression. It is an unholy alliance of power and pelf to dominate and enslave the human race.

The British people are conducting an active war against this unholy alliance. Our own future security is greatly dependent on the outcome of that fight. Our ability to "keep out of war" is going to be affected by that outcome.

Thinking in terms of today and tomorrow, I make the direct statement to the American people that there is far less chance of the United States getting into war, if we do all we can now to support the nations defending themselves against attack by the

Axis than if we acquiesce in their defeat, submit tamely to an Axis victory, and wait our turn to be the object of attack in another war later on.

If we are to be completely honest with ourselves, we must admit there is risk in *any* course we may take. But I deeply believe that the great majority of our people agree that the course that I advocate involves the least risk now and the greatest hope for world peace in the future.

The people of Europe who are defending themselves do not ask us to do their fighting. They ask us for the implements of war, the planes, the tanks, the guns, the freighters which will enable them to fight for their liberty and our security. Emphatically we must get these weapons to them, get them to them in sufficient volume and quickly enough, so that we and our children will be saved the agony and suffering of war which others have had to endure.

Let not the defeatists tell us that it is too late. It will never be earlier. Tomorrow will be later than today. Certain facts are self-evident. In a military sense Great Britain and the British Empire are today the spearhead of resistance to world conquest, and they are putting up a fight which will live forever in the story of human gallantry.

There is no demand for sending an American Expeditionary Force outside our own borders. There is no intention by any member of your Government to send such a force. You can, therefore, nail any talk about sending armies to Europe as deliberate untruth. Our national policy is not directed toward war. Its sole purpose is to keep war away from our country and away from our people.

Democracy's fight against world conquest is being greatly aided, and must be more greatly aided, by the rearmament of the United States and by sending every ounce and every ton of munitions and supplies that we can possibly spare to help the defenders who are in the front lines, and it is no more unneutral for us to do that than it is for Sweden, Russia and other nations near Germany, to send steel and ore and oil and other war materials into Germany every day in the week.

We are planning our own defense with the utmost urgency; and in its vast scale we must integrate the war needs of Britain and the other free nations which are resisting aggression. This is not a matter of sentiment or of controversial personal opinion. It is a matter of realistic, practical military policy, based on the advice of our military experts who are in close touch with existing warfare. These military and naval experts and the members of the Congress and the Administration have a single-minded purpose—the defense of the United States.

This nation is making a great effort to produce everything that is necessary in this emergency—and with all possible speed, and this great effort requires great sacrifice.

I would ask no one to defend a democracy which in turn would not defend everyone in the nation against want and privation. The strength of this nation shall not be diluted by the failure of the Government to protect the economic well-being of its citizens.

If our capacity to produce is limited by machines, it must ever be remembered that these machines are operated by the skill and the stamina of the workers. As the Government is determined to protect the rights of workers, so the nation has a right to expect that the men who man the machines will discharge their full responsibilities to the urgent needs of defense. The worker possesses the same human dignity and is entitled to the same security of position as the engineer or the manager or the owner. For the workers provide the human power that turns out the destroyers, the airplanes and the tanks.

The nation expects our defense industries to continue operation without interruption by strikes or lock-outs. It expects and insists that management and workers will reconcile their differences by voluntary or legal means, to continue to produce the supplies that are so sorely needed. And on the economic side of our great defense program, we are, as you know, bending every effort to maintain stability of prices and with that the stability of the cost of living.

Nine days ago I announced the setting up of a more effective organization to direct our gigantic efforts to increase the production of munitions. The appropriation of vast sums of money and a well coordinated executive direction of our defense efforts are not in themselves enough. Guns, planes, ships and many other things have to be built in the factories and arsenals of America. They have to be produced by workers and managers and engineers with the aid of machines which in turn have to be built by hundreds of thousands of workers throughout the land. In this great work there has been splendid cooperation between the Government and industry and labor, and I am very thankful.

American industrial genius, unmatched throughout the world in the solution of production problems, has been called upon to bring its resources and its talents into action. Manufacturers of watches, of farm implements, of linotypes, and cash registers, and automobiles, and sewing machines, and lawn mowers and locomotives are now making fuses and bomb packing crates, and telescope mounts and shells and pistols and tanks.

But all our present efforts are not enough. We must have more ships, more guns, more planes—more of everything, and this can only be accomplished if we discard the notion of "business as usual." This job cannot be done merely by superimposing on the existing productive facilities the added requirements of the nation for defense.

Our defense efforts must not be blocked by those who fear the future consequences of surplus plant capacity. The possible consequences of failure of our defense efforts now are much more to be feared, and after the present needs of our defense are past, a proper handling of the country's peacetime needs will require all of the new productive capacity—if not still more. No pessimistic policy about the future of America shall delay the immediate expansion of those industries essential to defense. We need them.

I want to make it clear that it is the purpose of the nation to build now with all possible speed every machine, every arsenal, every factory that we need to manufacture our defense material. We have the men—the skill—the wealth—and above all, the will.

I am confident that if and when production of consumer or luxury goods in certain industries requires the use of machines and raw materials that are essential for defense purposes, then such production must yield and will gladly yield to our primary and compelling purpose.

So I appeal to the owners of plants—to the managers— to the workers—to our own government employees—to put every ounce of effort into producing these munitions swiftly and without stint. With this appeal I give you the pledge that all of us who are officers of your Government will devote ourselves to the same whole-hearted extent to the great task that lies ahead.

As planes and ships and guns and shells are produced, your Government, with its defense experts, can then determine how best to use them to defend this hemisphere. The decision as to how much shall be sent abroad and how much shall remain at home must be made on the basis of our over-all military necessities.

We must be the great arsenal of democracy. For all this is an emergency as serious as war itself. We must apply ourselves to our task with the same resolution, the same sense of urgency, the same spirit of patriotism and sacrifice as we would show were we at war. We have furnished the British great material support and we will furnish far more in the future. There will be no "bottlenecks" in our determination to aid Great Britain. No dictator, no combination of dictators, will weaken that determination by threats of how they will construe that determination.

The British have received invaluable military support from the heroic Greek Army, and from the forces of all the Governments in exile. Their strength is growing. It is the strength of men and women who value their freedom more highly than they value their lives.

I believe that the Axis powers are not going to win this war. I base that belief on the latest and best information. We have no excuse for defeatism. We have every good reason for hope— hope for peace, yes, and hope for the defense of our civilization and for the building of a better civilization in the future.

I have the profound conviction that the American people are now determined to put forth a mightier effort than they have ever yet made to increase our production of all the implements of defense, to meet the threat to our democratic faith.

As President of the United States I call for that national effort. I call for it in the name of this nation which we love and honor and which we are privileged and proud to serve. I call upon our people with absolute confidence that our common cause will greatly succeed.

SHALL WE DO WHATEVER IS NECESSARY TO INSURE A BRITISH VICTORY? [6]

WILLIAM J. DONOVAN and ROBERT M. HUTCHINS [7]

This debate was one of "America's Town Meeting of the Air" programs, and was part of the Golden Jubilee celebration and national convention of the General Federation of Women's Clubs, at Convention Hall, Atlantic City, on May 22, 1941. More than 30,000 Americans, most of them delegates to the convention, made up the audience. It was "the largest Town Meeting" held since the beginning of that program, in May, 1935. The introductory remarks by George V. Denny, Jr., Moderator, explain the immediate setting of the debate and the importance of the speakers. [8]

MODERATOR DENNY: We are considering this evening the third and final question in a series on America's relation to World War II, in which we ask ourselves frankly and honestly, "Should We Do Whatever Is Necessary to Insure a British Victory?" This seems to us to state the issue clearly and definitely. We have talked about aid short of war; we have adopted the Lease-Lend bill; we have talked about convoys; and now we must face squarely up to the question, should we, the American people, do whatever is necessary to insure a British victory? Colonel William J. Donovan, the famous Commander of New York's Fighting Sixty-Ninth in the first World War, comes to us fresh from his observations of the European scene as an official observer for the Secretary of the Navy. It is our understanding that he answers tonight's question

[6] Reprinted from *Town Meeting, Bulletin of America's Town Meeting of the Air*, vol. 6, no. 28, May 26, 1941. Published by the Columbia University Press, 2960 Broadway, New York. By permission of the speakers and by special arrangements with Town Hall, Inc., and Columbia University Press.

[7] For biographical sketches see Appendix.

[8] For further comment on *America's Town Meeting of the Air*, see *Representative American Speeches: 1937-1938*, p. 52; *1938-1939*, p. 138; *1939-1940*, p. 234-6; and *1940-1941*, p. 209-10.

For further comment on Robert Hutchins as a speaker see *Representative American Speeches: 1937-1938*, p. 184; *1938-1939*, p. 199.

with a positive affirmative, and will give us his reasons therefor. Dr. Robert Maynard Hutchins, president of the University of Chicago, is an educator of international renown. He, too, was a soldier under fire in 1917-1918, but he answers tonight's question in the negative. Let us remember now and at all times that these discussions are presented to help you, the American people, make up your minds about a vital national issue. Opinions are strongly divided. This is a town meeting and not a mass meeting, and I have asked the audience to refrain from any prolonged demonstration of approval or disapproval of the remarks of our speakers. Reason rather than emotion must decide this question. I take pleasure in presenting at this time our first speaker, Colonel William J. Donovan, of New York City.

COLONEL DONOVAN: Ladies and gentlemen: Tonight we are to consider this question: Shall we do whatever is necessary to assure British victory? Let me meet that squarely. My answer is yes, and I give that answer with full knowledge of all the risks involved in doing whatever is necessary. But, having given that answer, we have not advanced very far.

With no intention of reflecting on those who prepared the question, I think the trouble lies with the question itself. It is the same difficulty that we find with so many of the questions bearing upon our position in this war. We have not been discussing, in my opinion, the primary question. We have been discussing questions like these: Shall we give aid to the British? If so, how much will we give? And then at what point shall we stop? Shall we convoy? Shall we declare war?

To me, all these questions are secondary questions. That does not mean that they are not important, but they are all subordinate to one fundamental question, which, if we answer the other questions, will nearly answer itself. That fundamental question is this: Are we in danger if Hitler wins, and, if so, how should we meet that danger? If we conclude that his victory carries no menace to us, then we do not need to bother with the second part of the question. But if it be shown that a Nazi victory would constitute a challenge to America, and the nature of that challenge is understood, I, for one, have no doubt that, despite all efforts from the outside to stimulate dissension among us, we would spring as a united people to meet that challenge.

So, while I feel we are a little late in coming to this question, it is better to do it now than not at all. I think, too, that we should deal with this question by argument and not by name calling, by understanding and not by invective.

So that my position is clear, I want to say to this audience that the head of the America First Committee, General Wood, is one of the real patriots of this country. While he and I are in disagreement, I know, coming as he does from a long line of soldiers, that at the first call to arms he would be in the front line. I have no doubt that those of his committee, who go about this country meeting their fellow citizens eye to eye, are sincere in their convictions and honest in their motives. Certainly all of us know that Dr. Hutchins has no other purpose in addressing the people of this country than to help them in deciding an issue which may determine our destiny and perhaps our very survival as a free people.

For those of us who differ with these distinguished gentlemen, let there be made but one claim: that in its critical hour, we, too, are trying to serve our country. We ought to examine this whole question of danger, and we ought to examine it with a completely open mind. We ought not to be diverted by the hearings and debates on the Lend-Lease bill, nor should we permit the issue to be confused by what was said in a political campaign six months ago.

We, as a people, must determine our course not by what somebody said or by what candidates promised, but by what it is necessary to do now for the safety of our country.

It seems to me that the question of danger can be fairly presented by these questions: What kind of world would we face if Hitler wins? What would Europe be under Nazi control? What will be the result for America, for each of us, if Hitler organizes all Europe's resources and all Europe's relations with the rest of the world?

Obviously, it is impossible here to fully explore the answer to these questions, but they are questions which I should like you to carry away with you. They are worth thinking about. They are the questions that I carried in my mind when I was lucky enough to have the opportunity to see, at first hand and with my own eyes, just what modern war is. I made two visits to Europe—first, shortly after the fall of France, and then from December to March of this year—on a journey of observation which included not only the British Isles, but also southeastern Europe, the Mediterranean area, Africa, and Asia Minor.

I want to make clear to you in discussing this question, because I had the good fortune to make such a personal reconnaissance, that I feel in no way qualified to talk to you as a military expert. On the contrary, I say with no false humility that because, in the last fifteen years, I have given some time and attention to visiting the critical places of the world, I feel that I can speak with less authority and with less dogmatism than if I had never gone there. You can understand this because you and I have heard statesmen assert that particular events could not happen, and yet they have happened with disconcerting regularity.

So the answers that I think I have found to these questions you may accept or reject in reaching your own decision. But I did find this, that the body of Nazi doctrine, confirmed by their writings and their laws, is that the German race is the master race; that the self-appointed destiny of the German race is to create a new Europe, and a new world, under Nazi domination; that force is the basis of all social relationship; that conquered nations and conquered areas must be reduced to a state of permanent inferiority, as in Czechoslovakia and Poland; and that the immediate result of a Nazi victory will be the organization of Europe as a single entity self-sufficient in foodstuffs, as a sure agricultural foundation upon which to base a firm Nazi military leadership—leadership that will be maintained because the cardinal pattern of Nazi policy will be to retain an iron hand over every industry engaged in the production of armaments of war. This doctrine is based upon the firm conviction that he who controls the industrial productive capacity of Europe will remain its future master, making impossible, in Europe, any successful resistance to the Nazi machine.

At the same time, the Nazis are attempting to destroy the intellectual leadership of occupied countries by closing all channels of free education and free expression. The intellectual elite in Czechoslovakia and Poland have been executed or driven into exile. Those who doubt that danger exists for us say, "Suppose all this is true, how is it going to affect us?" They say that those who believe it would constitute a danger must meet the burden of proof. I do not say that on the day after a Nazi victory in Europe that we would expect to find German transports off the Atlantic coast, but I do say that across the Atlantic we would have a great military empire which would have its whole industry under a comprehensive governmental system, able to lay down terms that we would be unable to meet.

But the greatest danger, not only to our economy, but also to our national security, would be that which strikes, indirectly, through South America. No one can doubt, I think, that Germany would attempt to deal with South America precisely as she has dealt, during the last ten years, with the Balkans. The only way any man can foresee the future is to examine it in terms of the past—in terms of the pattern of history, and the continuance of that pattern to the present, toward the future. There is a pattern of history in this matter which any observer can see. What happened to the Balkans is a prototype of what will happen to South America—first, economic protocols, then political penetration, then military infiltration. It will be a logical effort on the part of Germany to occupy strategic and outflanking positions against us, all of which would be justified on the ground that she must be protected against us.

If England falls, Germany has no one to interfere in Europe or the Middle East. She can deal with Russia at her leisure. She would obtain, at a stroke, every port, airdrome, and transatlantic terminus in Europe. We have seen, through the events of this war, that Germany always tries to outflank. By defeating England, she would outflank the Atlantic from Narvik to Capetown. She would obtain the French and the Italian fleets, and perhaps the British fleet as well—certainly the British fleet bases—and there, not only in Europe, but also in Africa, the possessions of the whole Atlantic seaboard would give her the bases to push her plans further. Meanwhile, in the Pacific, she would call upon Japan to fulfill her duty to the Axis. A beaten England means a threat to America from the East, the West, and the South.

Now, let us look at it from the present physical, military aspects of the war. Germany is making every possible effort to end the war this year. England is the last in a series of European obstacles that stand between Germany and her ambition. Hitler will certainly try to remove that obstacle either by direct invasion, or by throttling her shipping, or by both.

In the Mediterranean strategic area, we see the attack on Crete, the advance into Syria, the landing of troops at Iraq, and we see also, in the western Mediterranean, that Hitler has now the assistance of France—once an enemy, but now an ally. With assurance of French collaboration, the threat to the Spanish and Portuguese peninsula, and the closing of the Strait of Gibraltar, is a real threat. Once Hitler has obtained the Iberian Peninsula and French North Africa, his aircraft and submarines would be in a position to dominate the South Atlantic. Hitler will not only control the vital sea lanes of the British Empire by such a victory, but he will also control our own lines of trade with Brazil, Uruguay, and the Argentine. More than this, accepting the interpretation of the Armistice terms between Germany and France, as given by the French Ambassador in this country, Germany already has the right under those terms to establish her air bases at Martinique. For all we know, maybe Hitler has already done that very thing.

Don't imagine that, should Hitler beat England, we would not be in his way. Of course we would be in his way. We, the greatest industrial democracy in the world, and the last great obstacle to Hitler's world domination! He can't achieve his ambition as long as we stand in his way. Those who say that— in the face of these facts, in the face of the record of European history over the last eighteen months, over the last eighteen days —we are not in danger, have every factual presumption against them. The plain fact is that our vital interest will be affected by a German victory. We will be harmed if Hitler wins. Our outpost lines will have been destroyed. If Hitler wins, we will have to redraft our plans for the future; our concept of human life will be placed in jeopardy. We shall have to match Germany's military and naval power if we wish to continue our way of life.

I know that there are those who say that the way of life that we pursue is not a very perfect one and that we should concern ourselves with the improvement of our internal affairs rather than mess in concerns that are not our own.

Ladies and gentlemen, with a formidable, resourceful, and ruthless neighbor in our backyard and on our flank, we would have but little time for home concerns. But if, after an examination of the facts and after a full consideration of the possible worst that could happen, if, after all of this, we as a people believe that this statement I have made is unreal, that there is no danger, then I think there is but one course to pursue. If there be no danger, then certainly there is no reason for the maintenance of 1,000,000 men under arms; no reason to maintain our present aviation program; no reason to submit ourselves to the heavy burden of taxation in order to sink $7,000,000,000 in the ocean. If we are not prepared to see that the goods get to England, how can those who are against protection for those goods say that they are in favor of giving aid to England?

If we are going to give aid to England, we ought to be prepared to run the risk of getting it there, otherwise it is a useless and a cruel gesture. If we are not prepared to run that risk, we should be on the level with England and tell her we are through. That is not only the logic of the position of running no risk, it is the only square thing to do. The blow that we would give her by telling her that we would no longer help would be far less than the constant blows given her by uncertainty and indecision.

It is my belief that we should not aid England because she is in distress, and that we do it as an act of charity. We should aid England, if we do it at all, only because we recognize that she is a shield behind which we can learn to stand on our feet and equip ourselves as a self-respecting people. But if, from what I have said, a reasonable man would conclude that we are in danger, then our course is obvious. We should do each day what we think is right to do that day to avert the danger—not only for that day, but for the future. But whatever we do, we must do with the full realization of the risk involved, even though that risk may mean war itself. When I say this, I mean to say that I would not declare war. I do not think it necessary. We are not compelled to choose the alternative of neutrality or belligerency. I know it may be said that, if this plan be followed, war will be declared. I would be prepared to accept this risk, but I doubt if Hitler desires to rush into battle with this country. If he did, he has plenty of reason up to date. We should not be deterred from doing what we think best, by fear of war, once we recognize our danger. In common decency and self-respect we must do what we consider right, and be prepared to accept the consequences of our action. Then we must act with all speed, since we have seen, time and time again, that nations who have hesitated were lost.

MODERATOR DENNY: Thank you, Colonel Donovan. And now it is my pleasure to introduce our second speaker, Dr. Robert Maynard Hutchins, president of the University of Chicago.

DR. HUTCHINS: I am for aid to Britain. I am against naval or military intervention in this war.

For ten long years we tried one expedient after another to recover from a war. That war, for this country, had not been a bad one. But the effects of it, in terms of inflation and deflation, of delirium and depression, of hate and fear, were still being felt after twenty years.

Before 1917 the country had serious problems. The war settled none of them and produced some new ones we never dreamed of. From 1919 to 1929 we paid no attention to these problems, or to anything else, except the price of stocks. From 1929 to 1939 we thought of nothing but these problems. We applied a whole pharmacopoeia of desperate remedies and succeeded only in doing a few things that ought to have been done years before. We passed the Wagner Act, the social security legislation, and the Securities Exchange Act. We started the TVA. But there was little fundamental improvement. We were depressed and bewildered. We had some hope that some day we might get somewhere. We just couldn't see quite how.

When the war broke out, in 1939, the country recognized that its difficulties were still unsolved. Our liberals had been telling us for years that the first World War was accountable for many of them. They urged us not to be drawn into another conflict which could only aggravate diseases that had already proved nearly fatal. Leading businessmen warned us that there was nothing in war for business. They knew that though war business would be large, it might not be profitable; that if there were profits they would not last; and that the collapse of industry after the war would cancel them.

We wanted Hitler to be defeated. We knew all about him and didn't like any of it. We wanted the British to win. We like them. They speak the same language. They have an analogous constitutional system. We are accustomed to dealing with them. In 1939 we felt that a British victory would be advantageous to us. We did not believe that it was our only hope. We did not believe that our safety, or the integrity of our institutions, or the contribution we could make to the welfare of mankind depended on a British victory. Nobody offered the faintest suggestion that we should go to war. We knew too much about war to be deceived again.

How different is the spectacle today. Instead of working still to solve the problems resulting from the last war, we have been quivering for months on the brink of another. The President has been conducting a war of nerves against the Axis—and against his own people. The speeches of his representatives, from the Vice President down to Senator Pepper, have all the marks of a concerted campaign to frighten us into war. We have every reason to fear that we shall enter this war for democracy without resort to democratic processes. Because totalitarian powers do not declare war, but simply start shooting, this democratic nation, we hear, in its war for democracy should do the same thing.

We have stopped trying to make democracy work. The liberals now tell us that we cannot have democracy in this country unless the British Empire is preserved. Many leading businessmen hint that Hitler will starve us if he wins. Everybody tells us that Hitler will arrive in South America, or at the Panama Canal, or at New York City within a few minutes, days, months, or years after he has conquered England.

This, then, is the spectacle. It is the spectacle of a country with appalling problems, many of them resulting from the last war, about to plunge into another in the hope of ending its troubles that way. In the life of individuals this method of solving problems is known as suicide.

If we don't want to commit suicide, if we want to preserve our country, these problems must be solved. Let me recall a few of them: The problem of unemployment. Is the war a WPA project? The problem of social justice, justice to the Negro, to the sharecropper, to the migratory worker, to the exploited members of our economic system. The problem of clearing the slums and building 10,000,000 decent homes. The problem of the land, and of gaining access to it for the people. The problem of the machine, and how to direct it to the common good. The problem of starvation in the midst of plenty, politely called the problem of distribution. The problem of adequate medical care. The problem of agriculture. The problem of monopoly. The problem of capital and labor. The problem of political corruption. The problem of education. Last December, Mr. Walter Lippmann said "that the prevailing system of education is destined, if it continues, to destroy western civilization, and is in fact destroying it." If Mr. Lippmann is right, and I think he is, we would gain little by defeating Hitler unless we could reform education at the same time. But we obviously cannot guarantee a British victory and reform education, or anything else, at the same time. We cannot fight a total war and at the same time solve the overwhelming problems that must be solved if we are to make democracy work in this country.

We present a strange, and even an unprecedented, spectacle when we look at ourselves from the military point of view. We have not been attacked. We are not prepared. Hitler's public statements about this country, at least when compared with those of our leaders about Germany, have been characterized by moderation and reserve. Certainly no country ever entered a great war so unprovoked and so unprepared. Military nations have gone to war without provocation. Provoked nations have gone to war without preparation. For a nation to go to war as unprovoked and as unprepared as we are must be unique in history. We present the strange spectacle of a country dragging itself by its own bootstraps into a war which it did not begin, for which it is not responsible, for which it is not ready, and which, only a few months ago, it was determined never to enter.

I believe that we could win this war. I do not see precisely how we could win it, but I have faith that the vast resources of our land and the technological genius of our people would conquer in the end. But at how distant an end, and at how great a cost! On the basis of anything we know now we could not expect the end in less than five years. The cost is the sacrifice of the institutions we would be fighting to save. The cost is the sacrifice of millions of our youth.

But we are told we have no choice. Hitler will decide. Perhaps we shall be forced into bankruptcy, revolution, and totalitarianism at home. But we must make up our minds now to defeat Hitler or be defeated by him. If we are defeated by him, we shall have all this and Hitler too.

I insist that today we have a choice, that today we can decide. Will Hitler attack us? Not if we are prepared. Will he penetrate South America? Not if we deal justly and intelligently with her; not, for example, if we adopt Secretary Knox's proposal for an immediate customs union with the Latin American nations. Shall we be able to survive in a totalitarian world? The loss of all the foreign trade we have had in the last decade would cost less than one year of war. Shall we suffer the fate of Denmark and Norway? Not unless we stop building battleships and bombers; not unless the Atlantic Ocean is rolled back to make a pathway for the enemies of God.

Things will be bad for this country, and for the world, whether we go to war or not. They will be far worse if we go in than if we stay out. To stake the lives and fortunes of our people, and the hopes of the world, on the nightmares and bogeys that have been conjured up to scare us is to betray humanity. We know the horrors of war. They are obvious. They are inevitable. The horrors we are told we shall undergo if we stay out of war are the products of hypothesis and hysteria.

The United States must prepare to meet the totalitarian onslaught if, or when, it comes. We are working hard on military preparation. Military preparation suffices for defense. It suffices even for conquest. But for the peace that must come sometime, another kind of preparation is required. All we have to do is to recall our incompetence to deal in time of peace with those domestic problems that haunted us during the depression. With a multitude of gadgets, we were sinking into poverty. With a decreasing death rate, we had yet to discover what to do with our lives. With a love of liberty, we did not know how to use our freedom or how to free the economic slaves among our population. I have faith that we can gradually muster the military strength to win the war. I see no sign that we possess the moral, intellectual, and spiritual strength to write the peace.

I am not an isolationist. I have not joined the America First Committee. I do not like its name. I should like to join a committee for Humanity First. If the United States can serve humanity, it should do so, no matter what the cost in blood and treasure. The United States cannot serve humanity by making the totalitarian revolution world-wide. Yet if Hitler is really devoted to the totalitarian ideal, and is prepared to suffer personal defeat to realize it on a world scale, he should pray for America's entrance into this war. For it would follow, as the night the day, that a totalitarian banner would be raised over the Western Hemisphere.

But the peace—war is for the sake of peace. Since I believe that we shall have a totalitarian government after the war, I cannot see it writing a just and durable peace. But suppose that by some miracle we were to defeat the totalitarian powers without becoming one ourselves. Would we be prepared, even then, to write a just and durable peace?

We do not know what to do with ourselves. What shall we do with the Germans, Italians, and Japanese? Are we going to exterminate them? If not, we shall have to make them free and democratic, when we have not achieved freedom and democracy for ourselves. What shall we do with the British and the Chinese? Are we going to fight them to make them see things our way? What shall we do with Czechoslovakia, Poland, Latvia, Estonia, Lithuania, France, Luxembourg, Denmark, Norway, Belgium, Holland, Rumania, Jugoslavia, and Greece? Are we to restore the *status quo,* which contributed to this war, and simply hope that it will work next time? Until we know what to do with ourselves we can hardly venture to set the whole world right.

American imperialism I can comprehend. I can comprehend the position of those who want the United States to take charge of the world and run it at a profit. No member of the Humanity First Committee could favor such a course. I can neither comprehend, nor favor, a program by which the United States proposes to force the four freedoms on the rest of the world. We haven't got them. We don't understand them. And we don't really care very much about them. If we set out to impose our conception of them on the rest of the world, we can end only by establishing an empire. Empire means money and power. We may not understand or care about the four freedoms. We do understand and we do care about money and power. I have no more desire to see the world enslaved to the United States than I have to see it enslaved to Germany.

But, you say, suppose America is not perfect. Do we have to be perfect to be helpful? Aren't our ideals and our form of government better than those of the Axis? Wouldn't it be better for the world to have us write the peace, frail creatures though we are, than to have the gangsters of the Axis write it?

Our ideals and our form of government are better than those of the Axis. If we could persuade the Axis to adopt them, we would serve humanity well. But our form of government will not survive participation in this war. And our ideals will be unrecognizable by the time they have gone through a conflict in which we can succeed only if we have learned to hate everybody but the English, the Chinese, and the Latin Americans.

Our professed ideals and our theory of government are far better than those of the Axis. Our practice of life and government is better than that of the Axis. But our practice is not enough better to justify the hope that after we have won the war for democracy we can write a democratic peace. Our practice is not enough better to make the peace enough better to justify the slaughter of millions of men of all nations and the destruction of civilization and the hopes which all the world now places on America.

A fraction of our population have understood and tried to practice the four freedoms at home. Mr. Roosevelt has tried to practice them. Many liberals are now among the most earnest advocates of war. Their theory is that if we can only get rid of Hitler our problems will be solved.

We got rid of the Kaiser, and a worse than the Kaiser arose. If we get rid of Hitler, will not a worse than Hitler arise? The idealism and liberalism of Woodrow Wilson did not save us. When we had conquered, we did nothing to establish the four freedoms. We relapsed into "normalcy."

Those who have understood and practiced the four freedoms will not write the peace. Or if they do, why should they be any more successful in writing a just and lasting one than Wilson was? Randolph Bourne, the young poet who died during the last war, said, "If it is a question of controlling war, it is difficult to see how the child on the back of the mad elephant is to be any more effective in stopping the beast than the child who tries to stop him from the ground."

How can the United States serve humanity? It can serve humanity by resuming the long, hard fight for the four freedoms at home. We must translate them from rhetoric into practice. How we can do this is another speech, or a book, or a series of books. I doubt if I am competent to write them. The sole purpose of this speech is to show how not to get the four freedoms. We cannot get them by going to war. To get them we must put forth years, or even centuries, of unremitting effort. We must dedicate ourselves to service and sacrifice instead of to profit and power. If we would change the face of the earth, we must first change our own hearts. If we will fight for the four freedoms with the same devotion that total war demands, we have a chance to get them for ourselves and for our fellow men.

We are the only people who have. If we plunge into war, we shall deprive the world of its last hope. We shall rob mankind of its last chance.

ALL-OUT AID TO BRITAIN [9]

CLAUDE PEPPER [10]

Senator Claude Pepper gave this speech before the United States Senate on May 6, 1941. It was delivered in his usual energetic, extempore style, and it voiced his usual strongly pro-British attitude. The Senator was generally regarded as expressing the sentiments of President Roosevelt regarding steps to be taken for helping Great Britain.

At this stage in the development of World War II, the international issues that Congressmen grappled with included such problems as: Should U. S. naval patrols push out wherever necessary to warn ships on the way to England, to guide England in her attempt to avoid losing the "battle of the Atlantic?" Should United States merchant shipping be mobilized and thrown into the breach as a protection against British losses? Should American patrols return fire if fired upon? Should we regard the British Isles as vital for a military base, to be protected by America at all hazards? Will the outcome of the war depend on the United States? Should the President under the Lend-Lease Bill be allowed unlimited power? Should Congress enact legislation prohibiting convoys to England? Should we take steps to seize Dakar (or other points)?

At this time Knox, Stimson, Wickard, and others were busily speaking in favor of radical steps and in favor of an affirmative answer to practically all the questions suggested above. These talks, all of them widely aired over the radio, were assumed to be feelers to help the President mold public opinion to support his more active program, soon to be necessary when Germany either (1) drove through the Middle East, captured the Suez and Gibraltar, or (2) attacked England directly.

The Florida Senator, for more than a year, had been delivering speeches in Congress favoring "all-out aid" to Britain. The debate of June 17, 1940, to which the Senator refers in this later address, the editor received too late for inclusion in the volume of *Representative American Speeches: 1939-1940*. For a full understanding of the Senator's argument and thinking, however, the two arguments should be compared.

What of Senator Pepper's speech training, his methods of preparation and presentation? He had a course in public speaking at the University of Alabama, where he took his A. B. degree. He represented the University in the Southern Oratorical contest and was a member of

9 By permission of Hon. Claude M. Pepper, United States Senator from Florida. Text furnished through the courtesy of Senator Pepper and reprinted from the *Congressional Record*, vol. 87, no. 84, p. 3694-9, May 6, 1941 (daily edition), proceedings and debates of the 77th Congress, first session.

10 For biographical note see Appendix.

the campus debating society. At the Harvard Law School he had some experience in speaking as a member of the law class where practice appellate court work was carried on.

Concerning his Senate debates, he states (and his testimony is similar to that of practically every other Senator) that he seldom knows beforehand, in more than a general way, what he is to say. He generally formulates in his mind the "trend which I propose to follow in the discussion."

The text, as printed in the *Congressional Record,* he states "represents exactly what I said except for an occasional word or punctuation. It is a privilege regularly enjoyed by those who have spoken in the Senate to correct their remarks after delivery, but this relates only to minor and immaterial changes."

To young speakers, he advises, "Know your subject so thoroughly that it is a part of you; second, either formulate an outline and commit it to memory, or as you gain more experience, formulate some general scheme of your speech in your mind beforehand and prepare with more care the beginning, and still more care the conclusion; third, express in what you say and the way you say it utter sincerity; fourth, either practice before a mirror or have some real friend be frankly critical of your method of delivery so that you may avoid mannerisms or characteristics which would detract from a favorable and pleasant impression on the part of your audience. I cannot over-emphasize the importance of public speaking because by speech are people generally persuaded whether singularly, in groups or in crowds. He who has the gift of effective speech has many doorways open to him to render great service." [11]

Mr. President, a week ago today I stood at the Hermitage and gazed upon the tomb of Andrew Jackson. I walked over the spacious grounds where that brave man and his good wife had walked. I saw the slippers which had carried his restless feet. I saw the garment which had been wrapped around him in the last days of his life, and I saw the bed upon which he breathed his last. I could not come within the inspiring atmosphere of the life and the tomb of Andrew Jackson in this moment of crisis facing the country which he loved and for which he so often and so valorously offered his life without gaining some impression as to what Andrew Jackson would say to his beloved country in this sad hour.

[11] Letter to the author, June 19, 1940.

If there was anything distinctive about the character of Andrew Jackson it was the quality of positiveness and certainty that grew out of an unequivocal conviction. If there was anything he scorned, it was evasion and indirectness. If there was anything that marked Andrew Jackson the man, it was the manliness of all that he did. Therefore when this Nation is the last citadel of democracy standing in the world, and when the chief assault is not now in the Balkans, or even at the Dardanelles, or Gibraltar, or Suez, but upon the ramparts of American public opinion, it is well that we consider what America shall think and do in this troubled time.

I hope the Senate will not misunderstand me if I advert to the fact that about 10 months ago, on the sad day when the Republic of France fell, I ventured to make some comment in the Senate and to propose what I thought might be regarded as a constructive program containing seven points, which were:

First. Confer upon the President full wartime power to prepare and defend America;

Second. Universal defense service, so that every citizen may be best trained and placed for the country's defense;

Third. Confer upon the President power to suspend all rules, regulations, and statutes, including Army, Navy, and departmental seniority regulations, which, in his judgment, interfered with the maximum of the production, transportation, or manufacture of defense materials;

Fourth. Confer upon the President power to suspend the present debt limitation if in his judgment such limitation interferes with the maximum speed of the defense program;

Fifth. Grant the President the authority to aid in material or credit those countries and nations which, in his judgment, at this time constitute America's first line of defense;

Sixth. The President and the Congress to begin immediately the preparation and the adoption of a defense budget and a tax program adequate for the national defense; and

Seventh. Confer upon the President the power to take into custody for the duration of the defense effort all aliens whose freedom would, in his opinion, jeopardize the defense program.

Concluding those seven points was the reservation: These powers to last for the duration of the emergency only.

Mr. President, in the 10 months which have elapsed since those utterances were made here in this body the world has been made over. Those sinister forces which some thought had come to their culmination in that period 10 months ago have now grown even stronger, and they threaten even a larger area than that which was within the scope and compass of their thought then. Where their strategy at that time was Europe-wide, it has now become the grandest strategy ever conceived in the imagination of mortal man; it is as wide as the circumference of the globe itself; it touches every crucial point upon the face of the earth.

We know, of course, that now the Balkans lie supinely beneath the tyrant's heel; we know also that his army stands poised to strike at the Dardanelles, to take Gibraltar, and perhaps the Suez, almost at will, or within a relatively short time, and maybe possibly after a brief struggle. His power stretches even beyond that, for there is enough to convince any observer that there has been a solemn compact between Japan and Germany, and that, for the first time, the occidental and the oriental conquerors have covenanted to meet in India and bring into cohesion their old world-wide conquest.

A few days ago another significant event occurred. The Foreign Minister of the Japanese Empire came on a bargaining tour, pledging his troth to the highest and best bidder. Consequently, the Japanese renewed their ties of affection and fidelity not only to the Axis Powers, which they joined largely to coerce and threaten the United States of America, but they have added now into their orbit another force that for a time poised, we thought, upon a course of opposition to the Axis. I refer to the Russia of Stalin.

I have had a feeling since the beginning of this controversy that, since national policy is determined by national interest, there would come a time when Russia would move definitely into the orbit of the powers opposing the Axis. I think there has been great shortsightedness on the part, first, of Britain, and, then on the part of the United States of America in dealing with Russia. I think, if we had given greater assurance of strength to those ranks opposing the Axis, Russia would have been, perhaps, in a position to put up a little stronger front on their own part.

I venture to believe that an alternative was put to Russia when this war began: "Will you take a part of the loot of Poland or will you fight?" They very naturally said, "We will take a part of the loot and not fight." And when France was crushed an alternative proposal was again put to them: "Will you take a part of the loot of the Balkans or will you fight?" Again, seeing that England was hard pressed to survive and incapable of giving any aid, seeing that the policy of this country was still uncertain and equivocal, seeing that there was no ally in the Balkans of sufficient power to give them appreciable strength, again they said, not being entirely wedded to democracy, anyhow, "We will take part of the loot and still not fight." I think probably that the alternative is again being put to them: "Will you share the occupancy of the Dardanelles? Will you take part of the Near East? Will you carve up the Old World with us and take a share? Or will you fight?" And again without strength on the horizon apparently great enough to give them assurance of being able to stand out, they took the easy course, the way of least resistance, and said, "We will take the loot and still not fight."

How they salve their conscience, how they appease their judgment against the fateful day when they will have to answer to this Hitler who now breaks off little chunks of the earth and drops them into their supine lap, is a matter of their strategy and destiny, and not of ours. But now we have seen not just the Axis—Germany, Italy, and Japan—but we have seen beyond any question of a doubt that Russia has so much moved into the sphere of that constellation that she has even repudiated the sentiments of friendliness toward the opposing cause that she previously uttered.

We find the culmination of the whole scheme in the recent utterances of the Japanese foreign office, as given by one of their authoritative newspapers, as to what their aims are for a peace with the world. They say, of course, that our own defenses must be weakened; that we must reduce Hawaii to a naval base of relative impotence. They say that we and Britain must reduce the strength of our naval forces until they do not exceed those of the Axis. They say that the Monroe Doctrine shall be abrogated and that North America shall no longer claim the power to influence the destiny and the conduct of South America. Of course, they contemplate that Britain shall retreat from the east and from the Mediterranean and from the other points of advantage which the British hold upon the face of the globe. In other words, they lay down the ultimatum, "Retreat. Retreat. Retreat to your own shrinking sphere, or we will level at you the dastardly methods with which we have so gloriously succeeded in the months and the years past; and eventually you, too, shall crumble beneath this mighty effort."

And then we see Herr Hitler making a report to his Reichstag, which he calls, with sardonic hypocrisy, an elected body; and so he tells them that "the Reich shall live for a thousand years. There is no coalition possible upon the face of the earth that can stand against us." So does it appear, looking over the horizon that confronts the Fuhrer as he sits today, perhaps, upon his Olympian heights. As he stands where the brave Leonidas's men died and gloats over Thermopylae, which he has been able to conquer more gloriously than any tyrant of the past. It may be he will yet have the effrontery to stand on the Acropolis and try to claim for himself the glory of ancient Greece with the power of modern Germany. So this cruel pagan looks out upon the face of the earth and threatens all that comes within his sphere.

The question presents itself, Mr. President, to us, How much longer shall we wait to take the initiative away from the dictators? How many more miles shall we retreat? What other hiding places shall we seek? What new timidity shall clothe our efforts? What further uncertainty and doubt shall characterize our national policy?

Mr. President, how many sheep does a sheep-killing dog have to kill before he is branded as a sheep-killing dog? How many more nations besides the 15 he has already destroyed does Herr Hitler have to take to become the sheep-killing dog of the earth, to be destroyed like that dog which has castigated himself as unfit to live?

The question naturally presents itself to us, When shall we see enough to rouse us from our lethargy, and to make America for once take an affirmative and a positive course that will at last take the initiative away from these braggarts of the tyrannical world?

If modern war has proved anything, it has proved that the advantage lies with the party which takes and presses the initiative; yet in no case have we ventured to assume the initiative. We prefer to sit back here and make our materials, to let the whirl of our factories be indicative of our national effort, and then, fearing to venture upon the high seas against an assassin's weapon, let them go to a useless grave and destination. We prefer to see the world points of advantage seized, from which aggressors can leap at our throat, to wait until they are already there before we attempt to dislodge them or even to become concerned about their presence and the threat they make there.

* * *

Mr. President, in conclusion let me say that I have heard it said that America has a rendezvous with destiny. If we should not be permitted to experience that glorious destiny; if we shall be cut short before we reach the zenith of our glory and power; if that omnipotent God Who has always sheltered and nurtured us has an inglorious end in view for us; insofar as we are the masters of our own destiny, Mr. President, I prefer to see the last gallant American hand reaching, clutching at the standards of the enemy, his body fallen like Pickett's men across the ramparts of the foe and his last gasping breath shouting his sentiments of determination and purpose, and not to see a glorious people surprised in camp or slain supinely in bed.

AMERICAN NATIONAL DEFENSE

A STATE OF EMERGENCY EXISTS [1]

FRANKLIN DELANO ROOSEVELT [2]

President Roosevelt delivered this speech on the evening of May 27, 1941, from the White House. During May the international situation had shifted, to bring the war apparently nearer to the United States. The British battle-cruiser "Hood" had been sunk by the German "Bismark" in Western waters. (The British had taken quick revenge by destroying this largest of German war vessels.) The Allied defenses in Crete were beginning to collapse. In Iraq the forces of opposition to Great Britain were still resisting. German infiltration into Syria had begun. Admiral Raeder, chief officer of the German Navy, had warned America against using convoys. One hundred and forty Americans had been captured from the Egyptian liner "Zamzam" (most of them were later released). The Department of State was trying to ascertain the facts connected with Japan's seizure of ten million dollars worth of American goods in French Indo-China, and the American people wondered whether that incident was not the initiation of a move by Japan to seize that country. The President's personal secretary, Stephen Early, revealed that the White House believed that "the German Government was seeking to influence the President's speech."

Strikes as of June first on defense projects numbered fifty-three and involved more than 57,000 employees. According to the *United States News* (June 13, 1941), "The totals were the largest recorded for any week since the beginning of the defense program." Thus growing Nazi threats, need for maintaining British morale, a considerable tide of questioning on the part of congressmen who confessed that they were in the dark about the facts of the British situation and the urgency of convoys, and the upward curve of C.I.O. and A.F. of L. strikes in automobile, steel, mining, metal trades, and other areas producing war supplies, all furnished the immediate background in which the speech was prepared. From the White House came word that the President

---

[1] By permission of President Roosevelt. The text may be found in the *Congressional Record*, vol. 87, no. 100, May, 28, 1941, Appendix. Compare this text with that found in *Vital Speeches*, 7:508-12, June 1, 1941.

The author is indebted to F. Wilfred Fisher, a graduate student in speech at the State University of Iowa, for part of the data used in this introduction.

[2] For biographical note see Appendix.

"was devoting more time to the preparation of this speech than to any previous address" (*New York Times,* May 27, 1941, p. 4), and that he was rewriting in the light of changed conditions. The United States and even the entire world "awaited to hear the historical presidential utterance" (cf. *Time,* vol. 37, June 9, 1941; *New Republic,* vol. 104, June 2, 1941).

The speech was delivered before a visible audience of three hundred, including the governing board of the Pan American Union, the Canadian Minister, and their families. The invisible audience which the President directly addressed was "my fellow Americans of all the Americas." Sixty-five million Americans listened, and millions of others (the speech was short-waved overseas in fourteen languages). The eventual reach of the speech through newspapers of many countries and radio broadcasts was world wide. It is doubtful whether any previous speech in the history of mankind had been listened to or immediately read by so many human beings.

The speech was uncommonly well organized for a Roosevelt production. The first division stressed the growing Nazi menace to America; the second part, the expanding American methods of combatting this menace. Historic passages in the speech were those in which (1) Roosevelt declared that the Nazi occupation of the Atlantic islands, Iceland, Greenland, Cape Verde Islands, the Azores, would "endanger the freedom of the Atlantic and our own American physical safety"; (2) the United States would not wait until the Western Hemisphere was actually invaded before striking back; (3) goods would be delivered to Britain by whatever American aid (including navy and air forces) might be necessary; (4) help would also be given in full to China; (5) strikes in defense industries would not be tolerated; (6) a national emergency was proclaimed.

What was the public reaction? The dramatic climax with its declaration of national emergency was obviously for psychological effect. For the chief executive already had enormous powers under the Constitution and under the limited emergency. The real significance of the proclamation lay in the intention to apply those powers with more firmness. Roosevelt's policy was to make the public, labor, business, and perhaps the dollar-a-year administrators at Washington more conscious of the critical character of events with respect to Germany.

If voluntary response to the Presidential policies and requests at home should fail, then (so the speech implied) the full exercise of authority would be used. What were some of those Presidential powers? (1) Authority to increase the size of the regular Army and Navy, power to continue in service members of the Reserve and National Guard and the selectees in service; (2) authority to place defense orders in factories and plants and authority to commandeer factories refusing to accept such orders; (3) authority to establish prior ratings in allocating raw materials and in deferring the fulfilment of private orders; (4) authority in labor relations to suspend the eight hour day, to issue a "work or fight" order under the draft law, and to declare martial law and the use of the Army to terminate strikes; (5) authority to take over transportation of railroads, to requisition ships, and to seize and use foreign ships in U.S. ports; (6) power to control radio, telegraph, and telephone systems; (7) power to order public utilities to make interconnections and to take over power houses, dams, and reservoirs for making war materials; (8) power to supervise completely foreign trade; (9) authority to supervise completely banking operations, to engage directly in finance through government lending agencies; (10) authority to prosecute and convict foreign agents, spies, saboteurs; (11) indirect authority to control prices through power to requisition supplies and issue priorities; (12) authority as commander-in-chief of the Army and Navy to take almost any action "deemed advisable to defend the nation, and they (the powers) have seldom been challenged" (*United States News*, 10:12, June 6, 1941).

One immediate illustration of Presidential action following this speech was his sending soldiers with fixed bayonets into the North American Aviation plant at Inglewood, California, and of ending a strike in which the workers had directly defied the Federal Government.

The speech, moreover, was quickly followed by the closing of German and Italian consulates in this country and the severing of diplomatic relations with the Axis powers.

Most Americans listened soberly to the speech and endorsed fully its utterances. The nation's press gave their full approval to the President's stand (*United States News*, 10:12, June 6, 1941). Typical comments were: "The President struck a mighty blow for freedom" (*New York Times*); "This decision is the only decision possible for a people determined to maintain their way of life in a threatening world, and has been made now by the man delegated to make it" (Baltimore, Maryland, *Sun*).

The Executive Council of the American Federation of Labor "announced its agreement with President Roosevelt's declaration" (*New York Times*, May 29, 1941). The C.I.O. leaders, Philip Murray and John L. Lewis, made no comment. Abram Flaxer, of a C.I.O. union, criticised the address severely (*New York Times*, p. 7, May 30, 1941). Senator Wheeler and Colonel Lindbergh attacked the speech; Wendell

Willkie praised it. South American reaction was reserved. The next day, for example, Argentina's Acting President Ramón S. Castillo "reaffirmed" Argentina's neutrality and declared that that country was "friendly to all nations." The British press was naturally delighted. Official Japanese comment, because that country was not mentioned, was not unfavorable. German and Italian official criticism included such terms as "hypocritical," "nonsensical," "demogogic," "defamatory," "warmongering," "tactless," "confused," "unfair," "foggy," "alarmist" (*New York Times,* May 30, p. 9, Associated Press Dispatch, Berlin, May 29, 1941).[3]

My fellow Americans of all the Americas, my friends: I am speaking tonight from the White House in the presence of the governing board of the Pan American Union, the Canadian Minister and their families. The members of this board are the Ambassadors and Ministers of the American republics in Washington. It is appropriate that I do this. For now, as never before, the unity of the American republics is of supreme importance to each and every one of us and to the cause of freedom throughout the world. Our future independence is bound up with the future independence of all of our sister republics.

The pressing problems that confront us are military and naval problems. We cannot afford to approach them from the point of view of wishful thinkers or sentimentalists. What we face is cold, hard fact.

The first and fundamental fact is that what started as a European war has developed, as the Nazis always intended it should develop, into a war for world domination.

Adolf Hitler never considered the domination of Europe as an end in itself. European conquest was but a step toward ultimate goals in all the other continents. It is unmistakably apparent to all of us that unless the advance of Hitlerism is forcibly checked now, the Western Hemisphere will be within range of the Nazi weapons of destruction.

[3] For additional comment on President Roosevelt as a speaker consult previous volumes in this series: *1937-1938,* p. 11, 101; *1938-1939,* p. 25, 36, 97; *1939-1940,* p. 21, 26, 76, 117.

For our own defense we have accordingly undertaken certain obvious necessary measures:

First, we have joined in concluding a series of agreements with all the other American republics. This further solidified our hemisphere against the common danger.

And then, a year ago, we launched, and are successfully carrying out, the largest armament production program we have ever undertaken.

We have added substantially to our splendid navy, and we have mustered our manpower to build up a new army which is already worthy of the highest traditions of our military service.

We instituted a policy of aid for the democracies—the nations which have fought for the continuation of human liberties.

This policy had its origin in the first month of the war, when I urged upon the Congress repeal of the arms embargo provisions in the old Neutrality Law. In that message of September, 1939, I said, "I should like to be able to offer the hope that the shadow over the world might swiftly pass. I cannot. The facts compel my stating, with candor, that darker periods may lie ahead."

In the subsequent months, the shadows did deepen and lengthen. And the night spread over Poland, Denmark, Norway, Holland, Belgium, Luxembourg and France.

In June, 1940, Britain stood alone, faced by the same machine of terror which had overwhelmed her allies. Our Government rushed arms to meet her desperate needs.

In September, 1940, an agreement was completed with Great Britain for the trade of fifty destroyers for eight important offshore bases.

And in March, 1941, this year, the Congress passed the Lend-Lease Bill and an appropriation of $7,000,000,000 to implement it. This law realistically provided for material aid "for the government of any country whose defense the President deems vital to the defense of the United States."

Our whole program of aid for the democracies has been based on hard-headed concern for our own security and for the kind of safe and civilized world in which we wish to live. Every dollar of material that we send helps to keep the dictators away from our own hemisphere. And every day that they are held off gives us time to build more guns and tanks and planes and ships.

We have made no pretense about our own self-interest in this aid. Great Britain understands it—and so does Nazi Germany. And now—after a year—Britain still fights gallantly, on a "far-flung battle line." We have doubled and redoubled our vast production, increasing, month by month, our material supply of the tools of war for ourselves and Britain and China—and eventually for all the democracies.

The supply of these tools will not fail—it will increase.

With greatly augmented strength, the United States and the other American republics now chart their course in the situation of today.

Your Government knows what terms Hitler, if victorious, would impose. They are, indeed, the only terms on which he would accept a so-called "negotiated" peace.

And under those terms Germany would literally parcel out the world—hoisting the swastika itself over vast territories and populations, and setting up puppet governments of its own choosing, wholly subject to the will and the policy of a conqueror.

To the people of the Americas, a triumphant Hitler would say, as he said after the seizure of Austria, and after Munich, and after the seizure of Czechoslovakia: "I am now completely satisfied. This is the last territorial readjustment I will seek." And he would of course add: "All we want is peace, friendship, and profitable trade relations with you in the new world."

Were any of us in the Americas so incredibly simple and forgetful as to accept those honeyed words, what would then happen?

Those in the New World who were seeking profits would be urging that all that the dictatorships desired was "peace." They would oppose toil and taxes for more American armament. Meanwhile, the dictatorships would be forcing the enslaved peoples of their Old World conquests into a system they are even now organizing—to build a naval and air force intended to gain and hold and be master of the Atlantic and the Pacific as well.

They would fasten an economic strangle-hold upon our several nations. Quislings would be found to subvert the governments in our republics; and the Nazis would back their fifth columns with invasion, if necessary.

Now, I am not speculating about all this. I merely repeat what is already in the Nazi book of world conquest. They plan to treat the Latin American nations as they are now treating the Balkans. They plan then to strangle the United States of America and the Dominion of Canada.

The American laborer would have to compete with slave labor in the rest of the world. Minimum wages, maximum hours? Nonsense! Wages and hours fixed by Hitler. The dignity and power and standard of living of the American worker and farmer would be gone. Trade unions would become historic relics and collective bargaining a joke.

Farm income? What happens to all farm surpluses without any foreign trade? The American farmer would get for his products exactly what Hitler wanted to give. And the farmer would face obvious disaster and complete regimentation.

Tariff walls—Chinese walls of isolation—would be futile. Freedom to trade is essential to our economic life. We do not eat all the food we produce; we do not burn all the oil we can pump; we do not use all the goods we can manufacture. It would not be an American wall to keep Nazi goods out; it would be a Nazi wall to keep us in.

The whole fabric of working life as we know it—business, manufacturing, mining, agriculture—all would be mangled and crippled under such a system. Yet to maintain even that crippled independence would require permanent conscription of our manpower, it would curtail the funds we could spend on education, on housing, on public works, on flood control, on health. Instead, we should be permanently pouring our resources into armaments, and year in and year out, standing day and night watch against the destruction of our cities.

Yes, even our right of worship would be threatened. The Nazi world does not recognize any God except Hitler; for the Nazis are as ruthless as the Communists in the denial of God. What place has religion which preaches the dignity of the human being, of the majesty of the human soul, in a world where moral standards are measured by treachery and bribery and fifth columnists? Will our children, too, wander off, goose-stepping in search of new gods?

We do not accept, and will not permit, this Nazi "shape of things to come." It will never be forced upon us, if we act in this present crisis with the wisdom and the courage which have distinguished our country in all the crises of the past.

Today the Nazis have taken military possession of the greater part of Europe. In Africa they have occupied Tripoli and Libya, and they are threatening Egypt, the Suez Canal, and the Near East. But their plans do not stop there, for the Indian Ocean is the gateway to the farther East.

They also have the armed power at any moment to occupy Spain and Portugal; and that threat extends not only to French North Africa and the western end of the Mediterranean Sea, it extends also to the Atlantic fortress of Dakar, and to the island outposts of the New World—the Azores and Cape Verde Islands.

Yes, these Cape Verde Islands, only seven hours distance from Brazil by bomber or troop-carrying planes. They dominate shipping routes to and from the South Atlantic.

The war is approaching the brink of the Western Hemisphere itself. It is coming very close to home.

Control or occupation by Nazi forces of any of the islands of the Atlantic would jeopardize the immediate safety of portions of North and South America, and of the island possessions of the United States, and therefore of the ultimate safety of the continental United States itself.

Hitler's plan of world domination would be near its accomplishment today, were it not for two factors: One is the epic resistance of Britain, her colonies, and the great Dominions, fighting not only to maintain the existence of the Island of Britain, but also to hold the Near East and Africa. The other is the magnificent defense of China, which will, I have reason to believe, increase in strength. All of these, together, are preventing the Axis from winning control of the seas by ships and aircraft.

The Axis powers can never achieve their objective of world domination unless they first obtain control of the seas. That is their supreme purpose today; and to achieve it they must capture Great Britain.

They could then have the power to dictate to the Western Hemisphere. No spurious argument, no appeal to sentiment; and no false pledges like those given by Hitler at Munich, can deceive the American people into believing that he and his Axis partners would not, with Britain defeated, close in relentlessly on this hemisphere of ours.

But if the Axis powers fail to gain control of the seas, they are certainly defeated. Their dreams of world domination will then go by the board; and the criminal leaders who started this war will suffer inevitable disaster.

Both they and their people know this—and they and their people are afraid. That is why they are risking everything they have, conducting desperate attempts to break through to the command of the ocean. Once they are limited to a continuing land war their cruel forces of occupation will be unable to keep their heel on the necks of the millions of innocent, oppressed peoples on the Continent of Europe; and in the end their whole structure will break into little pieces. And let us remember the wider the Nazi land effort the greater is their ultimate danger.

We do not forget the silenced peoples. The masters of Germany—those, at least, who have not been assassinated or escaped to free soil—have marked these silenced peoples and their children's children for slavery. But those people—spiritually unconquered: Austrians, Czechs, Poles, Norwegians, Dutch, Belgians, Frenchmen, Greeks, Southern Slavs—yes, even those Italians and Germans who themselves have been enslaved—will prove to be a powerful force in the final disruption of the Nazi system.

All freedom—meaning freedom to live and not freedom to conquer and subjugate other peoples—depends on freedom of the seas. All of American history—North, Central and South American history—has been inevitably tied up with those words, "freedom of the seas."

Since 1799, 142 years ago, when our infant Navy made the West Indies and the Caribbean and the Gulf of Mexico safe for American ships; since 1804 and 1805, when we made all peaceful commerce safe from the depredations of the Barbary pirates; since the War of 1812, which was fought for the preservation of sailors' rights; since 1867, when our sea power made it possible for the Mexicans to expel the French Army of Louis Napoleon, we have striven and fought in defense of freedom of the seas, freedom of the seas for our own shipping, for the commerce of our sister republics, for the right of all nations to use the highways of world trade, and for our own safety.

During the first World War we were able to escort merchant ships by the use of small cruisers, gunboats, and destroyers; and that type of convoy was effective against submarines. In this second World War, however, the problem is greater, because the attack on the freedom of the seas is now fourfold: First, the improved submarine; second, the much greater use of the heavily armed raiding cruiser or hit-and-run battleship; third, the bombing airplane, which is capable of destroying merchant ships seven or eight hundred miles from its nearest base; and fourth, the destruction of merchant ships in those ports of the world which are accessible to bombing attack.

The battle of the Atlantic now extends from the icy waters of the North Pole to the frozen continent of the Antarctic. Throughout this huge area there have been sinkings of merchant ships in alarming and increasing numbers by Nazi raiders or submarines. There have been sinkings even of ships carrying neutral flags; there have been sinkings in the South Atlantic; off West Africa and the Cape Verde Islands; between the Azores and the islands off the American coast; and between Greenland and Iceland. Great numbers of these sinkings have been actually within the waters of the Western Hemisphere itself.

The blunt truth is this—and I reveal this with the full knowledge of the British Government—the present rate of Nazi sinkings of merchant ships is more than three times as high as the capacity of British shipyards to replace them; it is more than twice the combined British and American output of merchant ships today.

We can answer this peril by two simultaneous measures: First, by speeding up and increasing our great shipbuilding program; and second, by helping to cut down the losses on the high seas.

Attacks on shipping off the very shores of land which we are determined to protect present an actual military danger to the Americas. And that danger has recently been heavily underlined by the presence in Western Hemisphere waters of Nazi battleships of great striking power.

You remember that most of the supplies for Britain go out by a northerly route, which comes close to Greenland and the nearby island of Iceland. Germany's heaviest attack is on that route. Nazi occupation of Iceland or bases in Greenland would bring the war close to our continental shores; because those places are steppingstones to Labrador, Newfoundland, Nova Scotia, and the northern United States, including the great industrial centers of the North, East, and the Middle West.

Equally the Azores and the Cape Verde Islands, if occupied or controlled by Germany, would directly endanger the freedom of the Atlantic and our own physical safety. Under German domination they would become bases for submarines, warships, and airplanes raiding the waters which lie immediately off our own coasts and attacking the shipping in the South Atlantic. They would provide a springboard for actual attack against the integrity and independence of Brazil and her neighboring republics.

I have said on many occasions that the United States is mustering its men and its resources only for purposes of defense— only to repel attack. I repeat that statement now. But we must be realistic when we use the word "attack"; we have to relate it to the lightning speed of modern warfare.

Some people seem to think that we are not attacked until bombs actually drop in the streets of New York or San Francisco or New Orleans or Chicago. But they are simply shutting their eyes to the lesson we must learn from the fate of every nation that the Nazis have conquered.

The attack on Czechoslovakia began with the conquest of Austria. The attack on Norway began with the occupation of Denmark. The attack on Greece began with occupation of Albania and Bulgaria. The attack on the Suez Canal began with the invasion of the Balkans and North Africa. The attack on the United States can begin with the domination of any base which menaces our security—north or south.

Nobody can foretell tonight just when the acts of the dictators will ripen into attack on this hemisphere and us. But we know enough by now to realize that it would be suicide to wait until they are in our front yard.

When your enemy comes at you in a tank or a bombing plane, if you hold your fire until you see the whites of his eyes, you will never know what hit you. Our Bunker Hill of tomorrow may be several thousand miles from Boston, Massachusetts.

Anyone with an atlas and a reasonable knowledge of the sudden striking force of modern war knows that it is stupid to wait until a probable enemy has gained a foothold from which to attack. Old-fashioned common sense calls for the use of a strategy which will prevent such an enemy from gaining a foothold in the first place.

We have, accordingly, extended our patrol in North and South Atlantic waters. We are steadily adding more and more ships and planes to that patrol. It is well known that the strength of the Atlantic fleet has been greatly increased during the past year, and is constantly being built up.

These ships and planes warn of the presence of attacking raiders, on the sea, under the sea, and above the sea. The danger from these raiders is of course greatly lessened if their location is definitely known. We are thus being forewarned; and we shall be on our guard against efforts to establish Nazi bases closer to our hemisphere.

The deadly facts of war compel nations, for simple self-preservation, to make stern choices. It does not make sense, for instance, to say, "I believe in the defense of all the Western Hemisphere," and in the next breath to say, "I will not fight for that defense until the enemy has landed on our shores." And if we believe in the independence and integrity of the Americas, we must be willing to fight to defend them just as much as we would to fight for the safety of our own homes.

It is time for us to realize that the safety of American homes even in the center of our country has a definite relationship to the continued safety of homes in Nova Scotia or Trinidad or Brazil. Our national policy today, therefore, is this:

First, we shall actively resist wherever necessary, and with all our resources, every attempt by Hitler to extend his Nazi domination to the Western Hemisphere, or to threaten it. We shall actively resist his every attempt to gain control of the seas.

We insist upon the vital importance of keeping Hitlerism away from any point in the world which could be used or would be used as a base of attack again the Americas.

Secondly, from the point of view of strict naval and military necessity, we shall give every possible assistance to Britain and to all who, with Britain, are resisting Hitlerism or its equivalent with force of arms. Our patrols are helping now to insure delivery of the needed supplies to Britain. All additional measures necessary to deliver the goods will be taken. Any and all further methods or combination of methods, which can or should be utilized, are being devised by our military and naval technicians, who, with me, will work out and put into effect such new and additional safeguards as may be needed.

I say that the delivery of needed supplies to Britain is imperative. I say this can be done; it must be done; it will be done.

To the other American nations—twenty republics and the Dominion of Canada—I say this: the United States does not merely propose these purposes, but is actively engaged today in carrying them out.

I say to them further: You may disregard those few citizens of the United States who contend that we are disunited and cannot act.

There are some timid ones among us who say that we must preserve peace at any price—lest we lose our liberties forever. To them I say this, never in the history of the world has a nation lost its democracy by a successful struggle to defend its democracy. We must not be defeated by the fear of the very danger which we are preparing to resist. Our freedom has shown its ability to survive war, but our freedom would never survive surrender. "The only thing we have to fear is fear itself."

There is, of course, a small group of sincere, patriotic men and women whose real passion for peace has shut their eyes to the ugly realities of international banditry and to the need to resist it at all costs. I am sure they are embarrassed by the sinister support they are receiving from the enemies of democracy in our midst—the Bundists, the Fascists, and the Communists, and every group devoted to bigotry and racial and religious intolerance.

It is no mere coincidence that all the arguments put forward by these enemies of democracy—all their attempts to confuse and divide our people and to destroy public confidence in government—all their defeatist forebodings that Britain and democracy are already beaten—all their selfish promises that we can "do business" with Hitler—all of these are but echoes of the words that have been poured out from the Axis bureaus of propaganda. Those same words have been used before in other countries—to scare them, to divide them, to soften them up. Invariably, those same words have formed the advance guard of physical attack.

Your Government has the right to expect of all citizens that they take part in the common work of our common defense—take loyal part from this moment forward.

I have recently set up the machinery for civilian defense. It will rapidly organize, locality by locality. It will depend on the organized effort of men and women everywhere. All will have opportunities and responsibilities to fulfil.

Defense today means more than merely fighting. It means morale, civilian as well as military; it means using every available resource; it means enlarging every useful plant. It means the use of a greater American common sense in discarding rumor and distorted statement. It means recognizing, for what they are, racketeers and fifth columnists, the incendiary bombs in this country at the moment.

All of us know that we have made very great social progress in recent years. We propose to maintain that progress and strengthen it. When the nation is threatened from without, however, as it is today, the actual production and transportation of the machinery of defense must not be interrupted by disputes between capital and capital, labor and labor, or capital and labor. The future of all free enterprise—of capital and labor alike—is at stake.

This is no time for capital to make, or to be allowed to retain excess profits. Articles of defense must have undisputed right of way in every industrial plant in the country.

A nation-wide machinery for conciliation and mediation of industrial disputes has been set up. That machinery must be used promptly—and without stoppage of work. Collective bargaining will be retained, but the American people expect that impartial recommendations of our government conciliation and mediation services will be followed both by capital and by labor.

The overwhelming majority of our citizens expect their Government to see that the tools of defense are built; and for the very purpose of preserving the democratic safeguards of both labor and management, this Government is determined to use all of its powers to express the will of its people, and to prevent interference with the production of materials essential to our nation's security.

Today the whole world is divided, divided between human slavery and human freedom, divided between pagan brutality and the Christian ideal.

We choose human freedom—which is the Christian ideal.

No one of us can waver for a moment in his courage or his faith.

We will not accept a Hitler-dominated world. And we will not accept a world, like the postwar world of the Nineteen Twenties in which the seeds of Hitlerism can again be planted and allowed to grow.

We will accept only a world consecrated to freedom of speech and expression—freedom of every person to worship God in his own way—freedom from want—and freedom from terror.

Is such a world impossible of attainment?

Magna Carta, the Declaration of Independence, the Constitution of the United States, the Emancipation Proclamation and every other milestone in human progress—all were ideals which seemed impossible of attainment—yet they were attained.

As a military force, we were weak when we established our independence, but we successfully stood off tyrants, powerful in their day, tyrants who are now lost in the dust of history.

Odds meant nothing to us then. Shall we now, with all our potential strength, hesitate to take every single measure necessary to maintain our American liberties?

Our people and our Government will not hesitate to meet that challenge.

As the President of a united and determined people, I say solemnly:

We reassert the ancient American doctrine of freedom of the seas.

We reassert the solidarity of the twenty-one American republics and the Dominion of Canada in the preservation of the independence of the hemisphere.

We have pledged material support to the other democracies of the world—and we will fulfil that pledge.

We in the Americas will decide for ourselves whether and when and where our American interests are attacked or our security threatened.

We are placing our armed forces in strategic military position.

We will not hesitate to use our armed forces to repel attack.

We reassert our abiding faith in the vitality of our constitutional republic as a perpetual home of freedom, of tolerance and of devotion to the word of God.

Therefore, with profound consciousness of my responsibilities to my countrymen and to my country's cause, I have tonight issued a proclamation that an unlimited national emergency exists and requires the strengthening of our defense to the extreme limit of our national power and authority.

The nation will expect all individuals and all groups to play their full parts without stint, without selfishness and without doubt that our democracy will triumphantly survive.

I repeat the words of the signers of the Declaration of Independence—that little band of patriots, fighting long ago against overwhelming odds but certain, as we are now of ultimate victory: "With firm reliance on the protection of Divine Providence, we mutually pledge to each other our lives, our fortunes and our sacred honor."

OUR AIR DEFENSE [4]

Charles A. Lindbergh [5]

Colonel Charles Lindbergh appeared before the House Committee on Foreign Affairs, on January 23, 1941, to testify concerning H.R. 1776, known as the "Lend-Lease Bill," designed to give President Roosevelt authority to "sell, transfer, lend, lease, or otherwise dispose of" any defense articles to friendly powers.

Opponents of the bill, led by Senator Wheeler, argued that (1) it would give the President dictatorial powers, (2) it would allow the country to be led into the war, and (3) as a result of such participation it would wreck this country forever. Supporters argued that (1) the grant was needed, for speed was necessary, (2) the bill would give efficient help to England, and (3) the crisis was so great that only complete help would accomplish anything.

Senator Burton Wheeler, bitter isolationist, said that the bill would "plough under every fourth American boy," a statement that the President denounced as "dastardly," and "unpatriotic."

Before the House Foreign Affairs Committee, Secretary of State Cordell Hull opened the testimony for the bill. He talked for four and one-half hours. Secretary of the Treasury Henry Morgenthau, with a staff of experts, followed. Secretary of War Stimson, and others also appeared. Among those summoned who criticised the bill were Joseph Kennedy, Norman Thomas, and Charles Lindbergh.

The procedure of the committee hearing called for a formal statement, followed by cross-examination that sometimes lasted for hours. The atmosphere was informal. Testimony was sometimes interrupted by demonstrations by spectators. The committee usually applauded witnesses upon retiring. Committee discussion has served an important function in American Congressional government. The committee chamber has been the scene of highly important speaking as illustrated by the series of hearings on the lend-lease measure.

The principal questions under consideration were: (1) Does England face defeat? (2) Would American aid prevent such disaster? (3) Does it matter to the United States if England is destroyed? (4) Is the United States open to attack? (5) Will the proposed law mean war? (6) Will the proposed law give the President too much authority?

[4] By permission of Colonel Charles A. Lindbergh. Text taken from Hearings Before the Committee on Foreign Affairs, House of Representatives, 77th Congress, First Session, on H.R. 1776, p. 371-436.

[5] For biographical note see Appendix.

Colonel Lindbergh told the committee that the United States was not open to invasion by air, and upheld this assertion in cross-examination. He did not believe that, barring internal collapse in Germany, Britain, even with American aid, could win the war. He stated that he wanted neither side to win.

On February 5th he appeared before the Senate committee to testify. His remarks on these occasions caused much comment. Thomas W. Lamont, Secretaries Knox, Stimson, Ickes, and many other prominent Americans denounced him, and most of the newspapers as well. A prominent Texan proposed that he be deported, and President Roosevelt (in April) classified him as a "copperhead." (Lindbergh resigned as Colonel in the United States Army Reserve Corps.)

On the other hand, Senator Nye suggested that Lindbergh should go to Congress. His (Lindbergh's) position was hailed as "courageous" by Berlin and Rome officials and newspapers.

For some two weeks the House committee heard testimony, twenty-seven witnesses in all. The committee sent the bill to the floor of Congress, as did the Senate committee later. After brief debate in the House and much longer consideration in the Senate, the proposal was finally enacted into law in substantially its original condition.

During the period from February to July, 1941, especially after Colonel Lindbergh became active as a member of the America First Committee, he delivered a series of addresses in opposition to the Administration program of aid to Britain. Representative of these addresses were his speech at Madison Square Garden, New York City, on April 23, 1941, and the one at Minneapolis, on May 11, 1941.

Because of the frequency of his speaking appearances and the factual and comparatively unemotional character of his remarks, the question arose as to the possibility of whether a "ghost writer" prepared his manuscripts. In reply to a query from Senator Bennett Champ Clark, Lindbergh stated (See *New York Times*, February 7, 1941, p. 6): "No one has taken any important part in writing any of my addresses. I say no important part, but I always like to have my wife look over them. Beyond that no one has written a paragraph of them."

I understand that I have been asked to appear before this committee to discuss the effect of aviation upon America's position in time of war. I believe that this effect can be summed up briefly by saying that our position is greatly strengthened for defense and greatly weakened for attack.

I base this statement upon two facts. First, that an invading army and its supplies must still be transported by sea. Second, that aviation makes it more difficult than ever before for a navy to approach a hostile shore.

In support of these facts, I cite, for the first, the minute carrying capacity of aircraft in relation to the weight of equipment and supplies required for a major expeditionary force; and for the second, the experience of the British Navy off the Norwegian coast and in the North Sea.

I do not believe there is any danger of an invasion of this continent, either by sea or by air, as long as we maintain an army, navy and air force of reasonable size and in modern condition, and provided we establish the bases essential for defense.

How large our air force should be in actual numbers depends, of course, upon conditions in other parts of the world. Because of the existing European crisis, I should say that we would be wise to construct as rapidly as possible a total air force of about 10,000 thoroughly modern fighting planes plus reserves.

This number would, I believe, be adequate to insure American security regardless of the outcome of the present European war. Whether our air force should be increased or decreased in the more distant future will be decided by circumstances which we cannot now foresee. But an industry capable of building and maintaining a 10,000 plane force would, I believe, have adequate flexibility to meet any emergency with which we might be confronted in this hemisphere.

Accompanying this expansion of our air force should be the construction of aviation bases in Newfoundland, Canada, the West Indies, parts of South America, Central America, the Galapagos Islands, the Hawaiian Islands and Alaska. Secondary bases might be placed in parts of Greenland, but in my opinion Greenland is not of primary importance from the standpoint of aviation bases.

Since many people are discussing the possibility of an air invasion of America, I would like permission to bring a few points to your attention in this connection. It is first necessary to establish clearly the difference between an air invasion where troops are landed and a bombing raid where there is no attempt to establish a base on enemy territory. I will treat these two problems separately, for they are entirely different.

There has never been an invasion of enemy territory by air alone. The two outstanding examples of what might be called a partial air invasion were furnished by the German occupations of Norway and Holland. But in each of these instances the landing of troops by air was carried on simultaneously with a ground army invasion on a major scale. The maximum number of troops that could have been transported and supplied by air would have been ineffective without the immediate support of a ground army. If air invasion alone could be successful, it would have been used by the Germans against England many months ago.

It is important to note that the transport of troops by air in Europe has been over a distance of a few hundred miles at most. An air invasion across the ocean is, I believe, absolutely impossible at this time, or in any predictable future. To be effective in America, enemy aircraft would have to operate from bases in America, and those bases would have to be established and supplied by sea. Aircraft alone are not capable of carrying a sufficient quantity of material.

Claims have been made that America might be subject to air invasion by way of Alaska or Greenland, where the distance between land is short. But such claims overlook the difficulties of climate and terrain in these semi-arctic areas. If air routes to Asia and Europe through the North were preferable to the greater over-water distances farther south, they would have been used years ago by commercial airlines.

It is, of course, essential for us to maintain defense bases in Alaska. I believe that we should wage war with all of our resources if an invasion of Alaska or any other portion of America were attempted. But a sudden air invasion of this country by way of Alaska is out of the question. The conquest of Alaska would necessitate the movement of troops and supplies by ground and sea, the defeat of our own forces and the establishment of enemy bases. Even if that could be accomplished, there is little likelihood that the wilds of Canada could be crossed and the United States invaded by an army based upon remote Alaskan outposts of Asiatic or European powers.

If an enemy were planning on an invasion of America, I believe that the route over Greenland is one of the last he would consider. I spent several weeks in Greenland in the summer of 1933, surveying the coasts for air bases, and studying the conditions that would be encountered in operating a northern air route. I came to the conclusion that of all the possible air routes between America and Europe the one over Greenland would be the most difficult to establish and operate. Except for a rugged and mountainous strip around the coast, Greenland is covered with ice. The climate is uncertain and severe, the summer season is short, and the seas are filled with ice during the entire year.

The question of transoceanic bombing is, as I have said, entirely different from that of air invasion. It is, of course, perfectly possible today to build bombing planes that could cross the ocean, drop several tons of bombs, and return to their starting point. Transoceanic bombing raids could do considerable damage on peacetime standards, but they would have very little effectiveness on wartime standards. The cost of transoceanic bombing would be extremely high, enemy losses would be large, and the effect on our military position negligible.

Such bombing could not begin to prepare the way for an invasion of this continent. If England is able to live at all with bases of German air force less than an hour's flight away, the United States is not in great danger across the Atlantic Ocean. Not only is such bombing ineffective theoretically, but from a practical standpoint it is interesting to note that not a single squadron of transoceanic bombing planes exists anywhere in the world today.

I have, up to this point, attempted to show that aviation strengthens the defensive position of America. First, because it is impossible for an enemy to invade this continent by means of aircraft alone; second, because transoceanic bombing is indecisive; third, because our own air force makes it more difficult than ever before for an enemy to approach our shores.

However, I believe we are faced with the reverse situation when we contemplate sending our military forces abroad. Almost every advantage we have in defense would be a disadvantage to us in attack. It would then be our problem to cross the sea in ships and force a landing against the established air bases of our enemy.

If one studies the situation objectively, it becomes obvious that there are three great centers of air strength in the world today: the United States, Germany and Japan. Up to the present time we have led in the development of commercial aviation. Germany has led in the development of military aviation and Japan has led in the development of aviation in the Orient.

Since Oriental aviation is far behind that of Western nations, one might say that there are two great aviation powers; one in America and one in Europe. Personally, I do not believe it is possible for either America or Europe to invade the other successfully by air, or even by a combination of air, land and sea, unless an internal collapse precedes invasion.

In this sense aviation has added to America's security against Europe, and to Europe's security against America. One might sum the matter up by saying that aviation decreases the security of nations within a continent against each other, but increases the security of the continent as a whole against foreign invasion.

That aviation will have a great effect on the future relationship of nations is beyond question. But we in America are possibly the most fortunate of all peoples in this respect. We have a country and climate well suited to the development of aircraft. We have natural resources, great industries and a national psychology ideally adapted to the tempo of the air.

In conclusion, I would like to say that aviation is to us unquestionably an asset. It greatly strengthens our position and increases the security of this entire hemisphere from foreign attack.

WARTIME PRICE CONTROL [6]

Harold G. Moulton [7]

Dr. Harold G. Moulton delivered this address at the dinner meeting of the Maurice and Laura Falk Foundation, held in observance of its tenth anniversary, at the Hotel Schenley, Pittsburgh, Pennsylvania, September 24, 1940. Mr. Maurice Falk endowed the Foundation in 1929. The general purpose of the trust was for "the encouragement, improvement, and betterment of mankind." He stipulated that the principal and interest of the fund should be used within thirty-five years. The Foundation gave specific grants to competent economic organizations to finance definitive studies affecting the development of American industry, trade, and finance.

On the program besides Leon Falk, Chairman of the Board, Mr. Gow, and Mr. Moulton, were Leo Wolman, of the Research Staff of the National Bureau of Economic Research and Alfred P. Sloan, Jr., Chairman of the Board, General Motors Corporation.

The principles enunciated by Mr. Moulton in this address, although set forth in September, 1940, were even more timely in June, 1941. A great issue before the Administration at Washington, before American business, as well as the rank and file of the consumers, was, Would prices spiral under the huge national defense expenditures? Would inflation be inevitable? Early in 1941 President Roosevelt appointed Leon Henderson as price controller of the Defense Commission, or more popularly as "Price Boss."

Without much legal authority (as of June, 1941) except as he operated as part of the Executive branch, Henderson in attempting to control prices, relied largely on persuasion and patriotism rather than on coercion. He used as a club both "priorities" in the allocation of materials, and publicity. His economic philosophy was that (a) civil consumption should not be cut merely by allowing prices to rise; (b) that price increases in copper, steel, and other basic materials would not really develop much new capacity; (c) that to avoid inflation we should deal with heavy taxation (increase income taxes), various methods of compulsory saving, expansion of production, arbitrary control of prices (perhaps by congressional legislation). A long war, he believed, was in prospect. We must profit by the economic experiences with prices in 1917 (Bernard Baruch, chairman of the War Industries Board in the first World War was advising Henderson). The American

---

[6] By permission of Mr. Moulton. Text supplied through the courtesy of the speaker. Reproduced from *Proceedings of the Dinner Meeting of the Maurice and Laura Falk Foundation,* 1940, J. Steele Gow, Executive Director, Pittsburgh, Pennsylvania.

[7] For biographical note see Appendix.

problem was to "swamp Hitler with production while maintaining morale by avoiding inflation." Nevertheless, by July 1, 1941, food prices in the United States were skyrocketing, wages were higher than ever before in American history, and the outlook suggested a new wave of wage increase demands. Prices in general threatened to follow closely the trend of the first World War.

In view of such economic record since September, 1940, were the principles outlined by Moulton adequate to prevent disaster through inflation? Dr. Moulton, President of the Brookings Institution, has a reputation for sound thinking and solid research.[8] Also he is unusually effective as a speaker on economic themes.

At Albion College and at the University of Chicago he participated in intercollegiate debates and was elected to Delta Sigma Rho, intercollegiate debate society. For five years he was also coach of the University of Chicago debating team. (He was also professor of economics there until he became director of the Institute of Economics at Washington and later director of Brookings Institution.)

In the preparation of his addresses he finds it a "great help to prepare a series of key sentences which state precisely the thread of the argument." Another of his methods is to organize his entire address around a series of issues or arguments.

In delivering a written address he adopts several procedures: He writes the speech on half-size sheets. This arrangement keeps the "minimum possible amount of paper between the speaker and the audience." He reads the address over often enough so that he doesn't need to keep his eyes continually glued on the manuscript. He can "give at least two thirds of a sentence without looking at the manuscript." He is thus able to keep eye contact with all parts of his audience and project himself more effectively in his delivery. He sometimes amplifies his address in the light of the audience responses. "Frequently one will note from the response of the audience that the point needs emphasis or elaboration. In any case additions to the manuscript help to break the monotony of straight reading." And Dr. Moulton adds a bit of rare wisdom: "I make it a point not to tell stories which are unrelated to the field under consideration." [9]

The most striking economic phenomenon of every great war of modern times has been the enormous inflation in prices which has occurred. In the light of this history, the most insistent question of the present moment—when we are embarking on a defense program comparable in scope and potential economic effects to a major war effort—is whether a new era

[8] Those who study this address should also consult Dr. Moulton's "Fundamental Economic Issues in National Defense," Pamphlet No. 26, 1941, The Brookings Institution, Washington, D.C.

[9] Letter to the author, March 28, 1941.

of inflation is inevitable. Concern is intensified by the fact that the present war program begins at a time when the federal debt is 70 per cent higher than at the end of the World War and treasury deficits are already at wartime levels.

A glance at a price chart reveals that since 1800 there have been three great inflation periods—during the Napoleonic Wars, during the American Civil War, and during the World War. In each instance the general level of prices increased something like two-fold; and it is to be noted that the three price peaks of 1815, 1865, and 1920 were close to the same height. In between these mountain tops lie great price valleys. There were precipitate declines for some years after each war, then a flattening out into undulating plains, marked by occasional hills and hollows. Wartime price inflations have thus been the dominating influence in the great price fluctuations of modern times.

These price disruptions exert a profound influence upon the economic life of a nation. During the war the rise in prices works against the efficient mobilization of the nation's resources. This is because the inflation process affects prices, profits, rents, and wage rates very unevenly and thus creates arbitrary and useless changes in the distribution of income, resulting in a wholly irrational allocation of the war burden between different groups in the community. These developments lead to endless controversies involving losses in productive efficiency and the absorption of energies in trying to adjust or settle controversies and to maintain some semblance of national unity. The result is a slowing down of the mobilization program and a corresponding increase in the costs and suffering involved in a great war struggle. In some given case, moreover, it might well mean the difference between victory and defeat.

The postwar decline in prices exerts an equally important influence upon economic conditions. The deflation following the Civil War, for example, profoundly affected the position of all those who had contracted long-term indebtedness during the period of high prices and led to controversies and inflationary movements which lasted for a generation.

In the light of these facts, it is evident that the prevention of a wartime price inflation is of absolutely vital importance. It is not too much to say that the ability of this nation to ride the storms which now confront us and to come at last to calm harbors will largely depend upon the extent to which we are able to restrain the forces which make for wartime price inflation.

If we are to develop an effective control over prices it is necessary that we have a clear understanding of the sources of price disturbance. Analysis of price movements in past wars reveals that price distortions occur as a result of a number of operating factors. The principal factors conducive to price increases are the following:

The first factor is the placing of large government orders on a *competitive* basis. During the World War both the allied governments and different departments of our own government bid frantically against one another for scarce products, the result of which was to run up prices far beyond the level that would have been necessary under a system of coordinated buying.

The second force is the great increase of business orders for inventories or for plant expansion—in anticipation of coming shortages or expected price advances. Unless there happen to be large surpluses of basic materials or much un-utilized productive capacity this expansion of orders will shortly lead to a marking up of prices. In addition to advance buying by business organizations, there may also be extensive commodity speculation both on the organized exchanges and on the part of independent speculators.

The third factor promoting price inflation is the increase in wage rates. As the supply of labor, especially of skilled types, becomes scarce, business enterprises, government shipyard, etc. seek to procure workers by the lure of higher wages. At the same time labor organizations, taking advantage of the favorable labor market, make insistent demands for higher wages. Wage increases in war lines exert a pressure toward higher wages in non-war lines. This general increase in wage rates exerts a direct pressure, from the cost side, toward a universal rise in commodity prices. Moreover, once prices have advanced, whether because of the wage increases or for other reasons, an increase in wage rates is said to be made necessary by the rising costs of living.

It is commonly assumed that prices rise faster than wages and that in consequence the buying power of the working population is decreased, notwithstanding the increase in wage rates. This widespread belief is, as a rule, without foundation. During the World War period the earnings of labor constantly rose faster than the cost of living. This fact is clearly revealed by a chart showing the trend of weekly earnings of labor, wholesale prices, and retail prices during the war years. The rise in weekly earnings continuously ran ahead of the general cost of living index, which includes foodstuffs and rents, as well as general manufactured products. Weekly earnings lagged somewhat as compared with wholesale prices, but the significant comparison from the standpoint of purchasing power is the cost of living index. The increase in weekly earnings was due in part to advances in hourly rates and in part to the increase in the number of hours worked per week. *Family* wages per week, and especially per year, rose even more than the wages of individual workers, for the simple reason that, typically speaking, more members of the family became wage-earners. Family purchasing power ran far ahead of the increase in the cost of living.

The fourth major source of price stimulus is found in the expansion of consumer buying power. The increase in the total volume of production and employment leads to an increase in real wages, as already noted, and also in profits and dividends.

The resulting increase in consumer purchasing power leads to an increase in the demand for consumption goods, creating a "seller's market" conducive to price increases. Added to this increase in consumer purchasing power is the increase in government purchasing power—which is usually derived in no small degree from credit expansion—for reasons shortly to be discussed.

These interacting factors bring about in due course the familiar spiral of rising prices—rising costs—rising prices—etc. Once the movement is strongly under way it is impossible to check it through the machinery of price control—except by methods which would result in the crippling of the whole war program. This was the experience of the price-fixing authorities during the World War both in the United States and in European countries.

If we are to control prices in wartime it is obviously necessary to begin before the inflationary process is in full sweep; the inflationary forces must be checked at their sources.

First, the Army and Navy departments should not be given blank checks with which to compete against each other on a *price* basis for limited supplies of materials. Contracts should be made so as to yield a reasonable return to producers rather than on a basis of what a wholly abnormal market situation might make possible. I think we may safely assume that the mistakes along this line made in the last war will not often be repeated.

Second, the principle that prices should be allowed to rise to whatever height is necessary to call forth additional output from high-cost producers should not be adopted. This principle, or a modification known as the bulk-line principle, was extensively employed in the World War on the theory that high prices constituted the essential inducement to increased output, and that the resulting excessive profits of the lower-cost producers could readily be skimmed off by means of an excess profits tax. Experience showed that this policy enormously distorted the price structure and that the levying of high excess profits taxes was in no sense an adequate corrective. That is to say, not only could the excess profits tax not prevent the evil consequences of the distortion of the price structure, but it could not even satisfy the public that the industries of the country were not engaged in war profiteering. Instead of allowing a distortion of the price structure to insure the production of but a minor fraction of the total supply required, such additional output should be procured by means of subsidies or other direct methods.

Third, wage rates should not be increased except where necessary in the interests of health and efficiency. It should be carefully noted that in the early stages of a war, when the slack in the economic system is being taken up, wages will rise even though wage *rates* remain stationary. This is because the number of hours worked per week and especially per year increases. If price inflation can be avoided it is therefore unnecessary to increase wage rates in order to prevent a deterioration of living standards.

The payment of time and a half for over-time is of course equivalent to an increase in wage rates. This extra pay for the additional hours increases costs of production and exerts a pressure toward higher prices. In some lines the added labor cost may be absorbed, particularly in the early stages of a war, but in other lines it would mean immediate advances in prices. Once a movement for higher money wages is well under way no power exists which can prevent a development of the vicious spiral of inflation.

Fourth, the war should be financed just as far as possible without resort to credit expansion. We noted among the forces leading to inflation the expansion of consumer buying power, together with a great increase in government buying power. The expansion in consumer buying power arises, as we have seen, from the increase of wages and dividends resulting from the expansion of employment and production. Unless this increased buying power is diverted from consumer markets, the general public will be competing against the government for materials and supplies that enter into the war production program. If the government obtains its funds from bank credit expansion, the total money income available for expansion is increased relatively to the supply of goods and services and the resulting market competition is inevitably conducive to price advances.

For this reason it is of vital importance that the war should be financed just as far as possible from taxes and from loans paid for out of current income. By these means income which would otherwise be spent for consumer goods would be diverted to the Treasury and made available for expenditure by the government for the war materials required, thereby avoiding an expansion of money purchasing power relatively to the supply of available goods and services. This process, moreover, facilitates rather than retards the shifting of our productive energies into war lines. Such a policy is a fundamental part of any sound, comprehensive program of price control.

During the World War the financial methods employed were about as bad as it is possible to conceive. Not only was the tax program slow of development and inadequate in its scope, but the loan program was fundamentally faulty in its basic conception. Preoccupied with the naive view that money would win the war, that all that was necessary was to make sure that the Treasury had unlimited funds at its disposal, we raised vast sums by means of credit expansion. Not only were government bonds sold directly to the banks, but those sold to the public were paid for in no small degree with funds borrowed from the banks. In consequence the government had an abundance of funds but found it difficult to procure the essential supplies because of the competition of consumers whose incomes were expanding rather than contracting. At the same time, there were overly liberal extensions of bank credit to private enterprises, the only result of which was to

increase the capacity of particular companies to bid for inadequate supplies of materials and labor. Such loans were extended
to enterprises engaged in non-essential activities as well as to
those engaged in the production of war supplies. They were,
moreover, extended on a vast scale for speculative purposes,
particularly in the field of agriculture.

The control of prices along the lines suggested requires
the development of coordinated administrative machinery. It
cannot be satisfactorily accomplished by a series of price-control
agencies, operating independently of one another, nor can it
be accomplished by a central price authority unless such
authority envisages the problem in all its aspects and articulates
the whole in a unified program. Moreover, the program must
be coordinated from the very beginning of the mobilization
process.

The question must now be raised whether it is reasonable
to believe that a very substantial inflation of prices could
be prevented in wartime—even though the economic principles and administrative procedures adopted were of the
best. Does not a great war in the very nature of the case
necessitate such extensive readjustments of the economic structure and involve such a weakening or exhausting of resources
as inevitably to bring higher costs and prices? Putting the
matter another way—Does not the impoverishment which a
protracted war involves necessarily reflect itself in rising prices?

In a war involving extensive destruction of a nation's productive facilities by enemy forces, there can be no doubt that the
impairment of productive efficiency will result in higher costs
and higher prices. Moreover, in the case of a protracted war
of attrition there appears little question that the gradual weakening of productive power would manifest itself in rising prices.
But in a relatively short war in which the nation's territory is
not invaded or effectively bombarded by the enemy there is
no *underlying economic necessity* for an extensive inflation
of prices.

Applying these conceptions to the present American defense program there would seem to be little reason for assuming that an extensive rise in prices is necessary. The program was launched at a time when our production facilities—in most lines—were being utilized at much less than capacity. The program, as now projected, is of a magnitude smaller than the existing slack in the industrial system. National production is now running at about 70 billion dollars annually and we could perhaps produce as much as 85 billions. Making allowance for necessary concentrations of production it should still be possible to meet requirements in the main out of productive resources hitherto unutilized. This means that during the period when we are taking up the industrial slack we will be making a more effective use of our productive resources. In terms of energy we would be operating under conditions of increasing returns; real costs per unit of product would be declining. There would thus be no *necessity* for rising prices. In this connection it may be noted that business men have an opportunity to aid in maintaining price stability by refraining from advancing prices until forced to do so by rising *unit costs* —even though market conditions might be such as to make higher prices possible without loss of sales.

It is only when we reach the stage of shortages, involving the employment of less efficient labor, the utilization of obsolete or defective equipment, and the use of inferior materials, produced under unfavorable conditions because of war displacements, that costs, in real terms, begin to rise. In some lines of war production these tendencies may manifest themselves fairly early but in most lines they will be delayed for a considerable period. Moreover, they may in substantial degree be continuously offset by the prompt introduction of improvements in production technique. By utilizing all the technological knowledge and patented devices already available, the new installations of plant and equipment may largely offset the cost increasing factors to which reference has been made.

It is my considered judgment that there is no economic necessity for any substantial price inflation in connection with the present emergency defense program. If it occurs it will be because of a lack of adequate understanding of the sources of price disturbance or the adoption of unwise administrative procedures rather than because of any inherent economic impossibility of meeting defense burdens on the existing level of prices.

At the outset of this address attention was called to the fact that the present war emergency has come at a time when the federal debt is of an unprecedented magnitude and current deficits are at wartime levels. Are we not, therefore, inevitably faced with so rapid an increase in the public debt as to lead to financial disintegration which would be followed inevitably by inflation? Time permits but the briefest statement with respect to this problem.

It is my conclusion that it should be possible to finance the defense program without increasing the magnitude of current treasury deficits. An expansion of national income of 65 or 70 billions, the recent level, to from 75 to 80 billions might well be expected in 1941-42. (This is on the assumption that Great Britain is not defeated and that foreign demands will continue at something like present levels.) This rise in national income accompanied by increases in taxes should lead to a marked increase in federal revenues. At the same time the process will be accompanied by a very material reduction in the volume of unemployment, and hence in the amount of relief and kindred expenditures. Numerous other types of expenditures may and should be reduced in the interest of the most effective waging of the war. The fuller utilization of our national resources which the war program involves makes it possible to maintain fiscal stability. The outcome will depend primarily upon the degree of determination manifested by the fiscal authorities—congressional and otherwise—to maintain financial equilibrium.

THE PRESIDENTIAL CAMPAIGN OF 1940

ACCEPTANCE SPEECH [1]

Wendell L. Willkie [2]

Wendell Willkie in this address on Saturday, August 17, 1940, in Callaway Park, at Elwood, Indiana, accepted the nomination for the Presidency on the Republican ticket. The nomination itself was made on June 28, at the Philadelphia Convention of that party. Willkie had been put in nomination by Congressman Charles Halleck of Indiana, on June 26. On the first two ballots Thomas Dewey had led, with Robert Taft second; Willkie carried a majority of the votes on the sixth ballot. The nomination was generally regarded as one of "the people's choice" rather than that of the party politicians, and seemed to be the result of a spontaneous uprising of anti-Rooseveltians throughout the nation.

The audience was remarkable for its size. Elwood's 11,000 was reinforced by an army of 150,000 or 200,000. The crowd came in "60,000 autos, 63 special trains, 300 pullmans, 1200 busses." Many visiting delegations brought drum corps and bands; each group paraded through the streets. A Chicago delegation brought along an elephant; a group from Cincinnati brought three of these G.O.P. animals!

Thirty-five thousand persons sat before the speaker; three or four times that number stood behind and stretched far beyond the grove of the park. Observers agreed that it was the largest visible audience ever to hear a presidential acceptance speech, at least twice as large as the thousands upon thousands that listened to Roosevelt's acceptance speech at Franklin Field, Philadelphia, in 1936.

Mr. Willkie had come from Rushville on a private train that morning and had addressed a meeting of neighbors at Elwood High School. Representative Joseph Martin, minority leader of the House and chairman of the Republican National Committee, delivered the notification speech.

The speech, 6000 words in length, represented weeks of conferences and hours of writing. Mr. Willkie went to Colorado Springs on July 9 to rest and to prepare the address. At his hotel during the next thirty-seven days he is estimated to have talked with at

[1] By permission of Mr. Willkie. Reprinted from the *Congressional Record,* vol. 86, no. 150, p. 16108-11, August 19, 1940 (daily edition), proceedings and debates of the 76th Congress, third session.

[2] For biographical sketch see Appendix.

least "three thousand persons." Nevertheless he also found time for considerable research and general reading, including Carl Snyder's *Capitalism the Creator*, Morris Ernest's *Too Big*, Harold Laski's *The American Presidency*, *The Dissenting Opinions of Mr. Justice Holmes*.

"When Mr. Willkie arrived in Colorado Springs he was already planning the acceptance speech in his mind. Then he put a general outline down on paper. The many conferences helped to crystallize his thoughts, but he had outside help on specific sections. William Allen White, the Kansas editor; Lewis W. Douglas, former Budget Director, and General Hugh Johnson gave opinions on foreign policy. General Johnson also discussed national defense and conscription with him. For agriculture Mr. Willkie drew upon L. J. Taber, master of the National Grange; Earl Smith, head of the Illinois Farm Bureau, and many farm representatives he saw at Des Moines. Claude Baker, head of the International Typographical Union, helped on labor issues.

"The writing of the speech was the candidate's own. For research, aside from all the material gained in conferences, Mr. Willkie called in two of his campaign aides: Raymond Leslie Buell, former head of the Foreign Policy Association, and Russell W. Davenport, former managing editor of *Fortune*." [3]

The speech was obviously constructed to make political capital through (1) its proposal to make the campaign a crusade in favor of democracy; (2) its strong ethical proof by a detailed picture of the candidate's family, including his parents and ancestors, as the products and exemplification of the American system of freedom and of resistance to governmental tyranny, and through its suggestion that this candidate was essentially a "liberal"; (3) its clear statement that American democracy was to be defended against totalitarian threats; (4) its support of "selective service"; (5) its criticism of Roosevelt in his foreign policy because he had talked too much instead of "speaking softly and carrying a big stick"; (6) its strong declaration that the Roosevelt foreign policy was weak because it did not provide unity and economic health at home; (7) its enumeration of economic and social principles, including collective bargaining, free enterprise, Federal regulation, agricultural relief, the philosophy of plenty and of production, the philosophy of taxation for purposes of raising revenue, and of taxation in accordance with ability to pay; (8) its indictment of the New Deal because it had completely failed in these various economic and social aims; (9) its challenge for Roosevelt to debate the issues with Willkie; and (10) its plain statement that Willkie leadership would mean hardship and sacrifice.

According to *The New York Times*, Mr. Willkie deserved "the gratitude of all Americans" for the tone he set in his first speech of the campaign. "He has talked fairly to the American people. He has talked about real issues. He has met the test of a great occasion with courage and candor and foresight that do him honor." Herbert

[3] *New York Times,* Sunday, August 18, 1940, Section IV, p. 1.

Hoover praised the speech as a "call to our strength." Alfred Landon, A. H. Vandenberg, praised it. *Time* called the first half of it "heavy," and "disappointing," and added that "Willkie had much to learn as a speaker." New Dealers called it "the greatest political failure in history."

Columnist Ray Clapper asserted that the "people were filled with pain and disappointment at the bad delivery, but changed their minds as they read the speech." Added Clapper: "Not many major political utterances in modern times have rung with such courage as this Willkie acceptance speech."

One immediate result was the castigation of Willkie by Secretary of the Interior Harold L. Ickes (radio address of August 19). Asked Ickes: "By what grasshopper leap of the imagination does this candidate conclude that the President has not taken this country into his confidence on foreign policy?" Willkie was "the simple, barefoot Wall Street lawyer." Declared Ickes, "One cannot challenge the President of the United States to go about the country barnstorming, after the pre-radio fashion of the past century, without laying himself open to the charge that he is indulging in cheap bravado. . . . The President cannot adjourn the Battle of Britain in order to ride the circuit with Mr. Willkie. . . . The Presidency of the United States is no job for a mountebank."

Honorable Styles Bridges of New Hampshire replied to Ickes thus (radio address of August 20): " 'Honest' Harold Ickes' radio apology for President Roosevelt cost the Democratic National Committee around $7,500 last night. It would cost us nearly $4,000 for a reply with only half the time. Nothing Harold ever said or that Charlie Michelson could write for him could be worth that much. Refusing to chisel funds from New Deal business victims with a campaign handbook racket, we must save our funds for worthier purposes. . . .

"Who is this Ickes who talks so big—at a safe distance—about Hitler? In his own right Ickes is a Hitler in short pants. Like Hitler he hates the newspapers and freedom of press and speech and would ruthlessly control them. Like Hitler he is a professional rabble rouser who never succeeded at anything else; who is a political hatchet man. The New Deal regime that Ickes schemes for is nothing but an American form of nazi-ism. Like Hitler he is a common scold puffed up by high office. The resemblance is closest in their attitude toward the truth. Who is Ickes to make faces at Hitler? Doesn't he own a mirror?"

And *The New York Times* concluded editorially (August 21): "If the campaign is allowed to degenerate to this level the worst result will not be a loss of dignity, deplorable as that would be. The worst result will be to turn public attention away from the crucial national decisions that we must now make and involve it instead in stupid irrelevancies. If Mr. Willkie, for example, has lived at 1010 Fifth

Avenue, as Mr. Ickes pointedly remarks, Mr. Roosevelt has had a
home in a New York neighborhood at least as wealthy; and neither
fact has any bearing whatever on national policy."

The ceremony of an acceptance speech is a tradition of our
pioneer past— before the days of rapid communication. You
all know that I accepted at Philadelphia the nomination of
the Republican Party for President of the United States. But
I take pride in the traditions and not in change for the mere
sake of overthrowing precedents.

An acceptance speech is a candidate's keynote, a declaration
of his broad principles. It cannot possibly review the issues
in detail. I shall, however, cover each of them frankly during
this campaign. Here I give you an outline of the political
philosophy that is in my heart. We are here today to represent
a sacred cause—the preservation of American democracy.

Obviously, I cannot lead this cause alone. I need the help
of every American—Republican, Democrat, or Independent—
Jew, Catholic, or Protestant—people of every color, creed, and
race. Party lines are down. Nothing could make that clearer
than the nomination by the Republicans of a liberal Democrat
who changed his party affiliation because he found democracy
in the Republican Party and not in the New Deal party.

And as the leader of the Republican Party let me say this:
We go into our campaign as into a crusade. Revitalized and
reunited, and joined by millions who share in our cause, we
dedicate ourselves to the principles of American liberty, and
we shall fight this campaign on the basis of those principles,
not on the basis of hate, jealousy, or personalities. The
leaders of the Republican Party, in Congress and in the party
organization, have made me that pledge. I have given that
pledge to them. And I extend it to all who will join in this
cause. What we need in this country is a new leadership
that believes in the destiny of America. I represent here
today the forces that will bring that leadership to you.

There is a special reason why I have come back to Elwood, Indiana, to make this acceptance speech. I have an engagement to keep in this town. It was made a long time ago with a young man I knew well.

This young man was born and raised in Elwood. He attended the Elwood public schools. He worked in your factories and stores. He started the practice of law in your courts. As I look back upon him, I realize that he had plenty of faults. But he had also three steadfast convictions. He was devoted to the ideal of individual liberty. He hated all special privileges and forms of oppression. And he knew without any doubt that the greatest country on earth was the United States of America.

That boy was myself 30 or 35 years ago. I still adhere to those convictions. To him, to his generation, to his elders, and to the youth of today I pledge my word that I shall never let them down.

In former days America was described as a country in which any young man might become President. It is still that kind of country. The thousands of my fellow townsmen standing hereabout know how distant seemed that opportunity to me 30 years ago. We must fight to preserve America as a country in which every girl and boy has every opportunity for any achievement.

To the millions of our young men and women who have been deliberately disillusioned by the political influences I now oppose; to the millions who no longer believe in the future of their land—to them I want to say in all humility— this boy I knew started like you without money or position; but America gave him the opportunity for a career. I want to assure a similar opportunity to every boy and girl of today who is willing to stand on his own feet and work and fight.

I have more reason than most of you to feel strongly about this because the United States gave to my family their first chance for a free life. The ancestors of both my father and my mother, like the ancestors of millions of Americans, lived in central Europe. They were humble people—not members of the ruling or wealthy classes. Their opportunities were restricted by discriminatory laws and class distinctions. One was exiled because of his religion; another was persecuted because he believed in the principles of the French Revolution, and still another was jailed for insisting on the right of free speech.

As their descendant, I have fought from boyhood against all those restrictions, discriminations, and tyrannies. And I am still fighting.

My grandparents lived in Germany. They were supporters of the democratic revolutions in that country, and when the revolutions failed they fled to the United States. How familiar that sounds. Today, also, people are being oppressed in Europe. The story of the barbarous and worse than medieval persecution of the Jews—a race that has done so much to improve the culture of these countries and our own—is the most tragic in human history. Today there are millions of refugees who desire sanctuary and opportunity in America, just as in my grandparents' time. The protection of our own labor and agriculture prevents us from admitting more than a few of them. But their misery and suffering make us resolve to preserve our country as a land free of hate and bitterness, of racial and class distinction. I pledge you that kind of America.

My mother was born in this country. My father was three or four years old when his parents settled in northern Indiana. It was then a trackless forest. As a young man he helped to clear that forest. He worked his way through the Fort Wayne Methodist College, taught school, and became superintendent of schools here in Elwood. My mother was also a school teacher. Whenever they had time they both studied law, and eventually both took up the practice of law. I doubt if any two people ever appreciated or loved this country more than they.

As you who live here with them well know, they were fiercely democratic. They hated oppression, autocracy, or arbitrary control of any kind. They believed in the qualities that have made America great—an independent spirit, an inquiring mind, a courageous heart. At school they taught those virtues to many of you who are here today. At home they taught them to their children. It is a tribute to their teaching that when the United States entered the World War in 1917, three of their four boys were volunteers, in the uniform of the American forces, within one month after war was declared. They withheld no sacrifices for the preservation of the America of 1917. In an even more dangerous world, we must not withhold any sacrifice necessary for the preservation of the America of 1940.

Today we meet in a typical American town. The quiet streets, the pleasant fields that lie outside, the people going casually about their business, seem far removed from the shattered cities, the gutted buildings, and the stricken people of Europe. It is hard for us to realize that the war in Europe can affect our daily lives. Instinctively we turn aside from the recurring conflicts over there, the diplomatic intrigue, the shifts of power that the last war failed to end.

Yet—instinctively also—we know that we are not isolated from those suffering people. We live in the same world as they, and we are created in the same image. In all the democracies that have recently fallen, the people were living the same peaceful lives that we live. They had similar ideals of human freedom. Their methods of trade and exchange were similar to ours. Try as we will, we cannot brush the pitiless picture of their destruction from our vision or escape the profound effects of it upon the world in which we live.

No man is so wise as to forsee what the future holds or to lay out a plan for it. No man can guarantee to maintain peace. Peace is not something that a nation can achieve by itself. It also depends on what some other country does. It is neither practical, nor desirable, to adopt a foreign program committing the United States to future action under unknown circumstances.

The best that we can do is to decide what principle shall guide us.

For me, that principle can be simply defined:

In the foreign policy of the United States, as in its domestic policy, I would do everything to defend American democracy and I would refrain from doing anything that would injure it.

We must not permit our emotions—our sympathies or hatreds—to move us from that fixed principle.

For instance, we must not shirk the necessity of preparing our sons to take care of themselves in case the defense of America leads to war. I shall not undertake to analyze the legislation on this subject that is now before Congress, or to examine the intentions of the Administration with regard to it. I concur with many members of my party that these intentions must be closely watched. Nevertheless, in spite of these considerations, I cannot ask the American people to put their faith in me without recording my conviction that some form of selective service is the only democratic way in which to secure the trained and competent manpower we need for national defense.

Also, in the light of my principle, we must honestly face our relationship with Great Britain. We must admit that the loss of the British Fleet would greatly weaken our defense. This is because the British Fleet has for years controlled the Atlantic, leaving us free to concentrate in the Pacific.

If the British Fleet were lost or captured, the Atlantic might be dominated by Germany, a power hostile to our way of life, controlling in that event most of the ships and ship-building facilities of Europe.

This would be calamity for us. We might be exposed to attack on the Atlantic. Our defense would be weakened until we could build a navy and air force strong enough to defend both coasts. Also, our foreign trade would be profoundly affected. That trade is vital to our prosperity. But if we had to trade with a Europe dominated by the present German trade policies, we might have to change our methods to some totalitarian form. This is a prospect that any lover of democracy must view with consternation.

The objective of America is in the opposite direction. We must, in the long run, rebuild a world in which we can live and move and do business in the democratic way.

The President of the United States recently said: "We will extend to the opponents of force the material resources of this nation, and at the same time we will harness the use of those resources in order that we ourselves, in the Americas, may have equipment and training equal to the task of any emergency and every defense."

I should like to state that I am in agreement with these two principles, as I understand them—and I don't understand them as implying military involvement in the present hostilities. As an American citizen I am glad to pledge my wholehearted support to the President in whatever action he may take in accordance with these principles.

But I cannot follow the President in his conduct of foreign affairs in this critical time. There have been occasions when many of us have wondered if he is deliberately inciting us to war. I trust that I have made it plain that in the defense of America, and of our liberties, I should not hesitate to stand for war. But like a great many other Americans I saw what war was like at first hand in 1917. I know what war can do to demoralize civil liberties at home. And I believe it to be the first duty of a President to try to maintain peace.

But Mr. Roosevelt has not done this. He has dabbled in inflammatory statements and manufactured panics. Of course, we in America like to speak our minds freely, but this does not mean that at a critical period in history our President should cause bitterness and confusion for the sake of a little political oratory. The President's attacks on foreign powers have been useless and dangerous. He has courted a war for which the country is hopelessly unprepared—and which it emphatically does not want. He has secretly meddled in the affairs of Europe, and he has even unscrupulously encouraged other countries to hope for more help than we are able to give.

"Walk softly and carry a big stick" was the motto of Theodore Roosevelt. It is still good American doctrine for 1940. Under the present Administration the country has been placed in the false position of shouting insults and not even beginning to prepare to take the consequences.

But while he has thus been quick to tell other nations what they ought to do, Mr. Roosevelt has been slow to take the American people into his confidence. He has hesitated to report facts, to explain situations, or to define realistic objectives. The confusion in the nation's mind has been largely due to this lack of information from the White House.

As President, I plan to reverse both of these policies. I should threaten foreign governments only when our country was threatened by them and when I was ready to act, and I should consider our diplomacy as part of the people's business concerning which they were entitled to prompt and frank reports to the limit of practicability.

Candor in these times is the hope of democracy. We must not kid ourselves any longer. We must begin to tell ourselves the truth—right here and right now.

We have been sitting as spectators of a great tragedy. The action on the stage of history has been relentless.

For instance, the French people were just as brave and intelligent as the Germans. Their armies were considered the best in the world. France and her Allies won the last war. They possessed all the resources they needed. They had wealth and reserves of credit all over the earth. Yet the Germans crushed France like an egg shell.

The reason is now clear. The fault lay within France herself.

France believed in the forms of democracy and in the idea of freedom. But she failed to put them to use.

She forgot that freedom must be dynamic, that it is forever in the process of creating a new world. This was the lesson that we of America had taught to all countries.

When the European democracies lost that vision, they opened the way for Hitler. While Germany was building a great new productive plant, France became involved in unfruitful political adventures and flimsy economic theories. Her government was trying desperately to cover the people's nakedness with a garment that was not big enough.

The free men of France should have been weaving themselves a bigger garment. For in trying to pull the small one around themselves they tore it to pieces.

And in this tragedy let us find our lesson.

The foreign policy of the United States begins right here in our own land. The first task of our country in its international affairs is to become strong at home. We must regain prosperity, restore the independence of our people, and protect our defensive resources. If that is not done promptly, we are in constant danger. If that is done no enemy on earth dare attack us. I propose to do it. We must face a brutal, perhaps a terrible fact. Our way of life is in competition with Hitler's way of life.

This competition is not one merely of armaments. It is a combination of energy against energy, production against production, salesmanship against salesmanship.

In facing it we should have no fear. History shows that our way of life is the strong way. From it has come more wealth, more industry, more happiness, more human enlightenment than from any other way. Free men are the strongest men.

But we cannot just take that historical fact for granted. We must make it live. If we are to outdistance the totalitarian powers, we must arise to a new life of adventure and discovery. We must make a wider horizon for the human race. It is to that new life that I pledge myself.

I promise, by returning to those same American principles that overcame German autocracy once before, both in business and in war, to outdistance Hitler in any contest he chooses in 1940 or after. And I promise you that, when we beat him, we shall beat him on our own terms, and in the American way.

The promises of the present Administration cannot lead you to victory against Hitler, or against anybody else. This Administration stands for principles exactly opposite to mine.

It does not preach the doctrine of growth. It preaches the doctrine of division. We are not asked to make more for ourselves. We are asked to divide among ourselves that which we already have.

The New Deal doctrine does not seek risk. It seeks safety. Let us call it the "I pass" doctrine. The New Deal dealt it, and refused to make any more bets on the American future.

Why, that is exactly the course that France has followed to her destruction. Like the Blum government in France, so has our government become entangled in unfruitful adventures. As in France, so here we have heard talk of class distinctions and of economic groups preying one upon other groups.

We are told that capital hates labor and labor capital. We are told that the different kinds of men, whose task it is to build America, are enemies of one another. And I am ashamed to say that some Americans have made capital of that supposed enmity.

As for me, I want to say here and now that there is no hate in my heart, and that there will be none in my campaign. It is my belief that there is no hate in the hearts of any group of Americans for any other American group—except as the New Dealers seek to put it there for political purposes. I stand for a new companionship in industrial society.

Of course, if you start like the New Deal with the idea that we shall never have many more automobiles or radios, that we cannot develop many new inventions of importance, that our standard of living must remain about what it is, the rest of the argument is easy:

Since a few people have more than they need and millions have less than they need, it is necessary to redivide the wealth and turn it back from the few to the many.

But this can only make the poor poorer and the rich less rich. It does not really distribute wealth. It distributes poverty.

Because I am a business man, formerly connected with a large company, the doctrinaires of the opposition have attacked me as an opponent of liberalism. But I was a liberal before many of these men had heard the word, and I fought for many of the reforms of the elder La Follette, Theodore Roosevelt and Woodrow Wilson before another Roosevelt adopted—and distorted—liberalism.

I learned my liberalism right here at home in Elwood. From the factories that came into this town many years ago, large fortunes were made by a few individuals, who thereby acquired too much power over our community.

Those same forces were at work throughout the rest of the nation. By 1929 the concentration of private power had gone further than it should ever go in a democracy.

We all know that such concentration of power must be checked. Thomas Jefferson disliked regulation, yet he said that the prime purpose of government in a democracy is to keep men from injuring each other.

We know from our own experience that the less fortunate or the less skillful among us must be protected from encroachment. That is why we support what is known as the liberal point of view. That is why we believe in reform.

I believe that the forces of free enterprise must be regulated. I am opposed to business monopolies.

I believe in collective bargaining, by the representative of labor's own free choice, without any interference and in full protection of those obvious rights. I believe in the maintenance of minimum standards for wages and of maximum standards for hours. I believe that such standards should constantly improve.

I believe in the Federal regulation of interstate utilities, of securities markets and of banking. I believe in Federal pensions, in adequate old-age benefits and in unemployment allowances.

I believe that the Federal Government has a responsibility to equalize the lot of the farmer, with that of the manufacturer. If this cannot be done by parity of prices, other means must be found—with the least possible regimentation of the farmer's affairs.

I believe in the encouragement of cooperative buying and selling, and in the full extension of rural electrification.

The purpose of all such measures is indeed to obtain a better distribution of the wealth and the earning power of the country.

But I do not make my claim to liberalism solely on my faith in such reforms. American liberalism does not consist merely in reforming things. It consists also in making things.

The ability to grow, the ability to make things, is the measure of man's welfare on earth. To be free, men must be creative.

I am a liberal because I believe that in our industrial age there is no limit to the productive capacity of any man. And as I believe that I likewise believe there is no limit to the horizon of the United States.

I say that we must substitute for the philosophy of distributed scarcity the philosophy of unlimited productivity. I stand for the restoration of full production and re-employment by private enterprise in America.

And I say that we must henceforth ask certain questions of every reform, and of every law to regulate business or industry. We must ask:

Has it encouraged industries to produce? Has it created new opportunities for our youth? Will it increase our standard of living? Will it encourage us to open up a new and bigger world?

A reform that cannot meet these tests is not a truly liberal reform. It is an "I pass" reform. It does not tend to strengthen our system, but to weaken it. It exposes us to aggressors, whether economic or military. It encourages class distinctions and hatreds.

And it will lead us inevitably, as I believe we are now headed, toward a form of government alien to ours, and a way of life contrary to the way that our parents taught us here in Elwood.

It is from weakness that people reach for dictators and concentrated government power. Only the strong can be free.

And only the productive can be strong.

When the present Administration came into power in 1933, we heard a lot about the forgotten man. The government, we were told, must take care of those who had no other means of support.

With this proposition all of us agreed. And we still hold firmly to the principle that those whom private industry cannot support must be supported by government agency, whether Federal or State.

But I want to ask any one in this audience who is, or has been, on relief, whether the support that the government gives him is enough.

Is it enough for the free and able-bodied American to be given a few scraps of cash or credit with which to keep himself and his children just this side of starvation and nakedness? Is that what the forgotten man wanted us to remember?

What that man wanted us to remember was his chance—his right—to take a part in the great American adventure.

But this Administration never remembered that. It launched a vitriolic and well-planned attack against those very industries in which the forgotten man wanted a chance.

It carried on a propaganda campaign to convince the country that all business men are iniquitous.

It seized upon its taxing power for political purposes. It has levied taxes to punish one man, to force another to do what he did not want to do, to take a crack at a third whom some government agency disliked, or to promote the experiments of a brain trust.

The direct effect of the New Deal taxes has been to inhibit opportunity. It has diverted the money of the rich from productive enterprises into government bonds, so that the United States Treasury—and no one else—may have plenty to spend. Thus much of the money of the rich is invested in tax-free securities.

In this connection let me say that in its plan for tax revision the Republican Party will follow two simple principles. Taxes shall be levied in accordance with each one's ability to pay. And the primary purpose of levying them will be to raise money.

We must do it without inflicting on the poor the present disproportionate load of hidden taxes.

The New Deal's attack on business has had inevitable results. The investor has been afraid to invest his capital, and therefore billions of dollars now lie idle in the banks.

The business man has been afraid to expand his operations, and therefore millions of men have been turned away from the employment offices. Low incomes in the cities and irresponsible experiments in the country have deprived the farmer of his markets.

For the first time in our history American industry has remained stationary for a decade. It offers no more jobs today than it did 10 years ago—and there are 6,000,000 more persons seeking jobs. As a nation of producers we have become stagnant. Much of our industrial machinery is obsolete. And the national standard of living has declined.

It is a statement of fact, and no longer a political accusation, that the New Deal has failed in its program of economic rehabilitation. And the victims of its failures are the very persons whose cause it professes to champion.

The little-business men are victims because their chances are more restricted than ever before.

The farmers are victims because many of them are forced to subsist on what is virtually a dole under centralized direction from Washington.

The 9,000,000 or 10,000,000 unemployed are victims because their chances for jobs are fewer.

Approximately 6,000,000 families are victims because they are on relief.

And unless we do something about it soon, 130,000,000 people—an entire nation—will become victims, because they stand in need of a defense system which this Administration has so far proved itself powerless to create anywhere except on paper.

To accomplish these results, the present Administration has spent $60,000,000,000.

And I say there must be something wrong with a theory of government or a theory of economics by which, after the expenditure of such a fantastic sum, we have less opportunity than we had before.

The New Deal believes, as frequently declared, that the spending of vast sums by the government is a virtue in itself. They tell us that government spending insures recovery. Where is the recovery?

The New Deal stands for doing what has to be done by spending as much money as possible. I propose to do it by spending as little money as possible. This is one great issue in domestic policy and I propose in this campaign to make it clear.

And I make this grave charge against this Administration:

I charge that the course this Administration is following will lead us, like France, to the end of the road. I say that this course will lead us to economic disintegration and dictatorship.

I say that we must substitute for the philosophy of spending the philosophy of production. You cannot buy freedom. You must make freedom.

This is a serious charge. It is not made lightly and it cannot be lightly avoided by the opposition.

I therefore have a proposal to make.

The President stated in his acceptance speech that he does not have either "the time or the inclination to engage in purely political debate." I do not want to engage in purely political debate either. But I believe that the tradition of face-to-face debate is justly honored among our American political traditions. I believe that we should set an example at this time of the workings of American democracy, and I do not think that the issues at stake are "purely political." In my opinion, they concern the life and death of democracy.

I propose that during the next two and a half months the President and I appear together on public platforms in various parts of the country to debate the fundamental issues of this campaign. These are the problems of our great domestic economy, as well as of our national defense—the problem of agriculture, of labor, of industry, of finance, of the government's relationship to the people, and of our preparations to guard against assault; and also I would like to debate the assumption by this President, in seeking a third term, of a greater public confidence than was accorded to our Presidential giants—Washington, Jefferson, Jackson, Lincoln, Cleveland, Theodore Roosevelt, and Woodrow Wilson.

I make this proposal respectfully to a man upon whose shoulders rest the cares of the state. But I make it in dead earnest.

I accept the nomination of the Republican Party for President of the United States.

I accept it in the spirit in which I know it was given at our convention in Philadelphia—the spirit of dedication. I herewith dedicate myself with all my heart, with all my mind, and with all my soul to making this nation strong.

But I say this, too: In the pursuit of that goal I shall not lead you down the easy road. If I am chosen the leader of this democracy as I am now of the Republican Party, I shall lead you down the road of sacrifice and of service to your country.

What I am saying is a far harsher thing than I should like to say in this speech of acceptance—a far harsher thing than I would have said had the Old World not been swept by war during the past year. I am saying to you that we cannot rebuild our American democracy without hardship, without sacrifice, even without suffering. I am proposing that course to you as a candidate for election by you.

When Winston Churchill became Prime Minister of England a few months ago, he made no sugarcoated promises. "I have nothing to offer you," he said, "but blood, toil, tears, and sweat." Those are harsh words, brave words; yet if England lives, it will be because her people were told the truth and accepted it. Fortunately, in America, we are not reduced to blood and tears. But we shall not be able to avoid the toil and sweat.

In these months ahead of us, every man who works in this country—whether he works with his hands or with his mind—will have to work a little harder. Every man and woman will feel the burden of taxes. Every housewife will have to plan a little more carefully. I speak plainly because you must not be deceived about the difficulties of the future. You will have to be hard of muscle, clear of head, brave of heart.

Today great institutions of freedom, for which humanity has spilled so much blood, lie in ruins. In Europe those rights of person and property—the civil liberties—which your ancestors fought for and which you still enjoy, are virtually extinct. And it is my profound conviction that even here in this country, the Democratic Party, under its present leadership, will prove incapable of protecting those liberties of yours.

The Democratic Party today stands for division among our people, for the struggle of class against class and faction against faction, for the power of political machines and the exploitation of pressure groups. Liberty does not thrive in such soil.

The only soil in which liberty can grow is that of a united people. We must have faith that the welfare of one is the welfare of all. We must know that the truth can only be reached by the expression of our free opinions, without fear and without rancor. We must acknowledge that all are equal before God and before the law. And we must learn to abhor those disruptive pressures, whether religious, political, or economic that the enemies of liberty employ.

The Republican Party and those associated with it constitute a great political body that stands preeminently for liberty—without commitments, without fear, and without contradictions. This party believes that your happiness must be achieved through liberty rather than in spite of liberty. We ask you to turn your eyes upon the future, where your hope lies. We see written there the same promise that has always been written there—the promise that strong men will perform strong deeds.

With the help of Almighty Providence, with unyielding determination and ceaseless effort we must and we shall make that American promise come true.

IN SUPPORT OF WILLKIE [4]

JOHN L. LEWIS [5]

John L. Lewis, president of the Congress of Industrial Organizations (C.I.O.), delivered this address over the radio on Friday evening, October 25, 1940, from his headquarters in the United Mine Workers' Building in Washington, D. C.

The speech, sponsored by the National Committee of Democrats-For-Willkie, was broadcast over some 325 stations of the three national networks, at a cost of $45,000 (there was political speculation as to who would pay the bill), and was listened to by an audience estimated at 25,000,000.

The speech, coming as it did ten days before the election, and marking as it did the political break between Roosevelt and the head of a labor group representing perhaps four million unionists, marked a dramatic moment in the campaign.

Why had the dark-browed spokesman for mine workers, the auto, dock, lumber, and other large groups of workers, severed his alliance with the party to whom four years previously he and his fellow unionists had contributed $500,000 for campaign purposes? The gap had begun as early as 1937. By 1939 Lewis was vigorously condemning the New Deal for its failure to reduce unemployment, and its apparent reluctance to support labor fully through administrative rulings. During 1940 the president of the C.I.O. had repeatedly clashed with the Administration at Washington concerning labor policies. Lewis protested, for example, because labor had not been properly represented in the inner circles at the Capital. Furthermore he opposed conscription and other aspects of national defense, and he accused Roosevelt of inciting the American people to war. Lewis apparently was losing caste with the C.I.O. group as Sidney Hillman, vice president of the C.I.O. and labor coordinator for the National Defense Advisory Commission, gained in prestige. Lewis protested in vain because Bethlehem Steel Company, with $1,000,000,000 worth of government defense orders, was not complying with N.L.R.B. orders to disband a "company union."

Lewis also warned the voters against dictatorships and had come out early in 1940 against the third term. He hinted at the organization of a third party. At least one conference between Wendell Willkie and Lewis had been held before the announcement was made that the C.I.O. spokesman intended to endorse the Republican ticket.

---

[4] By permission of Mr. Lewis. Text furnished through the courtesy of Kathryn Lewis, Executive Secretary to Mr. Lewis.

[5] For biographical note see Appendix.

The speech was given by an orator described as "of first-rate quality, even of genius, perhaps. . . . He is bold. He is brilliant. He has on the whole displayed a rare capacity for growing in stature. . . ."[6] It was strong in ethical appeal in its opening vindication of Lewis as a labor and political leader; in its 2000-word indictment of Roosevelt for his international policy, for his seeking of continued power, for his failure to solve the unemployment problem; and in its 1500-word eulogy of Wendell Willkie ("he is a gallant American"); and in its closing appeal to laborers, farmers, youth, Negroes, military conscripts, churchmen, and women. As a political oration it was well organized, carefully composed, and impressively delivered. Magazine *Time* (36:18, November 4, 1940) observed that "Speaking like an old tragedian, he let his orotund words roll out. . . ." Lewis has natural eloquence even though it belongs more closely to the school of Bryan than of Franklin Roosevelt.

The immediate results were somewhat as follows: The leaders of the largest C.I.O. unions pledged their support of Roosevelt; many of the C.I.O. "left-wing" leaders followed Lewis, especially those promoting such unions as the Transport Workers, National Maritime Union, Packinghouse Union; most of the United Mine Workers' leaders still supported Roosevelt; the A.F. of L. affiliates attacked the C.I.O. president and stated that "a vote for Willkie is a vote for Lewis."

Significant was Lewis' statement that if Roosevelt was reelected, Lewis would regard the result as one of no-confidence in the president of the C.I.O. and stated that under such condition he, Lewis, would retire as president.

What part did labor play in the final vote for the Presidency? It was estimated that some 12,000,000 or 15,000,000 votes out of some 50,000,000 were cast by labor unionists and their families. The labor vote was especially heavy in Pennsylvania, New York, Ohio, Illinois, and Michigan, states which have been regarded as all-powerful in the size of their electoral vote. Before the Lewis speech the sentiments of the labor leaders, A.F. of L., C.I.O., railroad and independent unions, indicated that labor would go from 80 per cent to 90 per cent for Roosevelt.

Roosevelt won by 4,000,000 votes. It was generally agreed that labor helped to give him victory. But it is also generally agreed that the election demonstrated what previous political contests have shown— that labor leaders cannot deliver the labor vote. Labor has still a way of voting more or less independently, just as other population groups do. Lewis' influence was no doubt strong, but it could not turn the millions of minds that apparently had already decided to vote for Franklin Roosevelt. In November, 1940, true to his promise, Lewis resigned as president of the C.I.O.

I address all Americans. Our country is at one of the cross-roads of its political destiny. The issues run deep and will in-

[6] Harris, Herbert, *Labor's Civil War*, p. 257, Knopf, 1940.

evitably affect the well-being and lives of every American. They will also affect the population of every other civilized country, and may well determine the stability or instability of all the free institutions of our present-day culture.

I am conscious of the degree of responsibility which attaches to my words. I am a qualified representative of many organizations of labor, and other groups of citizens. It is not necessary to enumerate them, since my listeners are familiar with their identity. Suffice it to say that the direct and affiliated membership of these several organizations amounts to substantially ten million men and women. Adding to this number the numerical strength of their dependent families, there is achieved a sum total of human beings amounting to approximately one-fourth of the total population of our nation. Abandoning my right to speak officially for this great segment of our population, I choose to speak tonight only in the role of a citizen and an American. I do so in all the pride of my heritage, and with a desire to protect and preserve that heritage, and likewise the heritage of my peers. Accordingly, tonight, I do not speak for labor, but on the contrary, I speak to labor and to all my countrymen.

I do not control the vote of any one man or woman. I have no power and no influence, except insofar as those who believe in me may accept my recommendations.

On September 4th, 1939, in a public radio address, I said:

The nation cannot forever continue its appalling drift—thoughtless and sadly executed experimentation will not always suffice to beguile a suffering people. The internal national debt has already reached such proportions that it may never be liquidated by orthodox methods. In the face of the economic debacle in America, many of our statesmen are more concerned and agitated over the political quarrels in Europe. War has always been the device of the politically despairing and intellectually sterile statesmen. It provides employment in the gun factories and begets enormous profits for those already rich. It kills off the vigorous males who, if permitted to live, might question the financial exploitation of the race. Above all, war perpetuates in imperishable letters on the scroll of fame and history, the names of its political creators and managers.

The foregoing statement constitutes the first basis of my personal opposition to the reelection of President Roosevelt for a third term as Chief Executive of the Republic. Those who hear these words, and who have studied the public addresses of the President, from his Chicago "quarantine speech" to his Charlottesville "stab in the back" address, and thence to Dayton and Philadelphia, will understand his motivation and his objective. It is war. His every act leads one to this inescapable conclusion. The President has said that he hates war and will work for peace, but his acts do not match his words. I am opposed to any involvement of our country in foreign wars. I believe that every thoughtful and normal citizen is similarly opposed. They are willing, as I am willing, to contribute everything for any necessary defense of our geographical integrity, our families, our possessions, our liberties and our lives.

The flaming horror of the current war now engulfs many nations. Reason would seem to prompt a course of national action designed to restrict and abate the war, rather than to expand and intensify its scope and destruction.

The present concentration of power in the office of the President of the United States has never before been equalled in the history of our country. His powers and influence in this republic are so far-reaching that they intimately and vitally affect the lives and fortunes of every citizen. In like measure, they may affect the lives and fortunes of other nations and their populations.

How startling, therefore, is the spectacle of a President who is disinclined to surrender that power, in keeping with the traditions of the republic. The suggestion of a third term under these conditions is less than wholesome or healthy. Personal craving for power, the overweening abnormal and selfish craving for increased power, is a thing to alarm and dismay.

Eminent Americans have analyzed this principle in a manner that should bring conviction to the heart of every questioner. No citizen with the proper regard for the maintenance of orderly, temperate and considerate government should lightly endow any politician or statesman with a brief of authority that, for all practical considerations, runs in perpetuity.

Power for what? Personal and official power to what end? In all history, the unwarranted exercise of continuously vested authority has brought its train of political and social convulsions, for which humanity has paid an appalling price in loss of liberty, in disorder, tragedy and death.

America needs no superman. It denies the philosophy that runs to the deification of the state. America wants no royal family. Our forbears paid the price in blood, agony, privation and sorrow, requisite for the building of this republic. Are we now to cast away that priceless liberty, which is our heritage? Are we to yield to the appetite for power and the vaunting ambitions of a man who plays with the lives of human beings for a pastime?

I say "No." And whether I stand alone, or whether I am sustained, as I think I will be by the overwhelming number of American citizens, I should retain these convictions. It is time for the manhood and the womanhood of America to assert themselves. Tomorrow may be too late.

If President Roosevelt is reestablished in office in the forthcoming election, he will answer to no man, including the Congress, for his executive acts, that may create a dictatorship in this land. This election may be historically comparable to the controlled elections and plebiscites of some of the nations of the Old World. I ask my countrymen to pause briefly and think deeply before the die is cast on this grave issue.

On January 24, 1940, at Columbus, Ohio, in a public address, I said in part, as follows:

In 1936, a coalition was effected between the Democratic Party and organized labor. The resources of both interests were pooled—the objective being the return of the party to power in the election of the same year. Organized labor furnished money, speakers, party workers in every political subdivision and many millions of votes. It substantially financed the National Committee, various state committees, congressional committees, Labor's Non-Partisan League, the American Labor Party, the Progressive National Committee and the Good Neighbor League. Psychologically and politically, organized labor created the atmosphere of success that returned the Democratic Party to power with an ample margin of safety.

A political coalition, at least, presupposes a post-election good faith between the coalescent interests. The Democratic Party and its leadership have not preserved this faith. In the last three years, labor has not been given representation in the Cabinet, nor in the administrative or policy-making agencies of government. The current Administration has not sought nor seriously entertained the advice or views of labor upon the question of national unemployment or lesser questions affecting domestic economy, internal taxation, foreign trade, military and naval expansion, relations with foreign nations or the issues of war or peace. Labor today has no point of contact with the Democratic Administration in power, except for casual and occasional interviews which are granted its individual leaders. In the Congress, the unrestrained baiting and defaming of labor by the Democratic majority has become a pastime, never subject to rebuke by the titular or actual leaders of the party.

As the current year opens, the Democratic Party is in default to the American people. After seven years of power, it finds itself without solution for the major questions of unemployment, low national income, mounting internal debt, increasing direct and consumer taxation and restricted foreign markets. There still exists the same national unhappiness that it faced seven years ago.

The foregoing indictment has never been answered nor refuted, nor successfully denied by any single spokesman for the Democratic Party or the Roosevelt Administration. They cannot gainsay the cold, stark facts of that record. There is no spokesman in the Democratic Party, or in the Roosevelt Administration, intellectually capable of this task.

If this be true, what of the future? President Roosevelt is asking the American people to contribute to him at least four more years out of their individual lives. What will he do with those lives and this nation in the next four years, and how does he propose to do it? He has not said, and he asks from the people a grant of discretionary power that would bind him to no course of action, except the unpredictable policies and adventures which he may later devise.

After all, Americans are not a nation of guinea pigs, constantly subject to the vicissitudes of the economic and political experiments of an amateur, ill-equipped practitioner in the realm of political science.

One of the Commissioners of National Defense recently called public attention to the fact that there were forty-five million hungry people in America. In his subsequent press conference, the President rebuked the Commissioner for the statement and asserted that the condition had no relationship to the problem of national defense.

It is authoritatively stated that 20,000,000 people in the United States are able to spend only five cents per meal per person. Consider the astounding facts: 45,000,000 people in this land suffering from insufficient food and undernourishment, 20,000,000 of whom are required to live on an actual expenditure of fifteen cents a day. This, in a land of plenty, with its agricultural granaries, overflowing with surplus farm commodities, which the farmer is unable to sell. Where now are the tears for the "ill-housed, ill-clothed and ill-fed?"

The Roosevelt Administration is trying to create prosperity by the making of guns and lethal weapons. It points to the increased volume of production. It forgets to state that the productivity of the individual worker has vastly increased since 1929, and that increased volume does not correspondingly mean increased employment of workers. It forgets to state that there are 9,115,000 men and women in America still unemployed, and that the National Defense Program of production, when it reaches its maximum, will fall 5,000,000 short of providing employment for all. The Administration spokesmen forget to say what will happen to economic America when the 25,000,000 men now under arms in foreign nations, and the 70,000,000 citizens who service these armies, are returned to peacetime pursuits. The manufacturers of America and the workers of America will then have to compete in the remaining world markets with the quantitative production of foreign nations, whose workmen will occupy the relative economic and social status of chattel slaves.

Africa or the Orient. Surely, it is obvious that South American
Where will our country then sell its goods? Surely not in Europe, nor in the Baltic or Mediterranean areas. Surely not in

markets will be penetrated by the cheap labor products of the world commercial adversaries of the United States of America. What is being done by the Roosevelt Administration to safeguard our population from such an impending economic disaster?

What is being done to modernize the marketing methods of the United States in foreign trade territories, so as to compete with the changed rules of international commerce?

As a literal fact, the record of the last seven years is proof sufficient that the Roosevelt Administration is incapable of meeting this situation and maintaining this nation's rightful share of world commerce. And yet, this Administration in nonchalant and sprightly fashion, bluntly asks the American people to grant it at least an additional four years of power, so it can continue to toy with the lives of men and the destiny of nations.

If not Roosevelt, whom do I recommend to do the job of making secure our nation and its people? Why, of course, I recommend the election of Wendell L. Willkie as the next President of the United States.

He is a gallant American. He has opened his heart to the American people. He is not an aristocrat. He has the common touch. He was born in the briar and not to the purple. He has worked with his hands, and has known the pangs of hunger. He has had experience in various fields of American enterprise, and is an administrator and an executive.

Some sources have suggested that I should withhold my support of Mr. Willkie because Messrs. Grace, Girdler and Weir were allegedly supporting him. This is specious reasoning. One could as well suggest that the communicants of a particular faith should leave their church because of the presence of a hypocrite in their midst. Aside from this, these gentlemen must possess some virtue, because President Roosevelt has awarded them many fat and lucrative government contracts, at the expense of the public purse.

I may also add in passing, that it is a reasonable hope that these gentlemen, acting in their corporate capacities, will soon execute collective bargaining contracts with the C.I.O.

Wendell Willkie has said that he will put the unemployed to work; that he will abolish pauperism. He has said that he will increase the national income by working to increase the wages and incomes of those unemployed.

He says that he will enlist the representative brains of the nation to do this job. He says that he will take the representatives of labor into his Cabinet and into the policy-making agencies of government, to assist and cooperate in the economic rehabilitation of America.

He has said that he will reduce the cost of operation of our government, and thus reduce the taxes imposed upon individual citizens.

He has said that he believes in, and will enforce the right of labor to organize, and will promote collective bargaining between industry and labor.

He has said that he will preserve and maintain all social legislation previously enacted for the protection of labor and any other citizen.

Wendell Willkie has given his guarantee to the American people that if elected President he will not send the sons of American mothers and American fathers to fight in foreign wars. He avers that he will not use the power and influence of this mammoth nation to promote or create war, but rather exercise that power and that influence to abate war and promote and maintain peace between nations.

This statement of principles and objectives entitles Mr. Willkie to the support of every thoughtful citizen.

Can he accomplish such a task, many will ask. It is my considered judgment that if Wendell Willkie is elected President, this task can, and will be done.

Can we believe Mr. Willkie, some will ask. I reply that I have confidence in Mr. Willkie's integrity and honor. I do not think that he would wittingly deceive the people, or lead them astray for selfish purposes. He is a strong man. He is strong enough to enlist the services of other strong men to do the job of saving our nation, whether from attack by external foes, or disintegration from disunity within. For long years, I have served the men and women of labor. While serving them, I have ever sought also to serve my country and all its citizenry. I have been able to carry on, only because my acts were sustained by the confidence of the millions who stand behind me.

The words I utter tonight represent my mature conclusions and my sincere convictions. They are expressed, because I believe that the men and women of labor, and all other Americans, are entitled to know the truth as I see it.

I think the reelection of President Roosevelt for a third term would be a national evil of the first magnitude. He no longer hears the cries of the people. I think that the election of Mr. Wendell Willkie is imperative in relation to the country's needs. I commend him to the men and women of labor, and to the nation, as one worthy of their support, and as one who will capably and zealously protect their rights, increase their privileges and restore their happiness.

It is obvious that President Roosevelt will not be reelected for the third term, unless he has the overwhelming support of the men and women of labor. If he is, therefore, reelected, it will mean that the members of the Congress of Industrial Organizations have rejected my advice and recommendation. I will accept the result as being the equivalent of a vote of no confidence, and will retire as President of the Congress of Industrial Organizations, at its convention in November. This action will save our great movement, composed of millions of men and women, from the embarrassment and handicap of my leadership during the ensuing reign of President Roosevelt.

To the leaders of the C.I.O., its executives, staff officers and field representatives, I know, and have worked with each of you. Upon some of you, I have bestowed the honors which you now wear. Through the years of struggle, you have been content that I should be in the forefront of your battles. I am still the same man. Sustain me now, or repudiate me. I will not chide you, and will even hope that you will not regret your action.

To the Mine Workers of the nation, who know me best, and who have always been the shock troops in the forward march of labor, I say it is best for you, and for those you love, to help oppose the creation of a political dictatorship in free America.

To the steel workers, the automobile workers, the ship-builders, the maritime workers, the lumber workers in the far northwest, the textile workers, the white collar workers, and the men and women of labor in the miscellaneous industries, I say I have worked for you and have fought for you. Believe me now, when I say that your interests, and the interests of the families you support, lie in the acceptance of the truth of the words I speak tonight.

To the farmers of the nation, I say that I know something of your problems. I was born and reared in an agricultural state. You cannot be prosperous while the urban and industrial population is idle and debased. The national income must be increased, so that your crops will move to market at prices that will sustain you. Your interest lies in aggressive support of Mr. Willkie.

To the youth of America, many of whom will cast their first vote in November, I say that the road of opportunity for you lies in the election of Wendell Willkie for President. Surely, you wish to preserve the privileges, for which your elders and your forbears fought. Surely, you wish to widen the horizon of opportunity for yourselves and your contemporary citizens.

To the members of the Negro race in our northern states, I say your incomes as a group are the lowest; your living conditions are the poorest; your unemployment is the highest; discrimination against you is the worst. Surely, you have no cause to believe that President Roosevelt is an indispensable man; and surely you believe that Wendell Willkie can, and will do more for you than has been done in the last seven years. As a proven friend of the Negro race, I urge you to vote for Willkie.

You millions of young men, who have qualified for the peace military draft, have you cause to rejoice? You, who may be about to die in a foreign war, created at the whim of an international meddler, should you salute your Caesar? In cold, common sense, I think you should vote for Willkie.

You members of the Christian church, why should you vote for and support the man who ignores home considerations and practices the modern sorcery of war mongering?

Labor and the Christian church are the first victims of the social and political convulsions which follow war and one-man government.

To the women of our race, I say perhaps you can do the greatest part of all. May I hope that on election day, the mothers of our sons will, with the sacred ballot, lead the revolt against the candidate who plays at a game that may make cannon fodder of your sons.

For myself, it matters not. I do not fear the bravos of the Roosevelt Administration. I fear only for the people, and for our country. I am joining with Mr. Willkie in trying to do my part. I shall believe, my countrymen, that you will do likewise.

REPUBLICAN LEADERSHIP AND
NATIONAL DEFENSE [7]

Franklin Delano Roosevelt [8]

President Roosevelt delivered this major campaign address on national defense, on Monday night, October 28, 1940, in the Madison Square Garden, New York City.

The President, because of the international situation, laid down the rule that he would travel no further for speech-making in the campaign than an overnight journey from Washington. He also announced that he would do no more campaigning than to answer deliberate "falsifications of fact."

In line with this policy, aside from his frequent "defense inspection tours" with accompanying addresses, Mr. Roosevelt did not enter the campaign until October 23, when he spoke at Philadelphia. Here he was at his best as a campaign speaker. He followed with five other major addresses, at New York, Boston, Brooklyn, Cleveland, and at Hyde Park, the latter on election eve.

The President, in typical campaign form, spent the entire day of October 28 in traveling through fifty-eight miles of New York and Brooklyn streets, waving to the 2,000,000 wildly enthusiastic persons who lined the way.[9] Mr. Roosevelt gave seven short speeches during his tour, for example, at Hunter College, Fordham University, and at LaGuardia Field.

As early as three o'clock the crowd began to assemble at Madison Square Garden. More than 22,000 people jammed into the building and 25,000 more listened outside over the loud speakers.

Michael F. L. Walsh, Secretary of the State of New York, called the meeting together. Governor Herbert Lehman, Senators James R. Mead and Robert Wagner and others spoke. James A. Farley, "symbol of Democratic opposition to the Third Term," was on the platform.

Even as the President left Washington for his New York address the Italians with their potential army of millions had started their invasion of Greece, defended by some 150,000 troops. During the day in New York Roosevelt continued his telephone conversations with Secretary of State Hull and others at the Capital. The atmosphere of international events was tense.

[7] By permission of President Roosevelt. Text furnished through the courtesy of Stephen Early, Secretary to the President. The writer in this note is especially indebted to Helen Byse's, "A Comparison of the Speech Techniques of Franklin D. Roosevelt and Wendell L. Willkie in Two Major National Defense Addresses of the 1940 Presidential Campaign," a graduate study in the Department of Speech, State University of Iowa, 1941.

[8] For biographical note see Appendix.

[9] *New York Times,* October 29, 1940, p. 14, col. 3.

The public opinion polls had indicated that the Willkie cause was on the upswing. Republican strength was undoubtedly rising. The latest figures of the Gallup poll showed 53 percent for Roosevelt and 47 percent for Willkie—an exceedingly close race in view of the fact that the surplus Democratic majorities in the South would mean a requirement of some 52 percent for a Democratic victory.

Roosevelt's New York City campaign, therefore, was calculated to stem the rising Willkie tide and to rescue New York State from a threatened Republican victory. The aim was furthermore to strengthen the national support of the Administration policy of strong support of Great Britain.

The speech was a vigorous attack on the defense record of the Republican leaders and a recital of Roosevelt's own preparedness efforts since 1933. The issue the speaker stated clearly: "I now brand as false the statement being made by Republican campaign orators, day after day and night after night, that the rearming of America was slow, that it is hamstrung and impeded, that it will never be able to meet threats from abroad." Statements from Hamilton Fish, from Hoover, Vandenberg, and Taft were read to show that these men believed that America had been well prepared in both army and navy. Votes and speeches by McNary, Nye, and other senators, and by Representatives Martin, Barton, and Fish, were cited to illustrate their opposition to the bill for increase of the navy, repeal of the embargo on arms, against government taking over of manu-facturing plants refusing to cooperate in national defense. The speaker cited specific instances of the Democratic measures toward preparedness. Willkie, at Charleston, West Virginia, twenty-four hours later, attempted a refutation of the speech, but the President had the better of the argument in his citation of specific testimony.

Striking was the Roosevelt speech in its sarcasm and humor, and in its use of vivid language. Typical phrases or statements were, "those men of great vision," "with eyes on the good old ballot box," "our navy is anemic, our army puny," "their present barrage of verbal pyrotechnics," "On the radio these Republican orators swing through the air with the greatest of ease." To what extent did the President prepare this speech? We have no reason to doubt that his was the authorship. If we may speculate from the methods used in the composition of other Roosevelt addresses, the author in this instance, surrounded by his staff of research assistants and his other advisers, planned, rephrased, and reworked the speech—putting his personality into it so that (even though some critics suggested that the hand of Ickes was present) it was a Roosevelt production.

As usual Roosevelt had command of his audience. It continually cheered, laughed with the President, chanted with him "Martin, Barton, and Fish," booed the Republicans as Roosevelt castigated them. The delivery was as usual excellent—with clear enunciation, wide tonal range, pliancy, and with plenty of vocal enthusiasm. That "the change of pace was weak," and that "there was an over frequent use of the first personal pronoun," were perhaps justifiable criticisms.

What were the results? Those of us who listened over the radio noted the peaks of audience enthusiasm, the cheers and storms of approval, and especially the tremendous demonstration at the end. Said *Time* (36:12, November 4, 1940), "Only television could have shown the nation the relish, the skill of his performance. . . ." The *Des Moines Register* (October 30, 1940) agreed that Roosevelt had always been a "big armament man," but criticised him for "never really filling" the post of Secretary of the Navy after Swanson and for appointing as Secretary of War a man in whom he had no confidence."

However much these final Roosevelt campaign speeches determined the outcome, the fact remains that on November 5 some 26,000,000 voters cast their ballots for Roosevelt (with an electoral vote of 449) as against some 22,000,000 for Willkie (with 82 electoral votes).

Apparently Roosevelt had correctly gauged the temper of the nation when he made national defense against the Nazis the primary issue in his campaign and when he continually dealt constructively with that issue, supplementing his words with executive acts, that reinforced popular support for his point of view. The international turn of events in 1940 undoubtedly was a determining factor in the triumph of the "Third Term Candidate."

Tonight I take up again the public duty—the far from disagreeable duty—of answering major campaign falsifications with facts.

Last week in Philadelphia, I nailed the falsehood about some fanciful secret treaties, to dry on the barn door. I nailed that falsehood and other falsehoods the way, when I was a boy up in Dutchess County, we used to nail up the skins of foxes and weasels.

Tonight I am going to nail up the falsifications that have to do with our relations with the rest of the world, and with the building up of our army, navy and air defense. It is a very dangerous thing to distort facts about such things. If repeated over and over again, it is also apt to create a sense of fear and doubt in the minds of some of the American people.

I now brand as false the statement being made by Republican campaign orators, day after day and night after night, that the rearming of America was slow, that it is hamstrung and impeded, that it will never be able to meet threats from abroad.

That particular misstatement was invented about the time of the Republican National Convention. Before that, the responsible Republican leaders had been singing an entirely different song. For almost seven years the Republican leaders in the Congress kept on saying that I was placing too much emphasis on national defense. And now today these men of great vision have suddenly discovered that there is a war on in Europe and another one in Asia. And so, now, always with their eyes on the good old ballot box, they are charging that we have placed too little emphasis on national defense.

But, unlike them, the printed pages of the Congressional Record cannot be changed or suppressed at election time. And based on that permanent record of their speeches and their votes, I make this assertion—that if the Republican leaders had been in control of the Congress of the United States during the past seven years, the important measures for our defense would not now be law; and that the army and navy of the United States would still be in almost the same condition in which I found them in 1933.

I make these charges against the responsible political leadership of the Republican Party. There are millions of patriotic Republicans who have at all times been in sympathy with the efforts of this Administration to arm itself adequately for defense. To Washington in the past few months have come not two or three or a dozen, but several hundred of the best business executives in the United States—Republicans and Democrats alike. Not holding-company lawyers or executives, but men experienced in actual production—production of all the types of machines and tools and steel that have made this nation the industrial leader of the world.

I asked Mr. Knudsen and Mr. Stettinius and Mr. Harriman and Mr. Budd and the many others to serve because I believe they are certainly among the ablest men in the country in their own fields. I do not know their politics. I do not care about their politics. All I know is that they are cooperating 100 per cent with this Administration in our efforts for national defense. And this Government is cooperating with them—100 per cent.

All of these men—all of American industry and American labor —are doing magnificent and unselfish work. The progress today proves it. I shall have occasion in a later speech to tell more about the work they are doing, and about the progress which has been made in our defense.

When the first World War ended we were one of the strongest naval and military powers in the world. When this Administration first came into office fifteen years later, we were one of the weakest. As early as 1933 the storm was gathering in Europe and in Asia. Year by year I reported the warnings of danger from our listening posts in foreign lands. But I was only called "an alarmist" by the Republican leadership, and by the great majority of the Republican papers. Year by year I asked for more and more defense appropriations. In addition, I allocated hundreds of millions of dollars for defense work from relief funds, from Civilian Conservation Corps funds and from Public Works funds—as was understood by the Congress when the funds were voted.

Today our navy is at a peak of efficiency and fighting strength. Ship for ship, and man for man, it is as powerful and efficient as any that ever sailed the seas in the history of the world. Our army and our air forces are now at the highest level they have ever been in peacetime. But in the light of existing dangers they are not great enough for the absolute safety of America. While this great, constructive work was going forward, the Republican leaders were trying to block our efforts toward national defense. They not only voted against these efforts; but they stated time and again through the years that they were unnecessary and extravagant, that our armed strength was sufficient for any emergency.

I propose now to indict these Republican leaders out of their own mouths—these leaders who now disparage our defenses— indict them with what they themselves said in the days before this election year, about how adequate our defenses already were. Listen to this statement for instance. I quote: "The facts are that we have the largest and most powerful navy we ever had, except for two years after the World War, and the greatest air forces we ever had and a match for any nation."

Now who do you think made this statement in June 1938? It was not I. It was not even a member of this Administration. It was the ranking Republican member of the House Committee on Foreign Affairs, Republican leader, Hamilton Fish.

And now listen to ex-President Hoover speaking in that same year of 1938. I quote: "We shall be expending nine hundred million dollars more than any nation on earth," he complained. "We are leading in the arms race."

And now listen to Republican leader Senator Vandenberg, also speaking in 1938. He said that our defense expenditures had already bought us (and I quote) "an incomparably efficient navy"; and he said further "I rise in opposition to this super-super navy bill. I do not believe it is justified by any conclusive demonstration of national necessity."

And now listen to Republican leader Senator Taft—the runner-up this year for the Republican Presidential nomination—speaking in February 1940. I quote: "The increase of the army and navy over the tremendous appropriations of the current year seems to be unnecessary if we are concerned solely with defense."

There is the record; there is the permanent crystal clear record. Until the present political campaign opened, Republican leaders, in Congress and out, shouted from the housetops that our defenses were fully adequate. Today they complain that this Administration has starved our armed forces, that our navy is anemic, our army puny, our air forces piteously weak. This is a remarkable somersault.

I wonder if the election could have something to do with it. If the Republican leaders were telling the truth in 1938, then—out of their own mouths—they stand convicted of inconsistency today. If they are not telling the truth today, then they stand convicted of inconsistency in 1938.

The simple truth is that the Republican Party played politics with defense in 1938 and 1939. They are playing politics with national security today. The same group will still control their party policy in the Congress. It is the Congress which passes the laws of the United States. The record of these Republican leaders shows what a slim chance the cause of strong defense would have, if they were in control.

Not only in their statements but in their votes is written their record of sabotage of this Administration's continual efforts to increase our defenses to meet the dangers that loomed ever larger upon the horizon. For example, deeply concerned over what was happening in Europe, I asked the Congress in January, 1938, for a naval expansion of 20 per cent—forty-six additional ships and nine hundred and fifty new planes.

What did the Republican leaders do when they had this chance to increase our national defense almost three years ago? You would think from their present barrage of verbal pyrotechnics, that they rushed in to pass that bill, or that they even demanded a larger expansion of the navy. But, ah! my friends, they were not in a national campaign for votes then. In those days, they were trying to build up a different kind of political fence. In those days, they thought that the way to win votes was by representing this Administration as extravagant in national defense, indeed as hysterical and as manufacturing panics and inventing foreign dangers.

But now, in the *serious* days of 1940, all is changed! Not only because they are *serious* days; but because they are *election* days as well. On the radio these Republican orators swing through the air with the greatest of ease; but the American people are not voting this year for the best trapeze performer. The plain fact is that when the naval expansion bill was submitted to the Congress the Republican leaders jumped in to fight it.

Who were they? There was the present Republican candidate for Vice President, Senator McNary. There were Senator Vandenberg and Senator Nye. There was the man who would be the Chairman of the House Committee on Foreign Affairs, Congressman Fish. The first thing they did was to try to eliminate the battleships from the bill. The Republicans in the House voted sixty-seven to twenty against building them; and in the Senate the Republicans voted seven to four against building them.

The record is certainly clear that back in 1938 the Republican leaders were positive that we needed no more battleships. The naval expansion bill was passed; but it was passed by Democratic votes in the Congress—in spite of Republican opposition. Again, in March, 1939, the Republican Senators voted twelve to four against the bill for one hundred and two million dollars to buy certain strategic defense materials which we did not have in the United States. In March, 1939, the Republicans in the Senate voted eleven to eight against increasing the authorized number of planes in the Navy. In June, 1939, Republicans in the House voted one hundred and forty-four to eight in favor of reducing appropriations for the Army Air Corps. Now that proves this one simple fact. It proves that if the Republican leaders had been in control in 1938 and 1939, these measures to increase our navy and our air forces would have been defeated overwhelmingly.

I say that the Republican leaders played politics with defense in 1938 and 1939. I say that they are playing politics with our national security today. One more example: The Republican campaign orators and leaders are all now yelling "me too" on help to Britain. But last Fall they had their chance to vote to give aid to Britain and other democracies—and they turned it down.

This chance came when I recommended that the Congress repeal the embargo on the shipment of armaments and munitions to nations at war, and permit such shipment on a "cash-and-carry basis." It is only because of the repeal of the embargo law that we have been able to sell planes and ships and guns and munitions to victims of aggression. How did the Republicans vote on the repeal of this embargo. In the Senate the Republicans voted fourteen to six against it. In the House the Republicans voted one hundred and forty to nineteen against it.

The Act was passed by Democratic votes but it was over the opposition of the Republican leaders. And just to name a few, the following Republican leaders voted against the Act—Senators McNary, Vandenberg, Nye and Johnson; Congressmen Martin, Barton and Fish. Now, at the eleventh hour, they have discovered what we knew all along—that overseas success in warding off invasion by dictatorship forces means safety to the United States as well as to those smaller nations which still retain their independence and the restoration of sovereignty to those smaller nations which have temporarily lost it. One of the keystones of American policy is the recognition of the right of small nations to survive and prosper. Great Britain would never have received an ounce of help from us—if the decision had been left to Martin, Barton and Fish.

Let us come down to one more example—which took place just two months ago. In the Senate there was an amendment to permit the United States Government to prevent profiteering or unpatriotic obstruction by any corporation in defense work. It permitted the Government to take over, with reasonable compensation, any manufacturing plant which refused to cooperate in national defense. The Republican Senators voted against this Russell-Overton Amendment on August 28, 1940, eight to six. The bill was adopted all right—by Democratic votes. But the opposing vote of those eight Republican leaders showed what would happen if the national government were turned over to their control. Their vote said, in effect, that they put money rights ahead of human lives—to say nothing of national security. You and I, and the overwhelming majority of Americans, will never stand for that.

Outside the halls of Congress eminent Republican candidates began to turn new somersaults. At first they denounced the bill. Then when public opinion rose up to demand it, they seized their trapeze with the greatest of ease, and reversed themselves in mid-air.

This record of Republican leadership—a record of timidity, weakness and short-sightedness—is as bad in international as in military affairs. It is the same record of timidity, weakness and shortsightedness which they showed in domestic affairs when they were in control before 1933. But the Republican leaders' memories seem to have been short, in this, as in other matters. And by the way—who was it said that an elephant never forgets?

It is the same record of timidity, weakness and shortsightedness which governed the policy of the confused, reactionary governments in France and England before the war. That fact was discovered too late in France. It was discovered just in time in Great Britain. Please God, may that spirit never prevail in our land.

For eight years our main concern has been to look for peace and the preservation of peace. In 1935, in the face of growing dangers throughout the world, your Government undertook to eliminate the hazards which in the past had led to war.

By the Neutrality Act of 1935, and by other steps:

We made it possible to prohibit American citizens from traveling on vessels belonging to countries at war. Was that right?

We made it clear that American investors, who put their money into enterprises in foreign nations, could not call on American warships or soldiers to bail out their investments. Was that right?

We made it clear that we would not use American armed forces to intervene in affairs of the sovereign Republics to the south of us. Was that right?

We made it clear that ships flying the American flag could not carry munitions to a belligerent; and that they must stay out of war zones. Was that right?

In all these ways, we made it clear to every American, and to every foreign nation, that we would avoid becoming entangled through some episode beyond our borders. These were measures to keep us at peace. And through all the years of war since 1935, there has been no entanglement.

In July, 1937, Japan invaded China. On January 3, 1938, I called the attention of the nation to the danger of the whole world situation. It was clear that rearmament was now a necessary implement of peace. I asked for large additions to American defenses. I was called an alarmist—and worse names than that.

In March, 1938, German troops marched into Vienna. In September, 1938, came the Munich crisis. German, French and Czech armies were mobilized. The result was only an abortive armistice. I said then: "It is becoming increasingly clear that peace by fear has no higher nor more enduring quality than peace by the sword."

Three months later, at Lima, the twenty-one American Republics solemnly agreed to stand together to defend the independence of each one of us. The declaration at Lima was a great step toward peace. For unless the Hemisphere is safe, we are not safe. Matters grew steadily worse in Europe. Czecho-Slovakia was overrun by the Nazis. General war seemed inevitable. Yet even then Republican leaders kept chanting, "There will be no war." A few months later—on the first of September, 1939,—war came. The steps which we had carefully planned were put into effect. American ships were kept from danger zones. American citizens were helped to come home. Unlike 1914, there was no financial upheaval. The American Republics set up at Panama a system of patrolling the waters of the whole Western Hemisphere.

I ask you to support a continuance of this type of affirmative, realistic fight for peace. The alternative is to risk the future of the country in the hands of those with this record of timidity, weakness and short-sightedness or in the inexperienced hands of those who in these perilous days, are willing recklessly to imply that our boys are already on their way to the transports.

This affirmative search for peace calls for clear vision. It is necessary to mobilize resources, minds and skills, and every active force for peace in the world. We have steadily sought to keep mobilized the greatest force of all—religious faith, devotion to God. Your Government is working at all times with representatives of the Catholic, Protestant, and Jewish faiths. Without these spiritual forces we cannot make or maintain peace, and all three of them work with us toward that great end.

Shadows, however, are still heavy over the faith and hope of humankind. We—who walk in the ways of peace and freedom and light—have seen the tragedies enacted in one free land after another. We have not been blind to the causes, or to be the consequences, of these tragedies.

We guard ourselves against all evils—spiritual as well as material—which may beset us. We guard against the forces of anti-Christian aggression, which may attack us from without, and the forces of ignorance and fear which may corrupt us from within. We shall continue to go forward in firm faith. We shall continue to go forward in peace.

ATMOSPHERE OF THE SECOND WAR OF THE NATIONS

LET'S FACE THE FACTS [1]

DOROTHY THOMPSON [2]

The week of July 19th to July 26th, 1940, was marked by an interchange of speech-making on the international diplomatic front, "lightning-like in speed and vitriolic in content." President Franklin D. Roosevelt, in his acceptance speech of July 19th, sounded the keynote of his campaign and furnished the basis for his appeal to voters: "It [our choice] is the continuance of civilization as we know it versus the ultimate destruction of all that we hold dear, religion against godlessness, the ideal of justice against the practice of force, moral decency versus the firing squad, courage to speak out and to act versus the false lullaby of appeasement."

To this defiance of the Axis, Adolf Hitler, a few hours later, replied in a ninety-minute speech before the Reichstag, a speech translated into English by the Germans and broadcast widely. Hitler recapitulated the German successes since September, 1939, avowed Germany's interest in peace, and suggested in effect that it was not with the English people but with their leaders that he fought. "Neither in this world nor in the next can Mr. Churchill or M. Reynaud answer for the suffering they have caused by their counsels and decrees to millions of peoples."

Would this German broadcast, cleverly couched to undermine British morale, succeed? Three days later, on July 22nd, Lord Halifax in a radio address replied and proclaimed the continued solidarity of England and its rejection of anything resembling appeasement of the Nazis.

What would be the effect of the Reichstag speech on the continued war-determination of the British Commonwealth of Nations and of the Dominions? Certainly their loyal support of hard pressed England was imperative. At this juncture Dorothy Thompson, whether or not commandeered by Washington, took to the microphone and

[1] By permission of Dorothy Thompson. Text furnished through the courtesy of the speaker and by the cooperation of her assistant, Madeleine Clark. For the data of this introductory statement the author is partly indebted to a report (June 21, 1941) given by Elaine Nelson, a graduate student in speech at the State University of Iowa.

[2] For biographical note see Appendix.

addressed the Northern neighbors. She was "number one journalist, political pundit, ace columnist, and number one woman speaker." Her radio speech to the Canadians on July 21, 1940, was a direct reply to the Fuhrer and to his propaganda campaign.

What gave Dorothy Thompson special impetus for such a message? She had been a firm supporter of Roosevelt's foreign policy, had been expelled from Germany because of her journalistic activities, had for two years previously spoken continuously against that country, had repeatedly declared that a British defeat would be fatal to the United States, and had talked on the all-importance of a healthy morale in the winning of wars. As Nelson pointed out, "It was wholly natural that Miss Thompson should respond orally to this message instead of using just her syndicated column *On the Record*, which is read by 7,500,000 readers of 195 newspapers. She believes strongly in the efficacy of the spoken word, and she herself has written, 'The spoken word is probably more inflammatory than the printed word. The human voice is a more patent conveyor of emotion than the printed page.' "

The address is to be analyzed as an oration; it is one in the best sense of that term. Its occasion was a historic one; its theme, exalted; its structure, sufficiently articulated to ensure a flow of ideas without rigidity or ambiguity; its argument, impressive (from the point of view of pro-British Americans); its language, high-colored, figurative, original; its use of apostrophe and direct address (note the direct address to Churchill and to Hitler), repetition of language for emphasis, its parallel structure, illustration, invective, rhetorical question, always effective; its imaginative and emotional quality sustained. Its passages were more than mere rhetoric. The author, although a woman and without political portfolio, produced an oration that would compare not unfavorably with those of Churchill, Roosevelt, and other national leaders who were addressing world-wide audiences during this period.

What of Miss Thompson's oral effectiveness? She is in tremendous demand as a platform and radio speaker. Her voice is well pitched, often is tense, but well modulated. Her vocal diction, articulation and pronunciation, are excellent. She has been frequently described as "nervous" in her speaking activity, a "fault" of most superior speakers. In delivery she follows her manuscript somewhat closely,[3] but is a highly capable extempore speaker.[4]

MEN AND WOMEN OF CANADA: In speaking to you this evening over the Canadian Broadcasting Corporation, I am exercising the prerogative that is still enjoyed by the citizens of free

[3] Madeleine Clark in a letter to the author, April 2, 1941.

[4] For further comment on Dorothy Thompson's methods of delivery see *Representative American Speeches: 1937-1938*, p. 60; *Representative American Speeches: 1938-1939*, p. 87.

nations: the right to have an opinion of one's own, a view of affairs of one's own, and the right to express it. I am in the happy position of holding no public office, of speaking for nobody but myself. Yet what I think and feel is not unique. It is shared, as I well know, by many thousands of citizens of the United States.

This week we read of a peace offer that has been made by Hitler to Great Britain—made in his usual way of an open speech broadcast on the radios of the world, couched in now familiar terms, launched for purposes of international propaganda, and vague except for one thing.

It seems that Germany has no quarrel with Great Britain. Hitler's quarrel is exclusively with this particular British Government, and especially with its head, Mr. Churchill. If Mr. Churchill will only resign and a government come in which is acceptable to Mr. Hitler, he will be glad to make peace immediately. He has no desire to destroy the British Empire. The man standing in the way of peace is Churchill, and the so-called fifth columnists are "only honest men, seeking peace." That is Hitler's argument.

Now, of course, we have all become familiar with this. Mr. Hitler had no quarrel with Austria, only with Mr. Schuschnigg. So the moment Schuschnigg resigned he made peace with Austria by annexing it. He had no quarrel with Czechoslovakia, only with Mr. Beneš. So when Mr. Beneš resigned he made peace with Czechoslovakia by turning it into a Nazi Protectorate. He had no quarrel with any of the countries he has absorbed—only with those leaders who opposed the absorption. Mr. Hitler has no quarrel with traitors in any country on earth. They are his agents, and, as his agents, are honest men seeking peace. His quarrel is only with patriots.

I think we may expect that the whole force of the German propaganda in the immediate future will be concentrated on trying to break down Britain by removing her leadership. But in this struggle, as in all great struggles, nations do become embodied in the persons of the men who lead them.

In a poetic sense, I might say in a Shakespearean sense, it really is Hitler who faces Churchill. For if Hitler has made himself the incorporation of Germany, Churchill really is the incorporation of Britain.

These two men are the very symbols of the struggle going on in the world.

If we can detach ourselves for a moment from all the pain of this struggle, and look at these two men, we see one of those heroic dramas which literature can never approximate. On the one side is the furious, unhappy, frustrated and fanatic figure who has climbed to unprecedented power on the piled-up bodies of millions of men, carried and pushed upward by revolutionary forces, supported by vast hordes of youth crying destruction to the whole past of civilized man. Their upward surge in Germany was accompanied by the wailing and the groans of those "honest men of peace" who once lived in Germany, but were seized in their homes or on the streets and hurled into concentration camps or the barracks of the gangs, there to be beaten insensible with steel rods, or forced upon their knees to kiss a hated hooked cross. That is what Germany did to pacifists long before the war began. Out of Germany poured hordes of refugees, "scattered like leaves from an enchanter fleeing pestilence-stricken multitudes." The followers of Hitler laid their hands upon British and American money loaned to Germany to help her rebuild after the last war and with it began grinding out guns and cannons and ships and tanks and airplanes, crying war, crying revenge, crying dominion. Only when others reluctantly turned their hands to the making of hated cannon, did they yell, peace, peace. They stood in armor plate from their heads to their feet, their belts full of hand grenades, their pockets full of bombs, crying across their borders to those who, seeing, took a rifle from the wall: warmonger, warmonger!

He who stood atop this pyramid of steel-clothed men, stretched out his right hand and grabbed a province, and his left, and snatched another. The pyramid grew higher and higher. It made a mountain of blood and steel from the top of which the furious and fanatic one could see all the kingdoms of the earth. How small is the world, he thought. How easy to conquer. Look down upon these rich democracies. They possess most of the earth. Their youth play cricket and baseball and go to movies. Their life is a dull round of buying and selling, of endless discussion in silly parliaments and congresses. They have lost the will to power and domination. They have been scrapping their battleships and arguing against budgets for armaments. And for a quarter of a century in all their schools and colleges they have been preaching to their youth peace, fellowship, reconciliation. And he laughed, a wild laugh of thirsty joy, crying down to the serried rows on rows of uniformed fanatic youth: strike, and the world will be yours!

He looked across at Britain, and was satisfied. Britain was ruled by business men and bureaucrats. They were cautious men. The business men thought in terms of good bargains; the bureaucrats thought in terms of conferences and negotiations. They were decorous and they were old. They were very sure of Britain. Nobody has ever beaten Britain, not for hundreds of years. Britain was safe. The Germans were annoying again. The Germans were perennially annoying. But Britain was not a tight little island. Britain was a world, a good world, a free world. As it had been, so it would remain—world without end. Amen. And so they closed their briefcases and went fishing or shooting on week-ends. Nobody wanted war. War was unthinkable, really.

Yes, but in England there was a man.

Winston Churchill was no longer young. He was in his sixties. Yet, there was something perennially youthful about him, as there is always something youthful about those who have done what they wanted to do, and have been happy. He had had a good life, the best life any man can have: a life of action and a life of intellect. His father was the son of the Duke of Marlborough. His ancestors had served England and fought her wars and led her peace for as far back as one could remember. But he was the younger son of a younger son and therefore and fortunately, poor. What does a young man of spirit do, with quick blood in his veins, no money and a great tradition behind him? He goes to his country's wars. Young Winston was a soldier of fortune, a fighter on two Continents, a war correspondent, his heart mettlesome, his eye keen, living in his times, living in them up to the hilt, preserving every impression on paper, and seeing everything against the colored tapestry of the great history of Britain. O, yes, he was in love with life. He had no complexes and no neuroses. Shakespeare has described his kind. He called them "this happy breed of men!"

And what did he stand for in the history of England? Light and generosity; Home Rule for Ireland; tolerance and equality for the defeated Boers, generosity to the defeated Germans—he was no lover of the Treaty of Versailles; social reform and the rights of labor, as President of the Board of Trade; Imperial preference for the Dominions, for Canada.

He was no ascetic. He loved good food, good wine, pretty and witty women, gifted men, action and pleasure, color and sound. He was the great life-affirmer. Life was not buying and selling; life was not this margin of profit here or that margin of loss there; life was not the accumulation of riches; life itself was riches—the lovely sight of ships—nothing more beautiful than a ship, nothing more English than a ship, the ships of explorers, of traders, of fighters. To be First Lord of the Admiralty was a job for a man who loves ships, and because he loves ships, loves both their harbors and the oceans of the world.

The lovely forms of landscapes! Home from war and out of responsible office, he took himself a palette and colors and began to paint—like you, Mr. Hitler—to paint the world he loved. He loved this world with the catholic appetite of the artist of life.

For he was, and is, a soldier, a sailor, an artist and a poet. Is not a man rich if he is born with the English language in his mouth? What a language! A glorious and imperial mongrel, this great synthesis of the Teutonic and the French, the Latin and the Greek, this most hospitable of tongues, this raider of the world's ideas, full of words from the Arabic desert and the Roman forum and the lists of the Crusades. The English language fell from his tongue with that candid simplicity which is its genius, and with that grandeur which is its glory. But people said, "The trouble with Winston is he is too brilliant."

When a man is sixty, and has lived life to the fullest, when he has loved life and treated it gallantly, he has the right to retire, and be quiet, and cultivate his garden among his old friends. That is what civilized men have always done and always will do: "leave action and responsibility now to the young ones." That's what he thought.

Ah, but what was wrong with the young ones? The trained eye cannot be closed. The quick mind moves and thinks even if the body lies upon its back watching the clouds move lazily across an English sky. The poet sees what the commercial trader and the common politician do not. And suddenly the soldier-poet leaps to his feet. Something is about to happen! That which he loves more than food and wine and color and sound and action and rest and his garden; something that he loves more than life —that which is his life: his blood, his soul—that which is ancestry and friendship, family and friends, that which is the future —all the great past, all the stumbling present, all the future, the great future, of a language, of a race, is threatened. There is a cloud creeping over the landscape, the shadow of the growing pyramid grows higher. And the old passion for his greatest love wells up in the man's heart—the passion of his childhood, of his adolescence, of his youth, of his maturity, to which never for an instant was he fickle. For England! For Britain! For the Britain of the English soil and the far-flung Navy! For the Britain of the world language and the world commonwealth. For the Britain with her deathless attachment to law and to freedom.

What is this world, he thinks, if Britain falls? What will become of the ever expanding Commonwealth of Nations and the commonwealth of man?

It is too early to retire and cultivate one's garden. "If I forget thee, oh, Britain," he must have cried to himself, "let my right hand forget its cunning and my tongue cleave to the roof of my mouth."

So he puffed his way back to where the politicians were holding their conferences. Yes, he puffed his way. He was quite portly now, and not so young as he had been. But the tongue in his head was the old, great English tongue, and it had something to say.

Do you know what he said, Mr. Hitler? What Winston Churchill said? You once said something like that, too. You said, "Deutschland Erwache!" Germany Awaken! Churchill said, "England, Awaken!" You don't like Mr. Churchill, Herr Hitler. But you would have liked him, I think, if he had been a German.

But it was very hard to wake up England. Still, everybody listened to him—listened interestedly, admiringly, politely. You can't help listening to that tongue. Month in and month out he said, "Britain Awaken!" Month in and month out, with nothing but one seat in Parliament, and with words, he rediscovered for Britain what Britain in her greatest moments is: the parent of the world citizen; the home of the chivalrous; the defender of the faith. The defender of what faith? Of faith in God and in his common destiny, in his common right to citizenship on this planet.

Not in generations have such words of passionate love and measured indignation fallen from English lips as Churchill uttered in the series of speeches called "While England Slept."

And while he spoke to them, while he spoke mostly to unheeding ears, the shadow was lengthening and finally loomed so tall and menacing that all the world could see. And then, when it was over them with all the full darkness of its horror and destruction, the people of England, the common people of England, lifted Churchill on their hands, crying, "Speak and fight for us!"

It was very, very late, when Churchill took up his last fight for Britain. He inherited an unholy mess. Let us tell the truth. He inherited all that the men of little faith, the money-grubbers, the windy pacifists, the ten-to-five o'clock bureaucrats had left undone. But he said no word against them. He did not do what you, Hitler, have done to your predecessors—hold them up to ridicule and contempt. No word of complaint crossed his lips. He is half a generation older than Hitler, but he took up the fight for the sceptered isle, that precious stone, set in a silver sea; he took up the fight for the world-wide commonwealth of men, held together by the most slender thread of common language and a common way of life—and he fights his last fight, for the ways and the speech of men who have never known a master.

Why don't you take your hat off to Churchill, Mr. Hitler, you who claim to love the leadership principle? Why don't you take your hat off to a member of that race you profess to serve, the race of fair and brave and gallant northern men? By what irony of history have those who oppose you become those very men of the north, the Dutch and the Norwegians, Frenchmen, and those half-German, half-Norman folk who call themselves Britons?

Who is the friend of the white race? You, who have ganged up with Japan to drive the white race out of Asia, or Churchill who believes in the right of white men to live and work wherever they can hold their own on this planet?

You, who have waged war upon the white race, and attempted to divide it into superior white folks and inferior white folks, masters and slaves, or Churchill, who stands for the idea of commonwealth and equality?

Who is the prototype of the white man of the future, the world citizen, Churchill, or the world enemy? What do you hate in Churchill that you would not love in a German man? Do you despise him because he is a soldier, and a writer, and an artist? What has become of your charges of English money-grubbers in the face of this rosy old warrior-artist?

And who today is the plutocrat, who is the have nation, and who is the have-not nation?

The greatest have-not nation in the world today is the British Isles. Forty-two million people on an island assailed from the coasts of violated Norway, from the coasts of violated Holland, from the coasts of violated Belgium, and from defeated France, without resources of food or raw materials except as she can buy them or obtain them from her Allies across the oceans of the world. Does not the heroism of this embattled and impoverished Isle impress you, Hitler, you who praise heroism? Would you have more respect for some lickspittle or some cheap pocket imitation of yourself? Who is the plutocratic nation—Britain, in whose great house live today the children of the London slums, or Nazi Germany, the great *nouveau riche* kidnapper of provinces, collector of ransoms, stuffed with the delicatessen of the Danes and the Czechs and the Dutch, heavy hands spread out upon huge knees, with a gun like a gangster's diamond on every finger!

The plutocratic England you attack is today a socialist state— a socialist state created without class war, created out of love and led by an aristocrat for whom England builds no eagle's nests or palaces out of the taxes of her people, a man who cares nothing for money, or ever has, but only for Britain, and for the coming world that a free and socialist British society will surely help to build if ever it is built.

In your speech this week, Mr. Hitler, you said that it caused you pain to think that you should be chosen by destiny to deal the death blow to the British Empire. It may well cause you pain. This ancient structure, cemented with blood, is an incredibly delicate and exquisite mechanism, held together lightly now, by imponderable elements of credit and prestige, experience and skill, written and unwritten law, codes and habits. This remarkable and artistic thing, the British Empire, part Empire and part Commonwealth, is the only world-wide organization in existence, the world equalizer and equilibriator, the only world-wide stabilizing force for law and order on the planet, and if you bring it down the planet will rock with an earthquake such as it has never known. We in the United States will shake with that earthquake and so will Germany. And the Britons, the Canadians the New Zealanders, the Australians, the South Africans, are hurling their bodies into the breach to dam the dykes against world chaos.

I think that often in your sleepless nights you realize this, Mr. Hitler, and sweat breaks over you, thinking for a moment, not of a Nazi defeat, but of a Nazi victory.

And the master of the dyke against world chaos is you, Churchill, you gallant, portly little warrior. I do not know what spirits surround Hitler. I do not hear the great harmonics of Beethoven, but only the music of Wagner, the music of chaos. I do not see the ghost of Goethe nor the ghost of Bismarck, the last great German who knew when to stop.

But around you, Winston Churchill, is a gallant company of ghosts. Elizabeth is there, and sweetest Shakespeare, the man who made the English Renaissance the world's renaissance. Drake is there, and Raleigh, and Wellington. Burke is there, and Walpole, and Pitt. Byron is there, and Wordsworth and Shelley. Yes, and I think Washington is there, and Hamilton, two men of English blood, whom gallant Englishmen defended in your Parliament. And Jefferson is there, who died again, the other day, in France. All the makers of a world of freedom and of law are there, and among them is the Shropshire lad, to whom his ghostly author calls again: "Get ye the men your fathers got, and God will save the Queen."

And when you speak, Churchill, brave men's hearts everywhere rush out to you. There are no neutral hearts, Winston
Churchill, except those that have stopped beating. There are no
neutral prayers. Our hearts and our prayers say, "God give you
strength, God bless you. May you live to cultivate your garden,
in a free world, liberated from terror, and persecution, war, and
fear."

HITLER'S FIFTY-SECOND BIRTHDAY [5]

HANS V. KALTENBORN [6]

Hans V. Kaltenborn gave this address as part of his daily news commentary, over the National Broadcasting Company network, on April 21, 1941.

On that day Adolf Hitler celebrated the beginning of his birthday in a railway car, under the shadow of a Balkan mountain. The celebration, according to the official news agency, D.N.B., was one of "soldierly simplicity." Assembled for the celebration with Hitler were Göring, Goebbels, Ribbentrop, Keitel, Raeder, Himmler, and Hess. Just a few hours earlier the German troops had planted the swastika on Mount Olympus. The Jugoslavs were out of the war, having capitulated after twelve days of resistance. In Greece itself the Allied forces had repeatedly given way. The British, Australian, and New Zealand troops, five divisions at the most, fought valiantly day after day against more than forty German divisions. The German air force clearly dominated the British Royal Air Force and proceeded to destroy Greek village after village, including Larissa, Kalabaka, and other cities. More than fifteen hundred Nazi planes were in action.

To the left of the British from Mount Olympus to Corizza in Albania, the Greeks, who had resisted so heroically during the preceding months in their mountain stand against overwhelming Italian odds, were unable to resist the combined Italian and German pincer drives from the west and north. After the Greeks lost Corizza it was just a matter of a steady Nazi-Italian advance in the face of stubborn rear guard action. Presently the Germans had reached Thermopylae, one hundred miles from Athens and were still going strong. The British and Greeks had little to cheer them except the fact that they had slaughtered a considerable number of invaders. Furthermore the German airmen were already bombing British transports off Chalchis and were promising to make the English retreat from Greece a complete debacle, far worse than the Dunkirk retreat.

In such setting did Mr. Kaltenborn present his news commentary. Although this particular address bears the marks of efficient preparation, Kaltenborn has demonstrated throughout the past twenty years his unusual skill in last-minute extempore interpretation of the news. In 1922 he became the first of the radio news broadcasters to discuss current events. Since that time he has "built a solid, though unsensational, success, while other newscasters, rising on shouts of

[5] By permission of Hans Kaltenborn. Text supplied by the speaker.
[6] For biographical note see Appendix.

synthetic excitement, came and went." (*Reader's Digest,* 34:52-4, February, 1939, "Kaltenborn was ready," Powell, Hickman)

Said the magazine *Time* (32:42, October 10, 1938), commenting upon Kaltenborn's skill in reporting the capitulation of Czechoslovakia, "That he offered better comment on the crisis than anyone else was because he also offered a better combination of talent. . . . He had long trained himself in extemporaneous public speaking . . . and for the last eighteen years he has stepped to the microphone with only scribblings for script. . . . His comments throughout were calm, hopeful, accurate."

His speech concerning Hitler was in his best vein; he stated clearly and directly the latest events and then threw light upon them out of his years of experience as a newspaper editor, foreign correspondent, and general observer. He organized his material carefully, used language of distinction, gave quotations, which from the lips of other commentators might seem highly artificial, and presented the speech with fervor that stamped this performance as an example of an oration. (I use the word oration in the best sense of the term).

On leaving Russian soil today, Foreign Minister Matsuoka of Japan talked about his new Neutrality Pact with Russia. He said it was entirely unexpected and negotiated in ten minutes. Which means that Stalin needed it as a threat to Hitler, and Japan welcomed it as a threat to England and America.

Hitler's successes in the Balkans are having an important influence in Spain. An attack on Gibraltar through Spain is a logical next step for Adolf Hitler's troops. The Spanish press has suddenly turned violently anti-British and anti-American, which suggests that a Franco-Hitler deal has been made or is in sight.

Greece has a new Government under King George and Admiral Sakellarin. It was sworn in today. Rumania seems to be facing another revolution. Bulgaria is invading Yugoslavia. The Balkans are in for a long period of unrest, no matter what happens in Greece. German forces are steadily advancing closer to Athens. Only a military miracle can now prevent the German conquest of Greece. In North Africa the German advance has been stopped. In East Africa it is only a question of days before all Italian resistance ends.

Field Marshal Göring served today as spokesman for the German Army. In extending anniversary congratulations to

Adolf Hitler, he named the three things which made German victories possible. Those who think the Nazis have some miraculous recipe for military achievement might listen to Göring's enumeration of the three things that really count:

1) All kinds of arms; here he means particularly the latest types of planes and tanks produced in five years of complete concentration of German industry on military purposes. Today air superiority is essential to success on land or sea.

2) Training—In Nazi Germany this means the concentration of all education on the single purpose of creating a fanatically devoted, military minded, efficiently war prepared population.

3) Leadership—This refers to subordination of every other quality and purpose to the selection of indoctrinated individuals competent to lead soldiers.

And here is the greeting sent by the Pope today, not to Adolf Hitler but to mankind:

"The world does not need pride and violence, but instead it needs charity and love."

Adolf Hitler is 52 today. He celebrated his birthday somewhere in the Balkans near the scene of his latest Nazi victories. He did not go to the front. Hitler's associates do not permit him to take risks. They know that they need him. He is at once a symbol and a leader. Without his presence as mediator, without his decision in matters in dispute, they would quarrel among themselves—they would split the Party. Such factional disputes among Party leaders would soon divide the Army from the Party and pave the way for new controls. Thus it is self-interest that prompts today's abject worship by Göring, Hess and Goebbels at the Hitler shrine. They know the second-rate intellect, the frustrated spirit, the undeveloped body that is Adolf Hitler. But they also know him as one who has a shrewd instinct about the man he must mistrust. They know him to be unscrupulous and vengeful. They know, too, that he needs them and depends on them, that so long as they are content with their places in the hierarchy, they can remain safe and powerful while Hitler lives.

And, as dictators go, Hitler has lived long. Alexander died at 33 after a night of heavy drinking; Caesar died at 38 by the assassin's dagger and Napoleon died in exile at 51.

But Hitler differs from these men. They had military genius. Hitler has none, despite all his pretensions. Hitler has a genius for exploiting the hates and hopes of a defeated people. He is a truly great demagogue—unhappy Germany's Huey Long. Instinctively he knew that for the military minded, territorially ambitious Teutons he must provide the slogans of imperial glory.

Only a people nurtured in the democratic tradition could be misled by such a phrase as "Every man a king." "Deutschland erwache" gave Germans something to love. "Nieder mit den Juden" gave them something to hate. Master of mass appeal, Hitler once explained the three basic rules of his particular game: "Make it simple—say it often—make it burn."

Like most of the tyrants and demagogues of history, Hitler is utterly devoid of conscience, character or scruple. He violates the elementary rules of decent conduct among men and nations with cynical indifference. In this he is like most of the tyrants and dictators of history. Shakespeare describes the type in *Richard III*:

> For what is he they follow? truly, gentlemen,
> A bloody tyrant and a homicide;
> One rais'd in blood, and one in blood establish'd;
> One that made means to come by what he hath,
> And slaughtered those that were the means to help him.

But Hitler goes far beyond these simple, bloody crimes that mark the usurpers of all ages. He poisons and tortures men's minds as well as their bodies. When I first met Hitler a few months before he came to power, it was the bitterness of the man's spirit, the hatred of all those who dared oppose him that appalled me. I could then understand why he had just refused President Hindenburg's offer of an important position in a coalition cabinet. Here were a mind and spirit whose chief strength was inflexibility, rigidity of purpose—the utter inability to yield or compromise.

Of course, Hitler does change and he does compromise, but he refuses to admit this, even to himself. That is why you can truly say of Hitler, "He lies and does not even know that he lies." Or, as Lord Halifax once put it to me more politely when we were exchanging our impressions of the man Hitler, "Hitler," he said, "does not stay put."

Hitler already hated the United States when I first saw him in fall of 1932. Why? Because the United States defeated Germany, because Woodrow Wilson did not enforce his Fourteen Points, because he thinks ours is a land dominated by Jews. He rebuked me for daring to challenge his anti-Semitism. Did I not come from a country which excluded all aliens it did not care to admit? He said, in effect, "No American has the right to challenge anti-Semitism in Germany because the United States bars undesirable foreigners." This doesn't make sense, but it's a typical piece of Hitler logic. His appeal is to prejudice and passion; never to decency or common sense. He dreamed of a Nazi-dominated Europe long before he came to power. Mussolini once said, "Italian fascism is not an article of export." "Would you," I asked Hitler, "say the same of National Socialism?" "I don't need to export it," he replied truculently. "Emissaries are coming to me from all over Europe. They ask me how they can introduce the Nazi creed into their own countries. They will export it for me."

This agrees with what Hitler told Herman Rauschning after he came to power. If you want to know why Hitler will choose his own good time to make war on any country, consider what he has said again and again. His dupes and agents are now working night and day in the United States. They will go on working until he is ready to strike. Hitler is making war on us now, but he is doing it secretly. And he can accomplish far more against us in this way while diplomatic relations remain unbroken. Here is Hitler's own explanation of his method, as Rauschning quotes it in *The Voice of Destruction*:

Revolutionary propaganda must function before my Army acts. We have friends in the land of the enemy. They will help us. Confusion,

contradiction, uncertainty, panic—those are our weapons. I have
learned something from the Bolsheviks and I am not ashamed to
say so. Study intrigue and revolutions. Then you will know our
task. Seizure by surprise, terror, sabotage, attack from within—that
is the war of the future.

It sounds fantastic, but we know that it worked in Norway,
in Holland, in France, in Rumania, in Bulgaria and more recently
in Iraq. Hitler is disdainful of his generals except for immediate
military tasks.

"No generals rule me," he says. "Generals want to make war
like knights of old. I need no knights. I need revolutions. No
law, no treaty will keep me from using any advantage. I make
war."

It is difficult for decent human beings to admit that sometimes there is an immediate advantage for those who violate all
the rules of decent human conduct. That is why there are so
many Hitler dupes. There was a time when I was in danger of
becoming one myself. I, too, believed that since God works in a
mysterious way his wonders to perform, even a Hitler might be
His agent to undo the mistakes of the postwar treaties.

Now, I know better. Hitler has exploited the worst qualities
of the German race. But he has also known how to use in war
its habit of obedience, its scientific and military genius, its great
industrial power and its organizing capacity. By superior military attack from without and by exploiting the forces of decay
from within, he has made himself the master of Europe. Today
he is 52. Where will he stand at 53 or 54 or 55?

Primarily, that depends on America. He has grown too
strong for Britain to defeat him without our help. Sooner or
later, his conquests and those who helped achieve them will break
apart. But there is little comfort in the thought that Napoleon
kept Europe at war for more than a decade before ambition
o'erleaped itself. Only the United States holds that reserve of
political, economic and military power which can defeat Hitler by
the attack from without. Without our swift supply of all-out

help, stalemate and a decade of universal economic strangulation may lie ahead. One would like to appeal to Americans in the words of a great leader, who said:

"Do not believe that Hitler is a fortune-favored God. Among those men who seem attached to his interests there are those who hate him; others fear him; some envy him. Your delay and your negligence help bury these important truths. Think for a moment of the state to which you have been brought. This dictator has progressed to the point where you no longer have the free choice between vigilance and inaction. He has become a menace. He speaks in terms of arrogance. He can no longer content himself with what he has already conquered. Each day he enlarges his projects for the conquest of the world. He is surrounding you with tricks and traps while you delay and fail to act. When will you do what is needful to be done? When will we see you take decisive action? How long will it be before a direct menace faces your land? Failure to act in time is the most shameful sin of which we men can be guilty."

These words were spoken by Demosthenes to his fellow-Athenians in ancient Greece. I only changed one word, to substitute Hitler for Philip. For the Athenians of ancient Greece, like the Americans of today, were fond of ease and comfort and cherished a false sense of national security in the face of grave dangers from without and within.

It is true that Hitler is already 52 and has thus outlived the greatest conquerors of history. But we cannot and should not depend on death to defeat him. History may not repeat itself. Europe is a tired continent and may well be too tired to break its own chains.

Walt Whitman thought so, when he apostrophised the American Pioneers. "Have the elder races halted, wearied there beyond the seas?" he asked. And he answered with a challenge: "Ours then the task eternal." And what is that task? It is the task and duty of ensuring freedom—democratic freedom—for ourselves and for the world. For unless it is possible for men to be free and at peace in Europe, they cannot be free and at peace in America. The world has grown too small to be half slave and half free.

—Good afternoon.

SPRING COMES TO ENGLAND [7]

EDWARD R. MURROW [8]

Edward R. Murrow broadcast this address on March 9, 1941, at
2:30 o'clock Eastern Standard Time over the C.B.S. network.

Murrow, after his graduation from Washington State College in
1930, became, among other things, first president of the National Student Federation, visited 300 American colleges and spent some time
in Europe. He then became an assistant director of the Institute of
International Education. In 1935 he joined the Columbia Broadcasting System as director of talks in the department of special events,
and in May, 1937, became chief of the European bureau.

Before the outbreak of the present war he covered a large part
of Europe for C.B.S. Murrow, for example, chartered a 23-passenger
plane as "sole passenger to reach Vienna in time to describe the 1938
Anschluss."

His broadcasts from London have attracted a wide audience in
America. His reports illustrate how he has developed a new radio
reporting technique to cover this new kind of war. In giving a color-
ful, sensitive, behind-the-news account of Britain, Murrow "spent
every available moment, day and night, talking to the people of England, clerks, shopgirls, air-raid wardens, dockyard workers, housewives.
For these death is closer than it is to the men actually under arms as
the enemy concentrated on bombing raids over populous cities."

Murrow has recently (April, 1941, through Simon and Schuster)
published a collection of his broadcasts under the title, *This Is
London.* Elmer Davis,[9] the distinguished C.B.S. news analyst, states
in the introduction:

"We who work with Murrow are keenly aware of his excellence
as a reporter of pure news; indeed some of us—having, like most
radio news men, learned our trade in another medium—are perhaps
faintly scandalized that such good reporting can be done by a man
who has never worked on a newspaper in his life, and acquired his
basic experience of Europe, first as president of the National Student
Federation of the United States, and then in the service of the Institute
of International Education."

[7] Permission to reprint this broadcast was given by the Columbia Broadcasting Company. The text is taken from *Talks,* 6:1-6, April, 1941, a quarterly
digest of addresses broadcast over the Columbia network. "The reports of
foreign broadcasts which appear in *Talks* are ediphone transcriptions, and are
not compared with the original manuscripts."

[8] For biographical note see Appendix.

[9] See *Representative American Speeches: 1939-1940,* p. 63

This is London. Soon it will be spring in England. Already there are flowers in the park, although the parks aren't quite as well kept as they were this time last year. But there's good fighting weather ahead. In four days time the moon will be full again, and there's a feeling in the air that big things will happen soon.

The winter that is ending has been hard, but Londoners have many reasons for satisfaction. There have been no serious epidemics. The casualties from air bombardments have been less than expected. And London meets this spring with as much courage, though less complacency, than at this time last year.

Many ancient buildings have been destroyed. Acts of individual heroism have been commonplace. More damage has been done by fire than by high explosives. The things cast down by the Germans out of the night skies have made hundreds of thousands of people homeless. I've seen them standing in the cruel cold of a winter morning with tears frozen on their faces looking at the little pile of rubble that was their homes and saying over and over again in a toneless unbelieving way, "What have we done to deserve this?"

But the winter has brought sore conditions in the underground shelters. It has brought, too, reduced rations, repeated warnings of the imminence of invasion, shorter restrictions upon the freedom of the individual and organizations.

When spring last came to England the country was drifting—almost dozing—through a war that seemed fairly remote. Not much had been done to gear manpower and machinery to the demands of modern war. The story of the spring, summer and fall is well known to all of you. For the British it was a record of one disaster after another, until those warm cloudless days of August and September when the young men of the Royal Air Force beat back the greatest air fleet ever assembled by any nation. Those were days and nights and even weeks when time seemed to stand still.

At the beginning they fought over the English Channel, then over the coast of Kent, and when the German bombers smashed the advance fighter bases along the coast, the battle moved inland. Night after night the obscene glare of hundreds of fires reddened the bellies of the big awkward barrage balloons over London, transforming them into queer animals with grace and beauty. Finally the threat was beaten off. Both sides settled down to delivering heavy blows in the dark. Britain received more than she gave. All through the winter it went on. Finally there came bits of good news from the western desert. But even Tobruk and Bengazi seemed far away. Victories over the Italians are taken for granted here. Even the children know that the real enemy is Germany.

It hasn't been victories in the Middle East or promises of American aid that have sustained the people of this island during the winter. They know that next winter, when it comes, will probably be worse; that their sufferings and privations will increase. Their greatest strength has been and is something that is talked about a great deal in Germany but never mentioned here—the concept of a master race.

The average Englishman thinks it's just plain silly for the Germans to talk about a master race. He's quietly sure in his own mind that there is only one master race. That is a characteristic that has caused him to adopt an attitude of rather bored tolerance toward all foreigners and has made him thoroughly disliked by many of them. But it is the best thing that has closed his mind to the possibility that Britain may be defeated. The habit of victory is strong here. Other habits are strong, too. The old way of doing things is considered best. That is why it has taken more than a year and a half to mobilize Britain's potential strength, and the job is not yet finished.

The other day, watching a farmer trying to fill in a twenty-foot-deep bomb crater in the middle of his field, I wondered what would happen before he harvested the next crop from that bomb-torn soil. I suppose that many more bombs will fall. There will be much talk about equality of sacrifice, which doesn't exist. Many proud ships will perish in the western approaches. There will be further restrictions on clothes and food. Probably a few profiteers will make their profits.

No one knows whether invasion will come, but there are those who fear it will not. I believe that a public opinion poll on the question, "Would you like the Germans to attempt an invasion?" would be answered overwhelmingly in the affirmative. Most people, believing that it must be attempted eventually, would be willing to have it come soon. They think that in no other way can the Germans win this war, and they will not change their minds until they hear their children say "we are hungry."

So long as Winston Churchill is Prime Minister, the House of Commons will be given an opportunity to defend its traditions and to determine the character of the government that is to rule this country. The Prime Minister will continue to be criticized in private for being too much interested in strategy and too little concerned with the great social and economic problems that clamor for solution. British propaganda aimed at occupied countries will continue to fight without its heavy artillery, until some sort of statement on war aims, or, if you prefer, peace aims, has been published.

In the future, as in the past, one of the strangest sensations for me will be that produced by radio. Sometime someone will write the story of the technical and military uses to which this new weapon has been put; but no one, I think, will ever describe adequately just what it feels like to sit in London with German bombs ripping in the air, shaking the buildings, and causing the lights to flicker, while you listen to the German radio broadcasting Wagner or Bavarian folk music. A twist of the dial gives you Tokyo, talking about dangerous thoughts, an American senator discussing hemisphere defense, the clipped, precise accent of a British announcer describing the proper method of photographing elephants, Moscow boasting of prospects of the wheat harvest in the Ukraine, each nation speaking almost any language save its own. Finally, you switch off the receiving set in order that the sounds from the four corners of the earth will not interfere with the sound of the German bombs that come close enough to cause you to dive under the desk.

The bombs this spring will be bigger and there will be more of them, probably dropped from a greater height than ever before. Berlin and London will continue to claim that their bombs hit the military targets, while the enemy's strike mainly churches, schools, hospitals and private dwellings.

The opening engagement of the spring campaign is now being fought in the Atlantic. The Admiralty has taken over control of the shipyards in an effort to speed up production and repairs. Merchant sinkings will probably reach alarming proportions, but there will always be men to take ships out. The outcome of the battle in the Atlantic will be decisive. This island lives by its ships, and the ships will be carrying supplies from America.

There was no dancing in the streets here when the Lend-Lease Bill was passed, for the British know from their own experience that the gap between legislation and realization can be very wide. They remember being told that their frontier was on the Rhine, and they know now that their government did very little to keep it there.

The course of Anglo-American relations will be smooth on the surface, but many people over here will express regret that they believe America is making the same mistake that Britain made. For you must understand that the idea of America being of more help as a non-belligerent than as a fighting ally has been discarded, even by those who advanced it originally.

Maybe we shall do some frank, forthright talk across the Atlantic instead of rhetoric, but I doubt it. One thing that is not to be harvested will determine the pattern of events for a long time to come. British statesmen are fond of repeating that Britain stands alone as the defender of democracy and decency, but General Headquarters is now on Pennsylvania Avenue in Washington, D. C. Many Britishers realize that. Not all of them are happy about it, for the policies of Washington have not always been the policies of the Tory Party, which still rules this country. Presumably, the decisions of Washington will be taken in the full light of publicity and debate, and no mere radio reporter has the right to use the weight of monopolized opportunity in an effort to influence those decisions. We can only deliver to you an occasional wheelbarrow load of stuff, tell you where it comes from; and what sort of air-raid shelter or bastion you build with it is a matter for free men to decide. But since part of reporting must necessarily be personal, I'd like to end this with my own impression of Britain on the verge of spring and big events.

There's still a sense of humor in the country. The old feeling of superiority over all other peoples remains. So does class distinction. There is great courage and a blind belief that Britain will survive. The British aren't all heroes; they know the feeling of fear. I've shared it with them. They try to avoid thinking deeply about political and social problems. They'll stand any amount of government inefficiency and muddle. They're slow to anger, and they die with great dignity. They will cheer Winston Churchill when he walks through block after block of smashed houses and offices as though he'd brought them a great victory. During a blinding raid when the streets are filled with smoke and the sound of the roaring guns, they'll say to you: "Do you think we're really brave, or just lacking in imagination?"

Well, they've come through the winter, and they've been warned that the testing days are ahead. Of the past months, they may well say: "We've lived a life, not an apology." And of the future, I think most of them would say: "We shall live hard, but we shall live."

THE WHEEL OF JUDGMENT [10]

RAYMOND GRAM SWING [11]

This talk was given by Raymond Gram Swing as part of a regular broadcast on May 6, 1941, at 10 p. m., Eastern Standard Time. This special item, the reentry of Haile Selassie into Addis Ababa, was probably obscured by the more crucial events of the war: headline news concerned the continued activities of Nazi raiders in the battle of the Atlantic; the British struggle in Iraq to guard the oil wells and the approaches to the Suez; the continued withdrawal of the British rear guard from Greece after that melancholy collapse; the first official rumbles from Moscow that German troops were moving through Finland; the German blasting of Liverpool in Coventry fashion; Adolf Hitler's warning to America of Germany's war might; and Churchill under Parliamentary attack for the bad turn of events in the Mediterranean.

When Swing entered radio in 1934, he was regarded as "dull," "didactic," and "pedantic." His remarks over the air were without drama or comedy. His radio popularity came suddenly in September, 1939, with the German-Russian onslaught against Poland. Listeners liked his calm, analytical and yet optimistic handling of the events. Today he "reaches more listeners than any other person in the world who speaks over the radio, as he does, well and often." [12]

He broadcasts five evenings each week (except Saturday and Sunday) over some 110 stations of the Mutual Broadcasting System, and over short wave to South America and Australia (in which latter region the Australian Broadcasting Commission converts the transmission into long waves and "blankets the commonwealth"). Nine million Americans listen to him. In addition, he talks to England each week to an audience estimated to be 30 per cent of the British people, about nine million.

What of his background for his remarkable broadcasting success? (a) His father, Albert Temple Swing, was a Congregational minister, who later joined the faculty of Oberlin Theological Seminary; the mother taught German in Oberlin University. (b) Raymond had one year at Oberlin, studied music, vocal and church organ. (c) He had years of journalistic experience as reporter. He was Berlin correspondent for the *Chicago Daily News*, and reported from Berlin and through German-occupied Europe in World War I. After this war he was Berlin representative of the *New York Herald*, later in London as

---

[10] By permission of the speaker. Text furnished by Mr. Swing.

[11] For biographical note see Appendix.

[12] Jack Alexander and Frank I. Odell, "Radio's Best Bedside Manner." *Saturday Evening Post*. 213:14-15, December 14, 1940.

representative of the *Wall Street Journal* and other American papers.
After his return to this country in 1934 he managed to get a job as
broadcaster for the Columbia System; later he transferred to the
Mutual network.

Swing puts in twelve hours a day in preparation for his fifteen-
minute talk.   At ten o'clock in the morning he begins his digest of the
news and holds conferences with those who might supply data.   Once
he has decided on the main lines of his commentary, he checks his facts
by telephone or wire.   He calls up the Department of State at Washington, or some Wall Street investment firm, or other helpful source.
Often he converses with John Gunther, Dorothy Thompson, Vincent
Sheehan, and other erstwhile European journalists.

About 5 p.m. he begins typing his talk.   At six his portable has
produced some 500 to 2000 words.   After his evening dinner he
completes the talk,—about eight-thirty or nine o'clock.   "In the hour
that intervenes . . . he edits his manuscript, tearing out sentences and
phrases, and interlining copiously in a cramped, meticulous hand."
He reads aloud to himself his manuscript to get the feel of the material.
At ten minutes of ten he reports at the studio.

Sometimes late developments cause him to abandon much of his
talk and to refashion it as any daily paper does when unexpected
news appears.

He, like Kaltenborn, has a reputation for neat timing.   "Seated
at a desk, he turns the pages with one hand and holds a stop watch
with the other. . . .   He makes no gestures."   But he leans forward
with plenty of animation, all the while keeping his eye on the stop
watch so that he can close within a few seconds of the assigned time
limit.

His tones are well modulated, the syllables well rounded, each
vowel and consonant given its full value (perhaps overprecision).
His vocal training is apparent in his speech.   But he, different from
Kaltenborn, is in no sense dramatic and oratorical (I use that word in
a "good" sense).

He is careful in his selection of words.   He says, "And one thing
I am sure of, there can be no peace without communication, nor any
communication without honestly used words."

Also he is a mature philosopher, who frequently addresses visible
audiences, including college commencement exercises.   His doctrine of
the mission of democracy explains much of what he says over the air.
In his talk before the American Civil Liberties Union, February 12,
1941, he said:

"Democracy has many meanings to many men.   I know some who
think democracy is the capitalist system.   I know some who think it is
the open shop!   I know some who think it is financial oligarchy, which
is what Hitler calls it.   Some bitterly call it a fraud.   But all these
people think of democracy as an end-product, as the thing which is
built by the democratic process.   But democracy is not necessarily a
precise form of government, or a form of economic relationship.   It is

any system of society where the source of power is the individual, and whose laws safeguard the freedom of the individual. Democracy is the process of free individuals doing something with their freedom. If in his freedom an architect builds a poor house, the house is poor, not the freedom. And if modern democratic society is inadequate in some respects, that is not the fault of freedom. It is the poor use of freedom. And the cure for the poor use of freedom is not to abolish it, but to use it better."

The event of today, not in terms of day-to-day developments, but in terms of a deeper meaning, was the entry of Haile Selassie into Addis Ababa. He entered his capital formally, in the company of the British Commander, General Cunningham, and was received by his people with enthusiasm. No one with a sense of underlying propriety will fail to be stirred by the scene of this dignified and once abandoned ruler, coming again into his own. He does so as a by-product of a great war, but he ends his own cycle of tragedy with a fitting recompense. I must take you back to the day of June 30th, 1936, when Haile Selassie appeared before the Assembly of the League of Nations, like a figure out of the Old Testament, addressing men who were sheepishly ashamed to look him in the face. That was the day when the Italian journalists greeted him with a rowdy outburst of yelling and cat calls, and they had to be cleared from the gallery by the stupefied Geneva police. Haile Selassie then made a speech which rang with some of the soulful poetry of the Old Testament. "I pray to Almighty God," he began, "that he shall spare the nations the terrible sufferings that have been inflicted on my people, and of which the chiefs who accompany me here have been the horrified witnesses. It is my duty," he continued, "to inform the governments assembled at Geneva—responsible as they are for the lives of men, women and children—of the deadly peril which threatens them, by describing to them the fate which has been suffered by Ethiopia." Here was the knell of prophecy, if ever it has been heard in modern times. And the so-called Lion of Judah, humbled and wracked by the fate of his people, was not addressing the League as an outsider. His country was a full member, and it had been attacked by another member, Italy, and the League, it is well to repeat over and over again, did not see the need of bold loyalty to its principles. "The Ethiopian Government," said Haile Selassie that day, "never expected any other government to shed its soldiers' blood to defend the covenant when its own personal interests were not at stake. The Ethiopian warriors asked only means to defend themselves. On many occasions I have asked for financial assistance for the purchase of arms. That assistance has been constantly refused to me." Then he raised his final plea. "The problem submitted to the Assembly," he cried, "is much wider today than merely the question of settling the Italian aggression. It is collective security, it is the very existence of the League. It is the confidence which each state places in international treaties. In other words, international morality is at stake. Apart from the Kingdom of the Lord, there is not on this earth any nation that is superior to any other. Should it happen that a strong government finds that it may with impunity destroy a small people, then the hour strikes for the weak people to appeal to the League to give its judgment. God and history will remember your judgment. The aggressor has confronted the states with an accomplished fact. Are they to set up the terrible precedent of bowing before force? What measure do you intend to take? Representative of the world, I have come to Geneva to discharge in your midst the most painful duty for the head of a state. What reply have I to take back to my people?" The reply was silence. He could take away only the memory of embarrassed statesmen, of averted looks, of super-cilious smiles. Ethiopia was not aided or saved. But the wheel of judgment has made a turning. Today there is no League of Nations and today Haile Selassie reentered Addis Ababa. Today France is prostrate, Spain is starving, Holland, Norway, the Balkans are under the heel of the conqueror, and the city ports and industrial centers of Britain are scenes of desolation and grief. The world has chosen to learn the hard way. But Haile Selassie is back, as a witness that the wheel of judgment does make a turning. He is back through the aid that came too late, too expensively late, but it came.

SOVIET RUSSIA AT WAR [13]

WALTER DURANTY, LOUIS GOTTSCHALK, SAMUEL N. HARPER [14]

This radio discussion from the University of Chicago, over the Red Network of the National Broadcasting Company, was held on Sunday, June 29, 1941, at 1:30 p. m., Central Daylight Saving Time. The participants were Walter Duranty, foreign correspondent, *New York Times;* Louis Gottschalk, Professor of Modern History, University of Chicago; and Samuel N. Harper, Professor of Russian Language and Institutions, University of Chicago.

The war between Germany and the Soviet Union had broken out on Sunday, June 22, just one week before this broadcast. At once 2,000,000 or more Nazi soldiers, integrated with divisions, thoroughly mechanized, and with thousands of airplanes, attacked simultaneously on the Eastern front, from northern Finland to the Black Sea. Russia was apparently expecting the onslaught and rallied her millions as best she could, even though she quickly retreated through Poland, Latvia, Estonia, and other regions retaken in 1939-40. Real facts, after a week of struggle, had not yet emerged to throw much light on the probable outcome of the world's greatest battle. The strength of the Red army and air forces was still problematical. Many military observers predicted that the Stalin infantry and tanks and "Stalin Line" would quickly crumple. The questions which the Chicago Round Table conferees attempted to deal with were, How would the people of Russia react to this war? How strong was the political leadership of the Soviet Republics? Could the economic structure of this socialist state stand the strain of a major war?

The Round Table [15] was announced as "the oldest educational program continuously on the air." The broadcasts were entirely without a script and without an excessive amount of rehearsal. Subjects were chosen because of their social, political or economic significance. The speakers were experts and their remarks were usually aimed to provide information rather than to demonstrate heated controversy. The participants allegedly had "no ax to grind."

MR. GOTTSCHALK: Gentlemen, I think the Round Table is extremely fortunate in having two such experts as you as

[13] By permission of the University of Chicago and through the courtesy of the director of radio.

[14] For biographical notes see Appendix.

[15] For further comment on the Chicago Round Table see Introductory Note, *Representative American Speeches: 1939-1940,* p. 191.

its guests. Harper, if I am not mistaken, you have studied Russian affairs since long before the Revolution.

MR. HARPER: Since 1904.

MR. GOTTSCHALK: And you have been there about twenty times since then.

MR. HARPER: To be precise, eighteen times.

MR. GOTTSCHALK: Duranty, you have been in Russia for twenty years. I know that I have been reading your dispatches from there for a great many years.

MR. DURANTY: I lived there for thirteen years straight and have spent three or four months there every year since.

MR. GOTTSCHALK: That is fine for the Round Table, because we want to talk about *facts* this afternoon. We don't want to argue about intervention or nonintervention or about any of the other moot questions of the day. We want simply to have a factual discussion on Russia. Russia is definitely at war at last, and we want to know, Duranty, whether you think there is any chance of Russia's maintaining her position for any length of time.

MR. DURANTY: I think one point is not fully realized by some of the military experts, and that is that Russia has not yet begun to fight within the area of its own fortifications.[16] The fighting so far has been in that area which Russia seized deliberately as a glacis or outwork, or sort of bastion area, and where the fighting will be decisive will be on the old frontiers of Russia which have been prepared for the last seven years at least.

MR. GOTTSCHALK: Then it is a fact that there is some point in discussing Russia's situation, and it won't be ancient history before we get through. Do you think so, Harper?

MR. HARPER: No, I don't. I think it is too early to prognosticate on the military side, but I think it is very important that we discuss the internal setup.

---

[16] That is, within the area of the Soviet Union excluding the areas of land ceded by Finland in 1940 and those occupied in 1939 and 1940—Estonia, Latvia, Lithuania, the Russian segment of Poland, Bessarabia, and Bukovina.

MR. GOTTSCHALK: Good! In any war situation the morale of the people fighting the war is a very important factor, and I should like to start with that problem. Do you think the morale of the Russians is good at this time?

MR. HARPER: If we take it from the political point of view, I think we should note, first, that, while the promises of the new constitution given to the peoples of the Soviet Union in 1936 have not been carried out fully, nevertheless they have had elections.[17] I don't think they have been entirely as meaningless as a great many people thought. These elections are different from ours. On the basis of my long study of Russia from before the Revolution, I note that in these last years the Russian people and those in the Soviet Union have secured at last a channel of self-expression and self-assertion.

MR. GOTTSCHALK: Would you go so far, Duranty, as to agree with Harper that that would seem to indicate a certain growth of democracy inside Russia?

MR. DURANTY: I think the mechanism of democracy has been set up, but I still believe there has been a good deal too much of formal democracy. That is to say, they have learned at least the mechanism of voting, but I think, so far as self-expression is concerned, there has been a great deal of instructing the voters. That has occurred in other countries, too; but the voter is so thoroughly instructed in Russia that they vote 100 per cent, with no dissenting voice heard. I myself would be more impressed if the majority had not been 100 per cent and even in some fantastic cases where counting is a little careless (as one hears it has been in this great country occasionally), 102 and 103 per cent.

MR. HARPER: And in the Soviet system we must note The special position that the party holds.[18] You were in Moscow

[17] The new constitution was adopted in 1936, establishing the Union of Soviet Socialist Republics as a "socialist state of workers and peasants," composed of eleven constituent Soviet republics. It contained provision for wide democratic rights, including that of the secret election ballot for the Soviet citizen.

[18] That is, the Communist Party of about two million members.

at the time of the last and very important party conference in February of this year, were you not, Duranty?

MR. DURANTY: Yes.

MR. HARPER: And the party still holds the leading position?

MR. DURANTY: The party holds the leading position, but I would wish you to understand, Gottschalk, and you, too, Harper, that the position of the party in the last six months, let us say, has been modified very considerably for the better.

MR. GOTTSCHALK: In other words, I take it you are not quite agreed as to whether this constitutional experiment has promoted the morale of Russia or not. I would like to go on from that point and take up the question of economic morale. Has the productivity of the Russians tended toward a better military state in Russia?

MR. HARPER: There I would say very definitely, on the basis of my studies, that in the past year production has shown definite progress. Now, there has been recent legislation with regard to labor hours, imposing severe penalties for truancy and lateness. And there has been, if you wish, more regimentation. That is a very interesting question to raise, and it can't be answered.

MR. DURANTY: Wait a minute! There has been actually a definite conscription of labor with all that conscription implies in military terms. It is not so much a question of hours. Mind you, it is true that wages have increased in a commensurate degree, but there have been various penalties applied in the past year.

MR. GOTTSCHALK: The point I would like to ask in that connection is not so much whether that makes for greater efficiency—I assume it does—

MR. DURANTY: It does.

MR. GOTTSCHALK: —but whether it makes for a higher standard of living.

MR. DURANTY: Yes, I should say "Yes" again, undoubtedly. Labor has been paid overtime and possibly in some cases for a lot of work—Russia works on piece time—salaries have been raised. But don't forget that the standard of living in Russia depends not on wages but on supply. If there are enough goods, the standards will improve: not because salaries are raised but because goods are available for the consumer.

MR. HARPER: But, from the point of view of political morale, how does this "conscription of labor" operate?

MR. DURANTY: In the Russian system now it is virtually true that the worker is as thoroughly tied to his job as is the soldier to his job, and he has to be there on time. If he is not, he suffers a severe penalty. I remember that not long after the system began a man came to me and said, "My brother is in trouble. He has been late three times and is liable to be imprisoned, if not killed." He was only late a half-hour three times, and on two of those times, at least, he had a good excuse.

MR. GOTTSCHALK: They did not put him up against a wall and shoot him?

MR. DURANTY: Of course not. I said, "You will see what will happen is this: They will see whether your brother is a good worker or is a loafer, and, if he is a loafer, they will get rid of him." And he was not shot or backed up against the wall, but he was docked for the time lost.

MR. GOTTSCHALK: But the laws are very definite. Harper, you are an expert on the laws of Russia. The laws very definitely do imply capital penalty for a great many offenses.

MR. HARPER: I think we take those laws too literally in many instances. They are not applied in practice.

MR. GOTTSCHALK: That is to say, they are actually more an indication of what they want to correct rather than what they are going to do.

MR. HARPER: Yes, that is correct.

MR. GOTTSCHALK: Now, you mentioned the question of supply as the determining factor in the standard of living in Russia, Duranty, and I wonder whether the manufacture of consumer goods has increased to any extent in the past year or more.

MR. DURANTY: It has increased perhaps in actual volume but not in a ratio to demand. The real trouble has been that the Russian demands for the army, because of the very immense menace they knew was coming, have been so great that they have not been able to create consumer goods.

On the other hand, the Russians had a record harvest last year—the biggest harvest they have ever had—and so the food supply is better, and that, after all, is the most essential thing. Then housing has improved undoubtedly in the great cities.

MR. HARPER: In regard to the crop of last year, just as you had one or two of these severe measures of discipline with respect to labor in industry, there must have been a tightening-up of the frame-work of collectivism of agriculture. Now, if the crop was good last year, these measures have not been resented, and people have worked under them.

MR. DURANTY: Yes, undoubtedly. Only there is this point: The peasants have considerable surplus money and nothing to spend it on, and even in Russia babies need shoes, and that is one of the criteria by which countries decide their happiness or lack of happiness.

MR. GOTTSCHALK: In determining this question of prices and standard of living, not only supply and demand are necessary but, in talking about conditions in Soviet Russia at war, it seems to me very important that we talk about transportation. Duranty, you recently crossed the Siberian region, and I wonder if you had a chance to observe any of the transportation problems.

MR. DURANTY: Yes, and it was very interesting to me. I had heard that the Trans-Siberian Railroad had been double-tracked, but this time I saw it. I saw not only double tracks but double bridges.

MR. GOTTSCHALK: You mean they built two bridges every time they crossed a river?

MR. DURANTY: Yes, two separate bridges. If one is injured by bombing, the other one remains.

MR. HARPER: What about the supplementary track being built in the north that we heard so much about?

MR. DURANTY: I am not sure about that, although I have asked about it.

I had a rather interesting experience on my trip across the region of Siberia. I shared my coach three nights with a captain of the frontier guard, a young man, and there was a colonel in the same carriage. We had a good deal of talk together, and he gave me some very interesting information. First of all, I noticed that troops were moving westward, and I said, "I suppose they are going home for their Easter vacation." He said, "Not at all, we are moving troops steadily westward because we know that the enemy is there—the German enemy."

MR. GOTTSCHALK: The captain said that?

MR. DURANTY: Yes, and the colonel confirmed it. This was, I may say, before the neutrality pact with Japan [19] and long before the outbreak of war between Germany and Russia. And he said, what is more, "We can take care of the Japanese. Our frontier guards (he did not say, but which I imagine numbers about 350,000 men) and the local territorial division can handle the Japanese. They won't make any trouble. We have taught them two lessons already." [20]

MR. GOTTSCHALK: I don't want to interfere too much with the discussion of this problem of production and of industrial

---

[19] A neutrality pact was signed between Russia and Japan, April 13, 1941, guaranteeing each from attack in the rear should either be "the object of military activity on the part of one or several powers." The accord also guaranteed the territorial integrity of Japanese-dominated Manchukuo and Russia's Mongolian People's Republic (Outer Mongolia).

[20] In frontier fighting in recent years between the Manchukuoan and Mongolian puppet states referred to in footnote 19 and in the area southwest of Vladivostok at the junction of the Korean, Manchukuoan, and Russian borders.

relations, but I think we ought to discuss the "purges" in connection with the internal morale of Russia.

Have the purges, as far as you have studied them, created a situation in Russia which is rather hopeless with regard to industry and military affairs?

MR. HARPER: Well, I spoke of the failure of the complete fulfilment of the constitution, and I had in mind the purges. They represented another trend—a very negative trend. Those purges in 1937-38 definitely overreached. Since 1938—

MR. GOTTSCHALK: By "overreached" you mean they got too many people?

MR. HARPER: They got out of hand.

MR. DURANTY: They got out of hand, and it was collective madness. The thing became crazy. They were denouncing one another, slandering one another—people were having competition in doing that. All this came out in their own newspapers.

MR. HARPER: There was official recognition of that fact?

MR. DURANTY: Yes, it recognized definitely that the madness had existed, and they gave most astounding and fantastic figures on how this madness existed.

MR. HARPER: And it was stopped on the basis of that?

MR. DURANTY: It was stopped suddenly by the action of Stalin in July, 1938.

MR. HARPER: Of course, it was not possible to repair the damage done?

MR. DURANTY: Not to repair all the damage, but great efforts have been made. They printed the figures for four major provinces where reinstatements were made. They cannot revise the cases of the dead, but the number of dead was not very great, and the reinstatement was over 50 per cent in the four major provinces.

MR. HARPER: I know in 1939 I noted very clearly one effect of the purge. When I went around the institutions, I found young men in positions of responsibility. There were a few of the old, but it was largely a new generation—the generation trained by the twenty-two years of revolution—that had come up to positions of responsibility. You probably found the same thing last winter. Would you be willing to give your impression of these new men, whom we call "Stalin boys" sometimes?

MR. DURANTY: Yes, I found that, and I am not denying that some of these boys are energetic, tough, and hard. But you can't tell me that you improve the organization of any concern, no matter what it is—civil, military, or reportorial, or anything else—by cutting the organization all to pieces and putting in a lot of good new men, however good they are. And that is what they did.

I went to places and asked for people I had known before, and they said they had never heard of them. I thought they were lying or afraid, but the truth was they had not heard of them because the whole organization had been disrupted. It created a condition in which production went way down and stayed down, or, if it did not go down, it did not go up according to the curve of various plans. Actually, it went down in various branches.

MR. HARPER: For the last three years?

MR. DURANTY: Not for the last three years but up until the middle of last year.

MR. GOTTSCHALK: Military terror in the past—in the history of the French Revolution—had a desirable effect upon the army. It has gotten rid of the untrustworthy generals and the generals without initiative and put young and trustworthy persons in their place. Would you say that was true of the Russian terror?

MR. DURANTY: Well, it may have been, especially in the early days. I think there is no doubt that some of the early generals who were punished in the early days did have, if not conspirative action, conspirative conversations with people who were recognized to be for Germany, and for that they were punished. But the thing went too far, and I am sure a number of people were eliminated—and eliminated beyond recall—who today would be useful to the Soviet Union.

MR. GOTTSCHALK: Is it your impression that the army of Russia is not well led at the present moment?

MR. DURANTY: It is not my impression at all! I think it is undoubtedly led by good men and that, as you say, Harper, the younger men have come up and are possibly more energetic. I think they have a good, *excellent* strategy, but I think also they have lost men they would be glad to have back.

MR. HARPER: Also, in respect to the internal structure of the army, there have been in these last two years a reorganization and an introduction of a new form of discipline—a new form of leadership in the army. I am referring particularly to the elimination of that element which disturbed us outsiders a great deal—the political commissar sharing power with the military commander of a given unit.

MR. DURANTY: Now you come to a point of great importance: the division of power, the division of authority every soldier knows is ruinous to an army. That has been eliminated almost totally.

MR. HARPER: You mean since the Finnish war?

MR. DURANTY: Since the fighting in Japan, first of all. The lesson of the fighting in Japan was confirmed fully by the Finnish war.[21]

MR. GOTTSCHALK: You mean the political commissars have been wiped out, or they are simply reduced in status?

MR. DURANTY: No, not even "possibly reduced in status." Their status has been determined in accordance with military necessity, and they no longer have a divided authority. It is the same in civil life. The Communist and the Communist repre-

[21] December, 1939, to March, 1940, ending with the cession of certain Finnish territory around Lake Ladoga and in the north-central sections of Karelia to the Soviet, plus the leasing of other territories to Russia for the building of bases (such as that at Hango).

sentative in the factory can no longer interfere. They must cooperate.

MR. HARPER: To build up political morale.

MR. DURANTY: Yes, and to give what advice they can. They cannot alter orders.

MR. HARPER: That principle—the single responsibility of authority—is really being applied at last. They talked of it for years.

MR. DURANTY: Yes. I think it is being applied.

MR. GOTTSCHALK: I don't want to stop this discussion of the political effect of purges or other reforms inside Russia, but I do feel it is important that we go on to a discussion of the army, navy, and the air force of Russia in discussing this war situation.

You, Duranty, as a famous *New York Times* correspondent, and you, Harper, as the University of Chicago expert on Russian affairs, are probably not military experts, and yet I think an opinion from you would be valuable. Do you think the Russian army is any good?

MR. HARPER: My work has primarily been in the political side, and I followed with special interest the work of these political commissars, now eliminated in a moment of crisis. On the morale side I felt that Russia had a strong and patriotic army, but, particularly on the internal military side, I think Duranty is more qualified to speak, although I have always been interested in the statements of many of my friends among military experts on the spot who have seen the army. They have said, "This Red army is a tough army."

MR. GOTTSCHALK: Do you agree with that?

MR. DURANTY: I dare say, and I am no military expert. I had a year at the French headquarters at the end of the last war. I was with the Lett army fighting the Reds, and I have seen fighting in other parts of the world, so I know something about the way soldiers act and react.

Now, as a matter of fact, the Red army is well disciplined. You see it on parade and you see it in its ordinary social life, in groups in the street, etc.   In these big parades they handle difficult operations with success, and there is nothing more difficult to move than tanks and guns in a town.

Then take the military point of view.   After all, in Finland they started out with no thought that they were going to have a war at all.   They thought they were going to march in with banners, and some of them did march in with banners.   They thought it was going to be easy.   But, when they realized what they were up against, they marshaled their forces and drove through an extremely strong fortified line supported and held by an extremely gallant and powerful people.[22]

MR. GOTTSCHALK: The thing that interests me about the military situation is that now the English are close to German industrial centers.   The Germans planted their industrial centers so as to be far away from English airplanes, but now the English airplanes can fly across Germany and land in Russia, and Russian planes are very much closer to the German industrial areas to begin with.

But do the Russians have any planes that are worth counting on?

MR. DURANTY: Well, their planes are, I think, out of date to some extent.   That is to say, they are based on models older than the latest German planes, but they have a lot of them. They were the first people to use parachute troops.   They used parachute troops in large numbers in maneuvers in 1935.   They were the first people to use heavy tanks.   They are beginning to fight now in positions they have been preparing for seven years.   I think it is far too early to say that the Russians are inevitably beaten.

MR. HARPER: You may also call attention to the fact that Russia does not have what we call a "Maginot line" and, therefore, probably has not the "Maginot psychology."

MR. GOTTSCHALK: That raises an interesting question.   We have talked about production, purges, and army organization.   I

[22] The so-called Mannerheim Line, protecting Viborg and southeastern Finland from any military operations from Leningrad.

should like to raise the question of the Communist Internationale. Do you think this war will be fought as an international war rather than as a national war?

Harper, your political interest ought to lead you to an opinion on that.

MR. HARPER: It was interesting to note in Molotov's announcement of the war to the people of the Soviet Union last Monday that he emphasized that it was a "war for the fatherland." He used the phrase that was used in the war of 1812 at the time of the Napoleonic invasion. That is indicative of a definite rise of Russian nationalism, Russian patriotism, during these last years.[23]

MR. GOTTSCHALK: That is, emphasizing the old Russian national effort and successes?

MR. DURANTY: Precisely. One of the points that has been presented in reproach of Stalin by foreign political opponents (his own socialistic opponents) has been that he has betrayed the Revolution and has played the nationalistic game. I prefer to use the phrase "patriotic game," because the whole cult has been one of defense of Russia, of their own fatherland. Winston Churchill said exactly that in his speech: "the common men fighting for freedom." And as far back as 1935 we saw the new films—Peter the Great and other Russian pictures—all inculcating the idea of patriotism and patriotic defense as against what you might call socialism.

MR. HARPER: Reacting to that, in 1934 I was already using the phrase "economic patriotism."

MR. GOTTSCHALK: But Duranty's point apparently is that this is not economic patriotism but sentimental patriotism.

MR. HARPER: They are emphasizing that in the new building they have accomplished.

[23] V. M. Molotov, who resigned May 6 as premier in favor of Josef Stalin, is vice-premier of the Soviet Union and commissar for foreign affairs. In his statement of June 22, the day of the German invasion, Molotov said: "This is not the first time that our people have had to deal with the attack of an arrogant foe. At the time of Napoleon's invasion of Russia our people's reply was war for the fatherland, and Napoleon suffered defeat and met his doom."

MR. DURANTY: That is very true and also in the collective farms. Not all collective farms are successful, but a great many are, and they are proud of that and they are proud of their new "culture," because they have more schools than ever before, more doctors, more hospitals, more bridges, and more factories. Certainly, they are proud of that. It is quite true that it is pride of country, not a pride necessarily or primarily in socialism.

MR. HARPER: They always mention that it is a part of the building of socialism.

MR. DURANTY: Certainly.

MR. GOTTSCHALK: Then I take it both of you gentlemen are agreed that this is a nationalist war and not an international war as far as Russia is concerned.

MR. DURANTY: Certainly!

MR. GOTTSCHALK: I should like to go from this to the question of the effect of this war upon Russia's neighbors and, to begin with, on Russian substates. What would be your attitude?

MR. HARPER: You mean by "substates" those states which in the course of the past year have been subjected to the Soviet regime?

MR. GOTTSCHALK: During the past year or more.

MR. HARPER: The Baltic States and Bessarabia. I think very definitely that this will be a test of the Soviet system. What has been the result of the Sovietization of the past year? We can't answer that, but I think it is a question we should keep in mind. I would put it even more specifically. Will the Latvian peasant welcome back the former leader Ulmanis if backed by a German division and will the Bessarabian peasant welcome back the Rumanian landlord under Antonescu?

MR. DURANTY: I have been to Latvia recently and I know it well. I have talked about it a great deal, and I have written an article on the subject. The rank and file say they would prefer independence first, and they do not particularly want the Russians. I would bet that they would prefer, or would have preferred if they had had a choice, a German regime to a Russian regime. But they want independence first.

MR. HARPER: But you would not say the same about Bessarabia!

MR. DURANTY: I would not say that of Bessarabia. Bessarabia is sort of a stepchild of Rumania. The Bessarabians don't want the Rumanian officials back. They don't want the Rumanian landlord back. Rumania, after all, has never been noted very much for its excellence of government, and it did not treat Bessarabia very well.

MR. GOTTSCHALK: Recently?

MR. DURANTY: No, that has been going on for the last twenty years. Since the occupation of Bessarabia they have exploited the country, and the Russians were welcomed in Bessarabia, but I don't think they were welcomed in Latvia or Estonia.

MR. HARPER: Would you put Sweden and Finland in the same category as the. Baltic States?

MR. DURANTY: Finland and Sweden have been fighting against their fear of Russia for the last one hundred and fifty to two hundred years, and, when I was in Stockholm last—a year ago—I saw there the statue of Charles XII with his hand pointing eastward toward Russia.

MR. GOTTSCHALK: Time is getting short, gentlemen, and, in discussing the relation of Russia with her neighbors and her friends and enemies, I should like to raise the question of American cooperation. What would you say as to America's position?

MR. HARPER: Well, of course, the most important point there is the promise of aid to the Soviet Union that was made officially at the moment it was attacked by Germany. I would like to say very definitely that I don't think that promise of aid means alliance. Those who spoke of the Hitler-Stalin alliance now speak of the Roosevelt-Stalin alliance. In both instances the word is not applicable. I think it is a question of parallel action for respective national defense.

MR. GOTTSCHALK: You don't think, then, that Russia gave Germany the green light to start the war in 1939?

MR. HARPER: No, I don't. And I think it is particularly interesting to note that those who do tend constantly to repeat that statement are the very ones who support the thesis that Hitler's aim is world-domination. I have never been able to find that those two statements fitted in. It seems to me that they are in definite contradiction of each other.

MR. GOTTSCHALK: You have been to Japan recently, Duranty. What was the Japanese reaction to this declaration of war by Germany?

MR. DURANTY: I was there much before that. I left Japan six or seven weeks ago. But Matsuoka implied or would imply that they would wish to continue and, I think, to assist—

MR. GOTTSCHALK: Excuse me if I interrupt you, but there are only ten seconds left, and I should like to indicate how you gentlemen stand on this situation so far as I can interpret your stand. You two gentlemen contend that the internal morale of Russia is not so doubtful as many believe and that their military ability is still any man's guess. You at least, Duranty, think that they may yet surprise the military experts.

AMERICA'S WAR AIMS AND PEACE AIMS

FOUR HUMAN FREEDOMS [1]

FRANKLIN DELANO ROOSEVELT [2]

This address by President Roosevelt is the conclusion of his message to Congress, delivered in person to the two houses, on January 6, 1941. This is the only example of a Roosevelt speech in any of these volumes of *Representative American Speeches* to be given in part only. Space does not permit the reprinting of the entire message. For background of the address see introduction to Roosevelt's speech on "Preservation of American Independence," p. 19, in this volume.

In the future days, which we seek to make secure, we look forward to a world founded upon four essential human freedoms.

The first is freedom of speech and expression—everywhere in the world.

The second is freedom of every person to worship God in his own way—everywhere in the world.

The third is freedom from want—which, translated into world terms, means economic understandings which will secure to every nation a healthy peacetime life for its inhabitants—everywhere in the world.

The fourth is freedom from fear—which, translated into world terms, means a world-wide reduction of armaments to such a point and in such a thorough fashion that no nation will be in a position to commit an act of physical aggression against any neighbor—anywhere in the world.

That is no vision of a distant millennium. It is a definite basis for a kind of world attainable in our own time and generation. That kind of world is the very antithesis of the so-

[1] By permission of President Roosevelt. Text furnished through the courtesy of Mr. Stephen Early, Secretary to President Roosevelt.

[2] For biographical note see Appendix.

called new order of tyranny which the dictators seek to create with the crash of a bomb.

To that new order we oppose the greater conception—the moral order. A good society is able to face schemes of world domination and foreign revolutions alike without fear.

Since the beginning of our American history we have been engaged in change—in a perpetual peaceful revolution—a revolution which goes on steadily, quietly adjusting itself to changing conditions—without the concentration camp or the quicklime in the ditch. The world order which we seek is the cooperation of free countries, working together in a friendly, civilized society.

This nation has placed its destiny in the hands and heads and hearts of its millions of free men and women; and its faith in freedom under the guidance of God. Freedom means the supremacy of human rights everywhere. Our support goes to those who struggle to gain those rights or keep them. Our strength is in our unity of purpose.

To that high concept there can be no end save victory.

THE ONE ROAD TO PEACE [3]

Francis J. Spellman [4]

The Most Reverend Francis J. Spellman delivered this address on September 22, 1940, before the American Legion, at their annual convention in Boston, Massachusetts. The address was given from the shell of the Charles River Esplanade before an audience of 30,000.

This American Legion convention had a larger attendance "than at any previous annual session." More than 125,000 Legionnaires overflowed Boston. In their parade marched 100,000 for twelve hours before a crowd estimated at from 2,000,000 to 3,000,000 (*Time,* 36:19, October 7, 1940). In the parade was the new note of modern warfare—anti-aircraft guns, anti-tank guns, sky rifles, machine guns and other mechanized equipment.

The national setting for the convention was a sharp contrast to those of other years. Already the draft legislation was being prepared and the nation was apparently headed for immediate or early war. What attitude should the Legion take? For sixteen years the Legion had automatically adopted and readopted resolutions demanding American neutrality and isolation. Now the members adopted a resolution urging every practicable aid to Great Britain and China. Said the sponsor of the resolution, Warren Atherton, of the Legion's defense committee, "If we have to fight, let's fight beyond our shores before any foe can effect invasion."

In this local and national setting the Archbishop delivered an oration, avoiding direct discussion of the international events of the hour, but sounding the kind of idealism that Woodrow Wilson had so clearly and impressively voiced in 1917. Said the Archbishop, "We Americans want peace and we shall prepare for peace, but not for a peace whose dilemmatic definition is slavery or death." Without expanding his philosophy he stated it clearly: "The Highroad of Democracy . . . the road back to Christ and his teachings, in personal life, in national life, and in international life."

The address is a splendid example of an oration. It is well constructed, couched in emotional and imaginative language (suitable for delivery by students of public speaking); it sounds a theme of great concern, and is an address adjusted to the needs of his audience and of the occasion; it is an address, nevertheless, based upon the influence and role of the Church; and it was delivered with power.

[3] By permission of The Most Rev. Francis J. Spellman, D.D., Archbishop of New York. Text supplied through the courtesy of John J. Casey, Secretary to the Archbishop.

[4] For biographical note see Appendix.

The Archbishop spends much time and care in the preparation of formal addresses, as this example indicates. "However, his position is such that his presence is required at many formal functions, and at many of these he is called upon to speak, or he may feel that the occasion is such that he should address the gathering. On all these latter occasions he speaks extemporaneously." In the case of this Boston address he followed his manuscript completely.

With regard to special speech training, Archbishop Spellman had the training received "by every young man studying for the holy priesthood." [5] He was graduated from Fordham University, New York City, and prepared for the priesthood in the North American College, Rome, where he spent five years. On May 23, 1939, he was installed as Bishop of New York.

For further understanding of the Archbishop's attitude toward the international problem, students should read his "Address on the Occasion of his Installation as Bishop of New York," May 23, 1939, and especially his address at the time of his investiture with the Sacred Pallium, on Tuesday, March 12, 1940.

There is a fitness in your choice of this place for your assemblage on the first day of your national convention. You are gathered beside the Charles River, the river to which the poet Longfellow repaid with a song the help he had drawn for his spirit from its stillness:

> Thou hast taught me, Silent River,
> Many a lesson deep and strong.

We who crowd the margin of this stream on this autumnal night may also learn a lesson—that calmly and without hysteria we may prepare to preserve and defend the peace of our land. This, for us whose minds yield to its spell, is the admonition of the deep and quiet waters of this river "stealing onward like the stream of life."

We have met in the open with the sky as our roof. Looking upwards on this dark night of humanity's sufferings we seek hope in the heavens; and thence not merely a tiny ray but a whole flood of light descends upon us. On the same stars that now shine down on us looked St. Augustine centuries ago, and to his silent questioning they answered, "We

[5] Letter to the author from the Secretary to the Archbishop, April 3, 1941.

are not the God Whom thou seekest. He made us." Yes, the stars proclaim in luminous, inerasable language the existence of God. These stars navigate the firmament in a certain definite way and the plan, the progress and the order involved in their movements presupposes an intelligence which could not come from matter or from chance. And this intelligence vast enough to regulate the orbits of heavenly bodies we know by the name of God. God is that same first cause who designed our bodies, masterpieces resulting from the union of a hundred other master-pieces coordinated in such a manner that despite their separately complicated natures they function with an amazing harmony of action. Every fiber of our bodies, every power of our souls proclaims the existence of God, and though other pillars upon which our lives are based may have tottered, we still have God, the supreme master of order and firm is our confidence that through Him, out of the present turmoil, will come order and peace.

Lights lesser and nearer than the stars beam upon us. These are the lights of old Boston town, lights of hospitality and friendship and lights of freedom; for in convening in Boston we have come to an historic place where American independence was first asserted when, sped by lantern's flash, the midnight messenger of liberty raised the alarm, the sound of which at critical periods still rings and is heard in our land.

This river at the point where we are gathered is close to its outlet in the sea, and the sea for you of the American Legion is of epic memory. Gathered at the rim of ocean it is natural that your minds should go back in thoughtful retrospect to that heroic embarkation of your youth, upon the broad waters of the Atlantic so fateful for yourselves and so providential for our country. Beyond the seas was France where battle awaited you, into which you threw the strength and courage of your young manhood with such an impetus as to turn the whole tide of the war; nor did you rest until peace was returned to the world which at its announcement went delirious with joy.

When the combatants put down their arms, historians took up the pen to expose the origins of the sanguinary struggle, and many causes of the war were listed in books that have been published in the last two decades. By these authors the World War was explained in its beginnings by the rivalry of nations for power and wealth, their quest for territorial expansion and imperial domination, their seeking of new markets and outlets for capital investment, their competition in exploiting backward people, motives, all of them, materialistic, sordid and ignoble.

If these were the underlying causes of the World War you knew nothing of them. These were not the motives which stirred your minds and inspired you with the will for victory. Yours was an unselfish crusade. You fought for pure and high ideals. The spark that flamed you into patriotic fervor was flashed by the President of the United States, and you judged it your task, whatever the sacrifice, to bring to accomplishment the ardent hopes that our Chief Executive had formulated in matchless sentences vindicating the inviolability of small nations, the security of democracy and a world rid of the threat and actuality of war. Even though secretly mocked and later openly thwarted by foreign statesmen, these principles were sincerely proposed by President Wilson and by you as sincerely accepted.

Let historians, economists, sociologists and philosophers who explore human conduct decide among themselves the reasons for the outbreak of the World War; but for a confirmation of my recollection and my understanding of the reasons for our own involvement, I shall not resort to books. I shall turn to living witnesses, to you, men of the American Legion; and to my query why America threw its power into the contest, you will tell me as you have told your sons, that for them and for all the children of men you braved every peril that they might inherit and possess a world that would not know the evil of war, since the causes leading to war had by your determined valor been removed. For the disruption of peace, for the calamitous miseries that now oppress mankind, for the sorrows that we fear are yet to come, the responsibility must be placed on others. There can be no revindication against you; for you took no land that had to be reclaimed, you committed no economic wrong that had to be rectified, you suppressed no political liberties that only an uprising could restore. Your honor is forever secure. In military annals you belong to the company of the most knightly who fought without fear, without reproach, and without thought of personal gain or national expansion.

Despite the failure in the realization of our aims in the World War, we still remain idealists. To be otherwise is impossible for Americans. But experience has taught us a measure of realism. We know now that we cannot draw the boundaries of states on the map of Europe so that race will never transgress upon race. We know now that we cannot bestow our democratic institutions on peoples opposed by natural feelings and traditions to our political system. We know now that we cannot continue to remain unarmed when other countries have not imitated our peaceful example. We know now that it is our pressing duty to defend ourselves, our lives, our liberties and our institutions. Interventionists, isolationists and those whose political thought lies between these two extremes all agree and must agree on the policy of national defense.

What is worthless needs no guards set about it. The more valuable an object the more it calls for protection. . Treasure is kept in secret vaults. A city is patrolled by police. A home is locked and barred against intruders. If in this world there were no greed and envy, no violent actions to enforce illicit desires, these precautions would not be necessary. Nations do not differ from individuals and although we have envied none, have wronged none and have coveted nothing, although we have shared our abundance with a distressful world and have felt ourselves charged to do so before God and men, we have the fear that in many cases our charity has not been requited, our good will has not been reciprocated; we have the additional fear that our national wealth and our national way of life may have aroused envy in others and this envy might incite actual attempts to conquer us by force of arms, to take from us that which belongs to our people.

For who can gainsay as he envisages on the one hand the vast natural resources of our land and on the other hand the present rapacious temper that is abroad, quickened and emboldened by modern mechanical invention, that it would be worse than folly if we did not immediately proceed to build about ourselves a strong defense that will discourage any possible effort that might be made against us. It is better to have protection and not need it than to need protection and not have it. We Americans want peace and it is now evident that we must be prepared to demand it. For other peoples have wanted peace and the peace they received was the peace of death. Our good will and the sincerity of our desire for peace have been demonstrated to the extent of sinking our own battleships. We can no longer afford to be moles who cannot see, or ostriches who will not see, for some solemn agreements are no longer sacred, and vices have become virtues and truth a synonym of falsehood. We Americans want peace and we shall prepare for peace, but not for a peace whose dilemmatic definition is slavery or death.

Valuable as are our material possessions more precious still are our liberties. For these blessings of a higher kind no less than for our natural wealth are we indebted to God. This truth was forcefully enunciated by the Catholic Bishops of the United States assembled in the Third Council of Baltimore in the year 1837: "We consider the establishment of our country's independence," the Bishops said, "the shaping of its liberties and laws, as a work of special Providence, its framers building better than they knew, the Almighty's Hand guiding them. We believe that our country's heroes were the instruments of the God of nations in establishing this house of freedom." These are impressive thoughts prompting gratitude to God and a deeper appreciation of our inherited liberties. For religion, which traces the sources of all our blessings to a Divine Author, has always added its force to patriotism when our government has summoned our citizens to the country's defense so that those who have sprung up at the call have felt themselves doubly inspired and doubly armed.

Of this twofold influence of religion and patriotism have I been conscious in all the thoughts I have expressed to you on this occasion. The invitation to address you was directed to me as the Bishop of the Catholics in the Army and Navy of the United States, and in this capacity and as an American citizen have I spoken to you. I am proud to address the men of the American Legion and I believe in you. I believe you mean a great deal to America and that America means a great deal to you. You men cannot conceive the propriety of an organization calling itself "American" that challenges the constitutionality of a bill providing that no government position in a state may be held by anyone who believes in the overthrow of the government by force. And yet, there is such an organization. You cannot imagine an organization which openly teaches disrespect to the American flag and under the pretense of freedom of religion engages paid workers to go from house to house to attack the religion of others. And yet there is such an organization.

By vocation I am a man of peace. I am consecrated to Christ the Prince of Peace. Unceasingly day and night I pray and I ask my flock to pray for peace. "There is nothing to be gained by war that cannot be gained by peace," was the warning of Pope Pius XII on the eve of the outbreak of the present European conflict. I am a man of peace and I pray and hope and work for peace. Not knowingly would I injure anyone. I am a man of peace, but gone is my hope of building a world safe for democracy on such foundations as the Treaty of Versailles. Vanished, too, is the mirage of many philanthropic optimists who cherished the vision of a world united in peace and fraternal charity beneath the aegis of science divorced from religion and around the altar of Godless education. Blasted is the dream of a communistic universal brotherhood—blasted by the tell-tale rattle of machine guns and the roar of cannon over Finland.

Science, knowledge, communism, these three great hopes of men, these three great, deified abstractions have wavered and failed beneath the pressure of human prejudice and selfishness and the spirit of cruelty and wickedness in high places. A great scientist, himself a refugee from the deification of race and blood, has stepped beyond his depth and suggested that mankind abandon belief in a personal God. That is just what men have done and are doing and the net result is written in the bomb-mangled bodies and the decree-shackled minds of Europe's suffering millions.

What is the answer? There is only one road to peace that I know of, the Highroad of Democracy, the road marked by the sign posts of the Ten Commandments, the road back to Christ and His teachings, in personal life, in national life and in international life.

This is the road to peace. This is the road for America to take. This is the road our forefathers took when they lived and died for our national independence. This is the road you and your comrades took when they lived and died for the national independence of other countries. This is the road that we shall travel if we are to live in peace, a government of the people, by the people, for the people. If through indifference or negligence, if through penetration or permeation from without or corruption or disintegration from within, it shall come to pass that some day, some conqueror of democracy shall stand at the tomb of George Washington in Mount Vernon and with mock reverence and double-meaning cynicism salute our country's founder with these words: "Washington, we are here to finish your work!" God grant that I, for one, shall not be alive to know it.

May God bless the United States of America!

THE QUESTION OF PEACE [6]

HERBERT HOOVER [7]

Herbert Hoover delivered this address at the annual New Haven, Connecticut, Young Men's Christian Association dinner, on Friday evening, March 28, 1941.

Throughout the preceding months Mr. Hoover had been active as a public speaker, commenting at every point, as it was appropriate that an ex-President should do, on our foreign policy. On May 27, 1940, for example, he urged that his countrymen keep politics out of national defense; he outlined a specific program by which production could be speeded up under "centralization of executive responsibility," a plan which at the time this volume went to press had not been carried out. On June 25, 1940, he addressed the Republican National Convention on various issues, domestic and foreign. Later he raised the question of our foreign relations and took a definite isolationist attitude ("The immense task now is to shape our foreign policies to protect us from the conflagration in Europe and Asia."); he argued that our participation in the war would bring us only catastrophe and that "we cannot assure liberty in the Old World." He denounced President Roosevelt as a breeder of war and of hate. "It is not the province of the President . . . to create hate." And he raised the question of what would happen after the war (the genesis of his thinking in the New Haven speech). Notable in the speech was this paragraph:

". . . In time these world storms will blow themselves out. Perhaps it will be a long time. But the spirit of Luther, Goethe, Schiller, of Mazzini, and Garibaldi still live. And here upon our soil the temple of liberty must stand, that men may be inspired to return to its worship."

On October 31, 1940, he delivered a notable campaign address at Lincoln, Nebraska, in which he discussed again our foreign relations, criticised the President for his aggressive talk that seemed to be leading us to war, pled for maximum national defense, urged work rather than "talk," and advised the voters to support Willkie as less inclined to plunge us into war.

Outstanding also was his address before the Pennsylvania Society of New York, December 21, 1940, when he again urged preparedness to the limit, including intellectual defense, and put in a plea for feeding the "defeated democracies."

After the beginning of 1941 the clamor in the United States arose for a more specific statement of what should be the "peace objectives"

[6] By permission of Herbert Hoover. Text furnished through the courtesy of Mr. Hoover.

[7] For biographical note see Appendix.

of Great Britain (and of America). The significance of Hoover's address of March 28, 1941, is that it was one of the earlier attempts to outline such principles for the United States to follow at the next Treaty of Versailles (or of Berlin). Mr. Hoover was at pains to furnish his listeners with a full background of events of the first World War and of the "aftermath." (Note how he talked from his experience.) His analysis is clear and becomes embodied in his enumeration of "immediate questions."

This address, like the others in this volume, should be read against the international background of March, 1941. Germany was moving troops to Greece's frontier; Nazi raiders were blasting away at London; Yugoslavia at first agreed (apparently) to sign a pro-Nazi pact, listened to Hitler's ultimatum, and within a few hours after Hoover spoke, plunged into battle against the Germans.

Three days before this address Viscount Halifax, British Ambassador to the United States, had talked on "The War Aims of Great Britain." Shortly before President Roosevelt (March 15, 1941) in a nation-wide address had told the world Great Britain would get from America everything that was needed. Winston Churchill, on March 18, replied with profuse thanks for the promise of aid. Adolf Hitler, not to be outdone, addressed the world twenty-four hours after Roosevelt, and announced that "we will end this battle victoriously."

Throughout April, May and June, 1941, Mr. Hoover continued to talk as an "isolationist," but disavowed any connection with the official group sponsoring Lindbergh. Striking was Hoover's address of June 29, 1941, broadcast from Chicago, in which he denounced Russia, one week after that nation had felt the first impact of the Nazi Eastern blitzkrieg. He stated that Russia was one of the "bloodiest tyrannies" in history and denounced Stalin as one who "has taken advantage of the very freedoms of democracy to destroy them with the most potent fifth column in all history." He proposed (in line with his previous philosophy and speech-making) that the United States (1) give every aid to Great Britain and China, (2) arm for defense and keep out of the war, (3) see that Congress keep and exercise its authority to make war or peace, (4) abandon notions of "ideological" wars, (5) devote ourselves to promotion of the "four freedoms" in America, (6) go to the peace table with unexhausted reserves, and (7) abandon hates at the peace table.

Mr. Hoover continued to analyze national problems with much penetration. His voice quality, enunciation, and articulation were by no means those of Roosevelt. But Hoover's mental force, his strength of personality, gave weight to his addresses. Thousands upon thousands of Americans continued to listen to him and to respect his judgment even though he was not a speaker of the first rank.

I have been asked to speak to you and through you to a large group of young people on some of the moral and spiritual problems which now confront our country. Any discussion of them in these days involves questions of war and of the peace to come. And now they are the transcendent problems before youth. I shall therefore discuss for a few moments some of the moral, spiritual and social questions that dominate modern war and the making of peace.

Today we are pledged to give Britain the tools of war and our full economic aid. That is settled and done. Our national duty is to unite in making a good job of it. And to do it with good will.

The action of Congress has, however, enormously changed the shape of things. The aid to Britain combined with our own preparedness program forces us a long way into a war economy. Apart from these steps, our indignation at gigantic wrong to the democracies; the repugnance of free men for the whole totalitarian ideology; the steady impact of foreign propaganda; the constant agitation of a minority of our own citizens for all-out war—all press upon us the mental and spiritual attitudes of war. In a fog of emotions and appeals we are fast driving into the psychosis of war.

Whether we take the final fateful step or not, we have already made three positive appointments with destiny. One is that we will sit at the world's peace table. Another is that we face the problems of war emotions and war psychosis. The other is that we shall meet the financial, economic and social aftermath of a war.

America yearns for peace in the world. The freedom of men comes only in peace. It diminishes in war. The abolition of poverty and want comes only in peace. Poverty and want increase in war. Yet the world does not know, and we do not know how world peace can be made and maintained. The world does not know, and we do not know, how in the face of steady world impoverishment, we are to abolish want. We do not see our way. Today, over these questions, we are frustrated, confused, unhappy and fearful. Our unity of ideas extends only to a resolve to defend ourselves and a fervid wish that the struggling democracies shall win.

My purpose here is not to offer you a panacea for these confusions and problems. I wish to stimulate your thinking. For now is the time to think hard and think fast. We cannot wait until the appointments with destiny are upon us.

We joined in an exactly parallel war twenty-five years ago for the same purposes and under the same impulses. Even with victory, we failed to get either military, economic, or spiritual peace.

The failures of the last war to achieve peace root not only at Versailles but also in the forces generated in the war itself. They rooted deeper than that. They rooted in age-old hates and in the fires of imperialism. But we can get some light and some guidance from the experience and failures of that war and that peace making.

It is over twenty-two years since that World War ended. The youth of America today does not know of that war from its own experiences.

I am perhaps one of the few living Americans who had full opportunity from high places to see intimately the moving tragedy of the last World War. I saw it from its beginnings in 1914 all the way down through the long years which have not yet ended. I saw it not only in its visible ghastliness, but I lived with the invisible forces which moved in its causes and its consequences.

My country and foreign countries have honored me greatly over these years. There is nothing more in office or honor that the world could give to me. I can therefore add objectively to those experiences. I favored our entry into the last war so that I speak as neither a pacifist nor a militarist but rather as an analyst.

If we would see what the moral and spiritual forces are that we have to meet, we must consider the nature of total war.

The World War was the first total war of modern history. It was the first great war after the mechanical age. Prior to that time wars were more nearly contests between armies and navies. Civilian life proceeded with little interruption except near the actual scene of battle. The armed men represented a small part of the whole population. Their equipment was comparatively simple. Its preparation involved the energies of only a small part of industry. That last World War was the first time that the complete energy of the whole civil population on both sides was mobilized to fight and provide materials. It was total war.

Perhaps the most striking difference of total war from the old wars was that formerly armed men fought only against armed men. There were certain chivalries and sportsmanships. There was a real desire to keep women, children and noncombatant men apart from its shocks. In total war the basis has shifted in large measure, from war between armed men to war by armed men upon civilians. In the last war for the first time systematic and organized terrorization and killing of civilians became a part of this strategy. Cities, villages and homes were ruthlessly burned. Unarmed seamen and innocent passengers were drowned without a chance. Fire and explosives were rained on women and children from the skies.

Three times a day among 300 million people wherever a family gathered to eat they had less because of the enemy. Nowhere in Europe were people free of fear for their lives on land or sea.

In the course of that total war there developed in the civil population on both sides, three fierce and total emotions. These were hate, intolerance, and a spirit of exalting crusade.

From the sufferings of civilians blazed first indignation, and finally a fanatic hate. It enveloped the minds of every man, woman and child. And this hate was not directed solely to leaders of nations; it was poured upon every individual of the enemy nation. Soldiers fighting on the front held far less hate than civilians at home.

The second of these emotions from that total war was total intolerance. National unity was essential in the face of total national danger. But impatience at discussion rose rapidly to rabid intolerance. In the democracies part of that intolerance ran quickly to the suppression of free speech and free press. The democratic governments had no need to impose restraints on free expression. The crowd howled down the most objective statement, the most constructive criticism. They denounced it as the paid voice of the enemy. And intolerance went further. It persecuted inoffensive citizens.

The third great emotion of that war was a crusade of ideologies, of philosophies of government and of life. The ideology of Germany was much the same pattern as the one now in use. It was not so well perfected in phrases and method as this one. But they used most of the slogans we now hear. On our side we went to war to defeat "Might makes Right," and "The enslavement of the individual to the State." We said we would make the "world safe for democracy." It was to be "a war to end war." We said the end of war was that enemy nations must change their way of life to freedom and democracy and peace. The most sublime passions of our people were summoned in action and sacrifice for this purpose.

All these emotions were stirred on both sides of the conflict by the total power of government. That total war gave birth to governmentally organized propaganda. The hates of the people, their courage, and their aspirations could not be allowed to lag in the face of reverses and suffering. The atrocities and total wickedness of the enemy had to be constantly illustrated. All governments, including our own, engaged in it. The heads of those bureaus in most governments have written their confessions with pride in the lies they invented. Every government justified to itself that total emotion is essential to win total war.

To show how deeply these total emotions dominate total war, I may recall that after this had gone on for over two years in the last war President Wilson endeavored to bring about a negotiated peace. His representatives sought my views on its practicality. I felt that hope of negotiated peace was futile. The civilians on both sides cried out in hate and suffering for vengeance and crushing victory. I advised that no statesman or leader dared propose the necessary compromises which must be the basis of negotiated peace. And this proved to be the case.

And incidentally, I may observe another effect of these impelling emotions in total war between nations of large resources. Such war can apparently end only by exhaustion or revolution on one side or the other. And the victor in this race of exhaustion is only one lap behind the vanquished.

Once total war is joined it apparently can have no intermediate stops.

There are economic necessities in total war that create vast social aftermaths. The World War of twenty-five years ago was the first time the freedoms of business, labor and agriculture were suspended. Industry had to be expanded to meet war production. It had to be constricted in its service to civilian living. To direct these activities dictatorial authority had to be lodged in the governments. In the democracies we used soft phrases to cover these coercions. We talked of cooperation, voluntary action, but underneath we had to show "or else." The Government increased production both by going into business itself, and by government dictation to private owners as to what they must do. Whatever the fine phrases were in which we wrapped these actions, the cold fact was that government in business was socialism, and government dictation to private owners was fascism. The word fascism had not then been invented. The freedom of labor and the freedom of the farmer were driven a long way down that blind alley. Where people attempted to stand on their so-called rights, propaganda, intolerances and penalties of law were directed to drive them to cover. Taxes which expropriated savings, pressure loans and inflation were necessary. All that is the method of fascism.

Is it to be the tragic jeopardy of democracy that if it would go to war it must adopt the very systems which we abhor?

One of the emotional and intellectual currents of the last total war was the hope for peace that would make total war impossible again. The people of the democracies wanted armies and navies reduced if not abolished. They were reso-lute that some method must be found for justice between na-tions. A thousand ideas came forth. But there was no ade-quate discussion of how these ideals could be attained. The common expression was victory first. We had a daily reitera-tion of our high aims. Indeed within them was the hope of a better world.

With all these ideas and these emotions we went to the peace table. The American people at large were totally un-prepared for the problems of peacemaking. And hate sat at that table. Statemen were not free agents. The victorious peoples demanded revenge and reparations for their wrongs and sufferings. The men who represented England and France at that conference had just been elected on the slogans of "Hang the Kaiser," "Pay every farthing," "Revenge," "Reduce them to impotence forever." The allied leaders were con-sciously or unconsciously dominated by the bitterness of their people. They had to get their treaties approved at home. Reason could not be restored in the face of total emotion and total suffering. And although our American sufferings were far less than the others, yet we were slow to demobilize our war hates.

I recollect having had the temerity a few days after the surrender of the Germans at the Armistice to say we must at once take down the food blockade on their women and children. You would perhaps be surprised if you read the universal condemnation I received, not only in the Allied countries, but in America. They demanded more starvation after the war was over. Starvation is the mother of generations of hate.

Also remember Sherman's march to the sea. It has bred hate in our own Southern States for 80 years.

From all this the lesson is that hate, once aroused by the suffering of civil populations, outlasts even victory.

After the last total war the consequence was a treaty which in part sowed the dragons' teeth of the present war. President Wilson and his men sought valiantly to moderate it. The world hoped for a while that through the high-minded formula of the League of Nations the failures of the peace could be remedied when hates died. But the hates and fears lived on.

Then came the aftermaths of that total war.

Experience proved that liberty, freedom and democracy could not be imposed on nations by battle. All over Europe nations did come to the mourners' bench and appeared to be converted, but soon some were backsliders. Indeed, it was proved that intellectual ideas rooted in a thousand years of racial history cannot be uprooted with a machine gun.

Every nation was impoverished. There were millions of maimed and orphaned. Millions of homes and tons of ships were destroyed. War production had to cease, industry was dislocated, millions of men had to be demobilized. Unemployment and its thousands of miseries were inevitable.

The victorious governments which had some financial strength left carried through these burdens.

The vanquished governments could not do so. Their unemployment, starvation and a thousand miseries bred revolution. They staved off the day of economic retribution for a few years by financial legerdemain. But finally the former enemy countries collapsed and dragged even the victors into bitter depression. In the defeated nations the people in renewed misery demanded the existing system be turned out, whatever it was. In those countries the man on the soap box had the solution of all ills. His phrases contained only one idea in many formulas—to take away from those who still had something. And in the chaos of agony came the man on horseback. The treadmill of the world started all over again.

And at home it was a difficult task for the democracies to demobilize their wartime regimes. We had given no thought, had no plans for the moral and economic demobilization or the unemployment and financial aftermaths. We had no plan, no solution. It is easier to regiment a people than to unregiment them. Great vested interests and vested habits were created which pressed for perpetuity. Millions held government jobs. The thousands of people in authority were reluctant to give up power. Factories had thrived on government orders. Farmers liked the government prices. It was only the resolution of President Wilson and the men immediately around him who forced what we now call fascism to retreat. Nevertheless our Government remained in many kinds of business. And of more vital importance, the ideas of war fascism remained. When in later years confronted with difficulties, the people demanded that the Government resume these war methods. We saw many of them reappear in soft phrases to make them look like democracy.

All this is but a bare skeleton of the last total war. It takes no account of the millions who died.

In the present war pressure of starvation and air attack are far more diabolic than last time. Compassion is far weaker than even last time.

Today whether America joins in all-out war or not, we are faced with the same gigantic problems.

The great sacrifices which America will make are motivated by the hope of real and permanent peace.

And I urge upon youth that you study again these experiences for the light which they give upon our course for the future.

We will sit again at that peace table whenever it comes about. Hate will again also sit at the peace table.

The ghastly failures in peacemaking and in economic life after the last total war may be excused on the ground that those who lead the world were groping in the dark without the lamp of experience. We have had that experience. And these failures rise now with great questions that must be answered.

And in the study of these questions, let me suggest you examine the causes of failure of the Treaty of Versailles. You will find that a large part of them were failure to allay hate, failure of economic peace, failure to give opportunity of proper elbow room and of growth to the aspirations of peoples. It failed to secure disarmament and to prevent world inflation and bankruptcy. Peace must come from the prosperity and the hearts of men. It cannot be held for long by machine guns.

The immediate questions which arise are these:

Are we giving aid simply to assure the independence of Britain and the others who are fighting against aggression? Or are we extending our view to remaking the world?

How are we going to hold down destructive hate that makes constructive peace so difficult?

How are we to keep alight compassion for the injured and starving?

How are we going to settle the relations of the twenty races in Europe?

How are we going to be sure that liberty and freedom and democracy will be accepted by those races whose whole radical instincts rebel against it? Are we going to police the world?

How are we going to save a world ravaged by famine and pestilence?

How are we going to restore economic prosperity to an impoverished world?

How are we going to assure the proper elbow room for growing people?

How are we going to find refuge for the oppressed?

And here in America—

How are we going to hold down intolerance during this period which makes free speech and free press impotent to correct wrong and to develop constructive debate?

With far more difficulties than last time, how are we going to demobilize our war socialism and fascism in America and restore freedom again to men?

With far more exhausted resources than last time how are we going to provide for our own employment and economic recovery after this war?

In fact, how are we going to make a peace that will be a permanent peace?

These questions must be answered. Some of them need answers today. The others cannot be dismissed on the ground they must await the outcome of the war. There will be no time then. The answers are vital to the moral, spiritual and economic welfare of our youth. They will determine your whole lives. And to that end American youth should begin to think now, for it is you who are involved.

We cannot expect the British people in their desperation to devote much thought to these ends.

America, however, today stands a certain distance apart from that scene. We do not have the distraction, suffering and the engrossment closer to the battlefields.

I am one who prays with all my being that America's sons should not be sent to this war. If God grants that we become no more deeply involved than we are today we may be able to bring a more constructive and warning voice to the peace table. If our moral reservoirs are not drained by the full passions of war we may bring sanity and compassion. If our economic resources are still partly intact, we may be able to contribute something to restore another and better world. If our faith in democracy is held high amid the storms of war economy we may yet keep the lamp of liberty alight.

Whether the fates determine that we step fully into this war or not, these same questions must be answered. I bid you to think and think fast. For our common purpose must be that our country moves in the moral, the spiritual and the social paths that will keep it unimpaired in its freedoms, its Christian ideals powerful and impregnable.

SHOULD THE ENGLISH-SPEAKING
DEMOCRACIES UNITE NOW? [8]

DOROTHY THOMPSON and JOHN A. DANAHER [9]

This argument was presented on Thursday evening, February 13, 1941, as one of the regular Town Hall programs and was held in the Town Hall, New York. The moderator was George V. Denny, Jr. As the chairman explained, the discussion was based on the proposal of Clarence Streit (*Union Now*, Harper and Brothers, 1939, a book hailed as an American reply to Hitler's *Mein Kampf*) that the democracies form a common government based on the broad lines of the American Constitution. In 1940 Streit modified his program (in view of the collapse of numerous democracies after Nazi blitzkriegs) to encompass mainly the United States and Great Britain. Read, for example, his addresses of December 1, 1940, and of January 22, 1941. In 1939 he became chairman of the Interdemocracy of Federal Unionists. By June, 1941, the group numbered thousands, presumably recruited from the constituency that had carried forward the "Bundles for Britain" project.

Dorothy Thompson had been one of the original supporters of the Streit proposals. Senator Danaher, on the other hand, had a record as an isolationist and a critic of the Roosevelt foreign policy. He had vigorously opposed in the Senate and over the radio Roosevelt's spending program, the neutrality bill, releasing goods to England on credit, the Export-Import Bank lending authority program, the move to aid Finland financially, the use of American patrol vessels in aid to Britain, the transfer of destroyers to England, the Lend-Lease Bill, and similar bills aimed at collaboration with Great Britain.

The program was typical of Town Hall debates—a genuine two-sided argument rather than a panel discussion as exemplified in the Chicago Round Table.[10] Miss Thompson and the Senator, however, observed the amenities of good debate and proved, as did Glenn Frank and Robert Jackson the year before in a Town Hall debate,[11] that debaters can argue a point fairly, without resort to the strategic devices of school debaters or without commission of the fallacy of "ignoring the question" by undermining opposing personalities (a technique common in political debates).

[8] Reprinted from *Town Meeting, Bulletin of America's Town Meeting of the Air*, vol. 6, no. 14, February 17, 1941. Published by the Columbia University Press, 2960 Broadway, New York. (Single copies, ten cents; subscription to volume, $2.50.) By permission of the speakers and by special arrangement with Town Hall, Inc., and the Columbia University Press.

[9] For biographical notes see Appendix.

[10] See *Representative American Speeches: 1939-40*, p. 191.

[11] See *Representative American Speeches: 1939-40*, p. 233.

Senator Danaher's father was an eminent lawyer and able speaker and interested the son in speaking in the latter's high school days. Young Danaher engaged extensively in debates in the Meriden (Connecticut) High School. He had a short course in lectures on public speaking at Yale, but gained his real speaking experience after admission to the bar. He spoke at all sorts of public dedications, memorial ceremonies, in political campaigns, and did a considerable amount of jury trial work.

What of his methods of speech preparation? He attempts to analyze fully the question submitted him and attempts to build his remarks around a central theme which he "endeavors to analyze and to expound (I think) logically" so as to lead the audience to the conclusion he has in mind.

Generally he does not follow a manuscript. In this Town Hall Program, each speaker had twelve minutes for reading the prepared speeches.

To prospective speakers Senator Danaher suggests: "Like writing, speaking must be done over and over and over again. Knowledge of one's subject will naturally inspire confidence and make for ease of speaking. Thus, preparation is the real basis of successful public address, in my judgment. Thereupon, repeated practice will complete the necessary outline."[12]

For comment on Dorothy Thompson, see the introduction to "Let's Face the Facts," in this volume, p. 137.

MODERATOR DENNY: Good evening, neighbors! This is a sort of farewell to New York for six weeks while we go visiting around the country to show you our Town Meeting in action. Thanks to the generosity of the National Broadcasting Company, three more weeks have been added to our regular season, and Town Meeting will continue through May of this year, with a total of twenty-nine instead of twenty-six broadcasts.

Tonight we conclude our series on the question of aid to Britain with a discussion of what some may consider a radical proposal—the union of the English-speaking democracies. Most Americans are generally familiar with the Union Now movement originated by Mr. Clarence Streit, who spoke on the Town Meeting on this subject just before his book was published. As originally presented, Mr. Streit's plan called for a union of the then-existing democracies. It has

[12] Letter to the author, June 18, 1941.

since evolved into a proposal for a federal union of the English-speaking democracies. Hence, we are not discussing his original plan, but rather the more simple question, "Should the English-Speaking Democracies Unite Now?"

One of the original advocates of Mr. Streit's proposal was Miss Dorothy Thompson, one of the most influential women in the world of journalism and, we are happy to say, a member of Town Hall's Board of Trustees. Whether Miss Thompson approves entirely of the Streit Plan as it is now is a matter which she herself will reveal, but she does uphold the affirmative of tonight's question. Her friendly opponent is the distinguished United States Senator from the state of Connecticut, the Honorable John A. Danaher, whose speeches in the upper House are eagerly attended by all who can obtain seats in the Senate Chamber. I present our first speaker, Miss Dorothy Thompson.

MISS THOMPSON: Mr. Moderator, members of Town Hall: First of all, I am very happy to be here again after a long absence.

On everybody's tongue is the phrase: "When this war is over, nothing is going to be as it was before." That is a reasonable remark. For it must be quite clear that if everything before had been as it should have been, this war would not have occurred. A question that is harder to answer is: If things are going to be different, *how* are they going to be different?

I suggest that the following things must result from this war, unless it is to be followed by chaos very, very quickly: First, the world is going to be more greatly consolidated than it has been in the past. Second, the relationship between the United States and Europe must be settled in a manner that will endure for generations to come. Third, the relationship between the United States and the British Empire and Commonwealth must be put upon the firmest possible footing.

If you have two wars within one generation, something is wrong. What has been wrong for twenty-five years, in my belief, has been this: After the last war, we made a peace and did not provide adequate facilities for defending that peace. Previous to the last war, the peace of the world had been kept for over 100 years by the British Empire. I do not mean that during that time there was no war; I do mean that during that time there was no war involving the major powers of Europe or the major powers of the world at the same time. There was no world war for over 100 years. The last war was won for Britain and France by the intervention of the United States. The last peace was largely designed by the United States. In my opinion, that peace was a bad peace. Such has been my opinion for twenty years. I wrote about it for years before this war broke out, and for years I was sure that a war would break out as the result of the peace, and as a result of the fact that the United States had refused to accept the slightest responsibility either for enforcing the peace that we help to win, or changing it to fit changed conditions.

But whether the peace was good or bad, the fact of the matter was that the last war changed the power situation of even the victorious nations. It left Britain financially, economically, and militarily weaker than she was before it began. The only nation that really won the last war was the United States. We emerged as the relatively strongest single nation, financially, economically, and industrially, on earth. We refused to use that power in any constructive way. During the administrations of Mr. Harding, Mr. Coolidge, and Mr. Hoover, we made, in my firm belief, every political, financial, and economic mistake that could be made in regard to world policy.

We had not, mind you, refused to ratify the Peace of Versailles. We go around talking righteously about that, but it is not true. We concluded a separate peace with Germany which was, in effect, a separate ratification of the Versailles Peace. We refused to join the League of Nations and take full responsibility, but, since the affairs of Europe do actually concern us, as well as the affairs of the Far East, we were continual kibitzers in Geneva. On the other hand, we could never really throw our influence in any direction. We were, therefore, a completely unreckonable quantity in world politics.

Britain in her heyday maintained world peace by a supreme navy able to operate from key bases in the seven seas of the world; by using credit, money, and prestige as political instruments, for bargaining purposes; and by fostering free trade, and therefore contributing to a world which, for that century, and for that period of industrial development, was prosperous and in harmony with the interests of most nations. Not of all, but of most. Or at least of enough of them. She has not been able to do this since the last war.

Economically, under the three administrations that intervened between Wilson and Roosevelt, our policy was to promote the interests of the large corporations in this country, regardless of the over-all effect on the world economy. This country had become the creditor of all Europe. It was also protectionist. All the internal debts of Europe including reparations were keyed to our debt. No radical scaling down of the reparations could be made without a radical scaling down of the debts to us. No abolition of reparations could be made without the abolition of the debts to us. We could have maintained the debts, but that would have involved taking over the British role of promoting free trade. Or we could have remained protectionist and written off the debts. Instead, we tried to do both. That being impossible, we lent further money to Europe to the tune of $2,000,000,000, and more.

Meanwhile, following our lead, Britain and the rest of Europe went protectionist, and there was a huge debt structure with trade bottlenecks all along the line. It was like one of those Rhine wine bottles where the bottleneck begins at the bottom. The result was the complete collapse of the capital structure of both Europe and the United States in 1929. The revolution in Germany was the direct result of that collapse, and then Germany, under Hitler, cut herself loose from the international capital structure, using her butter and material economy to do it with. She armed for seven years, and then, convinced that France and Britain were weak enough to be forced to capitulate, started the series of adventures which precipitated the war. This war and its effects on America were predicted by Woodrow Wilson. He said, "Either we shall establish the League of Nations and really build it, or the whole business will have to be fought out again in twenty-five years." Well the twenty-five years are up, and here we are, and now we know—at least I think I know—what we all ought to have known all along: that the collapse of Britain would be a catastrophe for the United States. Everybody knows that, even Hamilton Fish. For even Hamilton Fish is suggesting lending Britain $2,000,000,000, something I could not have imagined from Mr. Fish a year ago.

The fact is that Britain and the United States are tied together with inseparable interests, tied together with a whole series of inseparable interests. For more than 100 years we have practically ignored defense in the Atlantic Ocean because the British fleet was there. The presence of that fleet and the fact that a war with Britain was unthinkable saved us billions of dollars in taxation. Although we have looked carefully for naval and air bases in the Pacific—in Hawaii, in the Philippines, Guam, Wake Island—we haven't had a single base of any kind between here and the British Isles, until we acquired them from Britain in Newfoundland, since the war began. The cold fact is that the British Isles are our Philippines in the Atlantic.

Add to this the interdependency of our trade. In the year 1938—a year before this war began—roughly 76 percent of our exports and 79 percent of our imports were to and from the British Isles and the British Empire.

Add to this the fact of our common language and our common institutions. Language is the greatest bond between men in this world. Even Hitler, with his race theories, has to admit it; when it comes to a showdown he defines a German as any white man who speaks German unless he happens to be a Jew. As for our institutions, they have been progressively approaching each other. Britain and America have been farthest apart when the extreme tories have been in power in Britain, with their love for the caste system. But social advances in Britain have been breaking down this system with extreme rapidity, and the war is going to break them down altogether. In fact, some Americans who love the British upper classes and the stately homes of England to the exclusion of the 40,000,000 other Britons, are now beginning, like Mr. Mark Sullivan, to worry lest Britain become a little too democratic and a little too socialistic. Well, it's about as much of either as the New Deal is. I think we are rather keeping pace with each other. As for the British members of the free Commonwealth—Canada, Australia, South Africa, New Zealand—our relations with them are friendlier, if anything, than with the United Kingdom. Our soldiers found that out in the last war.

Now, this entire English-speaking world is threatened. And with it, we are threatened. The threat against Britain is changing your life, and mine, and the life of everybody in this room; because of that threat to Britain, my stepson, aged twenty-three, is in uniform; and because of it my tax bill is going to take another big jump. And because of it, in one way or another, we are intervening in Europe again, and this time not with men, only because of the changed nature of war. But this time we have got to think up something better and more constructive than intervening in Europe and then pulling out again, or leaving our affairs to Great Britain in peace and then jumping in, in war.

One cause of war has been the inability of European nations to unite. Behind Napoleon and even blindly behind Hitler is the urge of the Continent of Europe to unite. But Britain, being neither of Europe nor out of it, has been unable to look upon any form of a united Europe with a friendly eye. Her coasts are too vulnerable. She has really been safe only as long as Europe was divided into numerous sovereign states with which she could make alliances. Hitler will never be able to unite Europe except as he turns it into a colony for German exploitation and domination; that is his dream. But a new dream is dawning all over Europe, in all the countries, in all the states— the dream of a federated free Europe, of a United States of Europe.

But such a federated Europe needs both the impetus of an example and a picture of how it could adjust its affairs to the British Empire and the United States. Britain would either have to go with that Europe or with us. I am presuming the best possible outcome of the war, namely, that Britain wins it. She would have to go, even in the best case, with Europe or with us; and in the worst case, she would have to go with Mr. Hitler. And so I propose that she go with us, that we make a voluntary federation of the English-speaking world confined, to start with, to only the following things, because I am very much against blueprints, and that is perhaps where I differ with Mr. Streit; I think we should start with a few very simple things and see how they work out:

A common defense; a common naval defense; a common currency; a common economic policy in regard to trade and the disposal of surpluses; and free immigration between ourselves. India and Egypt ought to be given dominion status, and the opportunity to enter this federation if they so desired. And furthermore, I would leave it open to anybody to enter it, who so desired.

The center of such a federation would be in North America, not in the British Isles. That is obvious. Our land area, industrial resources, and position between the two oceans make that inevitable. Such a federation would, in effect, mean the liquidation of the British Empire into the complex of an English-speaking unity or commonwealth of states. And such a federation would have nothing whatever to fear from the unity of

Europe. With a federated Europe, along a pattern somewhat similar to our own, we might make an interlocking federation; and, at any rate, we could make a peace that would endure for 500 years. The Anglo-Saxon world, which has carried the banner of liberty and freedom on every hemisphere for centuries, would be able to raise it again, in a better way than it has ever been raised before, and set the example to all nations.

This, in my belief, is the only constructive answer to Hitler. It says: You do not need war and conquest to create greater unities, greater commonwealths. All you need is human imagination and democratic will. Actually, the democratic world has been perishing because of a lack of vision.

If the menace of Hitler can lead us to something as constructive as this, I shall be willing to contribute to a monument for him—to the man who scared us into acting with courage and imagination. Thank you.

MODERATOR DENNY: Thank you, Miss Thompson. Now, I take pleasure in presenting our second speaker, United States Senator John A. Danaher, of the State of Connecticut.

SENATOR DANAHER: Mr. Denny, Miss Thompson, and fellow Americans:

The question before us for consideration is evidence of a plot to get our nation into the war. "Unite now" does not mean after the war, it means now. This question, shall we unite *now* with an empire at war *now,* presents fairly and squarely to the American people the very nub of the agitation over the conduct of our affairs for the past two years.

The agitators for this proposition contemplate a *new nation,* of which the United States of America would be only a part, just as the state of New York is a part of the United States. Let there be no mistake, therefore, on two fundamental points: First, that to unite now means for the United States a war now. Second, that our nation would become part of the British Empire under a new name.

First, to unit now with the United Kingdom and the British Empire means that our nation necessarily would be bound to guarantee the continued existence of the other six so-called democracies. Since they are already at war, a war which Great Britain declared for whatever purpose, we would at once and *now* become engaged in that war. There are millions of reasons why we should not take that step, and these reasons are personified by the lives of the millions of Americans who would enter that war. To unite now means war now, a war to the death, a war in Europe, a war in Africa, in Asia, in all the far-flung reaches of the world.

Second, the proposal is un-American, for it will necessitate the adoption of a new form of government for us; it will result in the subordination of our government as an independent entity.[13]   For us to unite now means that the United States would lose its international status and would become a mere component in a new union with the separate nations now comprising the British Empire, while we would become citizens of the newly formed nation.

Third, there would be a permanent commitment of the people of the United States, not only to defend, but to support the coeval so-called democracies. Our new union would have no tariffs among the member components, so that one-fourth of the world would then have the American market, and the inhabitants thereof would compete against all American workers. Again, we have it on the authority of Secretary Morgenthau that Great Britain has no more available assets. We would be bound permanently to sustain our bankrupt associates, for there could be no withdrawal from the new union. That this course would involve the prospective total economic collapse of our own country suggests billions of reasons why we should not endorse this proposed unity; reasons, this time, in the form of dollars, perhaps silly, foolish dollars, to be sure, but American dollars,

[13] Moreover, we would automatically be aligned against every other nation and every other people speaking any other language. The plan is aimed designedly at the United States.

none the less, and they're all we have, produced from the toil and the effort of Americans. The war effort for Great Britain alone would cost a minimum of $1,000,000,000 per month, not to mention her staggering debts, and the continuing cost of her future support.

So, let's examine this question, to gain a proper perspective. What steps have been taken in the past two years that we should now be asked to unite our fate and our fortunes with those of the British Empire?

From that day when Mr. Anthony Eden visited us, in December, 1938, our every official act has been in the direction of this union we have been hearing about. Senator Pittman, on January 3, 1939, inserted Mr. Eden's speech in the *Congressional Record,* just before the President made his "methods short of war" speech. Both talked about democracies, much as you have heard Miss Thompson tonight. By almost daily utterances the nation was prepared for the repeal of the embargo on arms so that we might become the arsenal of the democracies, in the war yet to come.

The arms embargo was repealed in November, 1939, and on the President's insistence the cash and carry plan was inserted in its place, and we began to ship munitions to the allies. From the very beginning Great Britain took out arms export licenses in only a small fraction of the total being taken by France. Was it to be up to us, the United States, to play our part to supply Great Britain with the planes and munitions she would need? The full import of the plan, now embodied in H.R. 1776, has not even yet been realized by our people.

In October, 1939, we established in the Atlantic, a neutrality patrol. In December, Mr. Early from the White House announced that the American cruiser "Tuscaloosa" came upon the liner "Columbus" in a sinking condition, afire from stem to stern, while a British destroyer stood by in the vicinity. But, in January, when the Chief of Naval Operations appeared before our committees, he told us how successive patrols of American warships daily followed the "Columbus" from the time she left Vera Cruz until she went to her watery grave. We learned from him that our naval aviators were patrolling upwards of 1,000,000 miles per month.

In May came the formation of a Committee to Aid the Allies, founded by leading internationalists, including Colonel Stimson, who, after his speech in New Haven demanding the opening of our ports to Great Britain's Navy, was appointed Secretary of War. With Colonel Stimson came conscription of our youth, with cries of emergency. The National Guard was ordered into Federal service. We heard plans for an army of 1,300,000 men, then for an army of 4,000,000 men, notwithstanding the Chief of Staff shortly before had told the Congress that an army of 400,000 would be ample. But the orders for 4,500,000 soldiers' identification tags were placed in October.

Everyone knows of Mr. William Allen White and of his frank and outspoken story of the "smartest trick" he and his committee played in building up the transfer of the fifty destroyers. Everybody knows that he openly said the committee he headed was a propaganda organization. Everybody knows that his associates, many of them sponsors of Union Now, finally made such demands for war that it got too hot for Mr. White and he resigned at white heat, saying he had never intended to go to war in the first place. But he told us he had done his work when the internationalists succeeded in getting Mr. Willkie nominated at the Republican Convention. Indeed, as Mr. Walter Lippmann said only a few days ago, if Mr. Willkie had not in advance pledged all-out aid to England, he never would have received the nomination. Mr. Willkie, before the Convention, told of his position at the dinner at Mrs. Ogden Reid's, so Mr. Julius Ochs Adler swung his *New York Times* into line with the *New York Tribune* in support of Mr. Willkie. The President's control of the Convention which renominated him for a third term is well known. The internationalists couldn't lose, for neither candidate would or did discuss what should have been the fundamental issue before the American people in 1940.

Meanwhile, on every hand our people were bombarded by a campaign of fear; the Congress was practically told that if we didn't pass all of these bills, one after another, the Germans would be coming up the Potomac by tomorrow afternoon at a quarter after two. Away went our destroyers; away went our flying fortresses. Colonel Stimson reported to the Congress in January, as the law requires, that last year the American Army furnished Great Britain with rifles, machine guns, and light artillery for a military force of upwards of 1,000,000 men.

But the campaign of fear progressed week in and week out, day in and day out, over the air, in the moving pictures, in the press, until the American people became inoculated with the virus of panic. Under its cover, there was imposed upon the American people, through legislation, the machinery for a blocked currency system, controls over our exports and imports, diversion of our stabilization fund, the nationalization of our industry, and similar measures. Still not a word to the American people, to explain to them that they must unite with the British democracies, except the nationwide newspaper advertising and radio campaign being conducted with the support of Mr. Streit, Miss Thompson, Mr. Russell Davenport, and others for Union Now, backed also by the same people who were sponsors of the League of Nations movement twenty years ago.

Mr. Ernest Lindley, the President's biographer, wrote in *Newsweek* for September 30, 1940:

> British talk about a union with the U. S. is just a morale booster and the start of a buildup for some postwar semi-alliance. Washington, of course, wouldn't touch the idea with a ten-foot pole now. Both President and Mrs. Roosevelt are deeply interested in the general idea of some *eventual* alliance and have had several private discussions with Clarence Streit, author of *Union Now.* Naturally, however, the Administration wouldn't openly broach the subject until there had been long public discussion and much further decline in isolationist sentiment.

Because of the election campaign, just as Mr. Lindley said, "naturally . . . the administration wouldn't openly broach the subject until there had been long public discussion. . . ." Then came the fireside chat, and finally the address of the President on the state of the union on January 6th. No longer is there talk of "measures short of war." Now we must stamp out Hitlerism, we are told. Now we must establish four freedoms everywhere, whether people want them or not. The President said: "No issue was fought out on this line before the American electorate." He was right; you never did have a chance to decide the issue.

By January 20, 1941, *The New York Times* quoted Doctor Felix Morley, formerly editor of the *Washington Post* as saying that President Roosevelt "is feeling his way" toward an Anglo-American union. Doctor Morley declared "that the Lend-Lease Bill pointed toward a policy of a 'definite political union' with the British Commonwealth of Nations. . . ."

Finally, Mr. Willkie went to England, bearing a letter from the President of the United States to Mr. Churchill. It remained for Mr. Churchill to tell us that it contained a poem which the President had said in the letter "applies to you people as it does to us." The lines the President wrote commence, according to Mr. Churchill,

> ". . . sail on, O Ship of State!
> Sail on, O *Union,* strong and great!'"

The lack of time precludes a complete resume; but do you think these things are just accidents? Do you think for one minute that day in and day out we can safely say we don't want war, while every day we do the things which are taking us into it? These events are planned. These events have been planned. They explain the third term. They explain Mr. Willkie. They explain conscription. To those of us trying to save the United States, who have seen these things day by day and month by month, the trend was obvious, the end result almost inevitable.

But it is *not* inevitable. We need not buy this war. We need not form a union now. If our people have a rendezvous with destiny, it can still be a destiny of our own making. As an

American, I glory in our nation, her institutions, and her people, and believe that we should not surrender them to the formation of a new union now. When our founders dissolved the political bands which once before linked us with the British Empire they declared that we should "assume among the powers of the earth the separate and equal station to which the laws of nature and of nature's God" entitled us. To our continued maintenance as a free and independent nation, I propose that with our founders in the Declaration of Independence, we Americans "pledge to each other our lives, our fortunes and our sacred honor."

NATIONAL ATTITUDES

THE FUNCTION OF DEMOCRACY [1]

WILLIAM O. DOUGLAS [2]

This address was given on June 20, 1941, before the Common-wealth Club of San Francisco, California. It is included in this volume as an excellent exposition of American principles of government. Judge Douglas was appointed a Justice of the Supreme Court of the United States in 1939.

There probably have been but few generations which have felt as poignantly as ours the challenge in the poet's dictum that—

> "Each age is a dream that is dying
> Or one that is coming to birth."

We know that we are more than mere spectators on a world revolutionary scene. We know that those revolutionary forces are infections in the world blood stream and that we shall be profoundly affected even though that disease will not ultimately triumph.

For these reasons we are all thinking deeply and profoundly about our responsibilities in this present world crisis.

Not so long ago I heard a professional group cheer the boast of a speaker that he had not mentioned once in his address the word "democracy."

Democracy, however, is no empty word, no mere shibbo-leth. It is a word to fill the heart with pride.

It reflects the faith of nations in the common sense of the common man.

[1] By permission of Associate Justice William O. Douglas. Text from *Congressional Record*, vol. 87, no. 124, July 3, 1941, Appendix, A3488-9.
[2] For biographical note see Appendix.

It carries the precious cargo of equal justice under the law, the right freely to speak and write and to worship God, the right of free assembly, and equality of political and social opportunity.

It is the way of life which respects the dignity of man, which recognizes no special class of citizenship based on wealth or poverty, or color, race, or creed.

These are commonplaces to us. We are inclined to take them for granted as we are the sun, and moon, and stars. But in these days of world upheaval unguarded assumption of the permanency of any institution is hazardous.

For these reasons, now is the time for open avowal of our faith, not for silence. Now is the time to utilize vigorously our constitutional rights so as to preach and practice incessantly the truths of democracy.

As Francis Hackett has put it, "We, the democrats, have not supposed that we must assert ourselves aggressively. Our faith has been sapped because of that." (*I Chose Denmark,* 1940) Aggressive assertion of an unbounded devotion to this way of life not only replenishes the people's faith—it helps create the alertness in thought and action necessary to transform that faith into a work-a-day creed.

With the world on fire we know it is not enough for us to vote and pay taxes and earn a living. Fifty years ago the thought was current that the nation could afford the luxury of having little skill in government because it required the use of its best brains and talents in the development of the country. But we know that we can ill afford any such diversions from active participation in this current campaign.

The needs of democracy cannot be filled merely by service within the normal orbit of our daily lives. Those needs must also be satisfied through civic, municipal, county, state, and national activities. And, somehow or other, our contributions must be made through those channels by devoting at least a part of our reserves of energy to public enterprises.

We have it in our power, by giving only a part of our lives, to provide a leadership in thought and action which will create a genuine—a spiritual—renaissance of the democratic faith. Those millions of Americans who have a real appreciation of the blood and sweat and sacrifice which through the centuries have ingrained into our present society the noblest ideals of mankind are the strongest sort of bulwark against those forces which would dislodge society from its moorings.

1. We must make sure that our citizens retain their old tradition of participating in the important decisions which affect their lives, their property, their ideals. The gap between local democracy and national representative government must not be allowed to widen. The people must remain part of an integrated national system, so that they feel an intimate contact with their government, so that it does not become a thing apart—removed and remote from them. One of the ways of maintaining that bridge is through the many articulate but unofficial groups concerned with some aspect of our social, economic, or governmental problems. Through them many a citizen can become an active participant in the body politic and actually share in the decisions which affect his own welfare. Such groups help make democratic government the imperishable possession of each citizen. Hence they are strong underpinning for an aroused and alert democracy. May the leaders of community thought, devoted to democratic ideals, assume responsibility for making them effective agencies through which the people may undertake active daily roles of citizenship.

2. The function of democracy, unlike totalitarian governments, is to train men—little men as well as big men—not for subjugation but for independence. We know that therein lies the great strength of democracy. We know that only in that way can the great spiritual values of a whole people be cultivated and preserved. Yet we also know that that requires great skills in view of the complexities of a technological age. It means that every citizen must have a stake in his country

adequate to justify in his eyes the sacrifices which any contingency may entail. It means that some way or other big men and little men must work as partners in our national endeavors. It means that powerful men and weak men must be joint venturers in preserving America in its own image. It means that government must serve a whole people—regardless of lines of wealth or poverty, strength, or weakness. And our endeavor must be not the detection of motes in each other's eyes but an objective, united assault on common problems.

To integrate the energies of little men and big men, share and share alike, into all local, state, and national undertakings is a task which requires continuous statesmanship. But success in that effort is a permanent achievement. It means that no caste system takes root. It means that equality and fraternity are given practical recognition. It means that men from all walks of life will find common adventure and thrills in serving jointly a great cause. It means that the eyes of men will be lifted from mean objectives to lofty ideals.

The sense of fraternity, the desire for service, the adventurous instinct are deep in the soul of America. They have been successfully appealed to before by offer of far less noble causes than the democracies now tender.

3. There must not grow up in this country any second or third or fourth class of citizenship.

There is only one class of citizenship in this nation. There is no room for any inferior grade. Where one has been allowed, the result has been the downward spiral of disunity. Then hate and intolerance have been incorporated. Under those conditions the enemies of democracy invariably have risen to power. Under those conditions there is an insistence on a conformity which is the beginning of a disintegrating process.

Every nonconformist who is beaten, every practitioner of the right of free speech who is jailed, every unpopular exponent of a religious faith who is deprived of his constitutional rights bring every free man a step closer to incarceration or punishment, or discreet and frightened conformity. Infraction of the Bill of Rights knows no terminal points. We know from the experience of other peoples that what starts as suppression of an unpopular minority swings as easily to persecutions on the right or on the left, until few can afford to be nonconformists. Those who started as instigators of oppression of a minority often turned out to be the next victims. We know that the concentration camps of Europe are not operated on racial, economic, social, or intellectual lines.

We should ever be mindful that all the battles for freedom are not won in the courts. "Only a persistent, positive translation of the liberal faith into the thoughts and acts of the community is the real reliance against the unabated temptation to straitjacket the human mind." (Frankfurter, *Law and Politics*, p. 197.) Vigilant patrol of the domestic scene against infraction of these fundamental constitutional rights will guarantee that the American sense of fair play will carry the day.

4. A contemporary observer has said that as a result of the incredible sophistries and the brutal and ruthless attacks by totalitarian leaders on the democratic processes, "The Declaration of Independence may now be referred to without apology, and even policemen on the beat are becoming dimly aware that there is such a thing as the Bill of Rights."

Certainly, those assaults have made us all realize more keenly than ever before that there is only one liberty, and that is liberty within the law. Without that cementing element there can never be confidence in order—the real basis of all security. And without a common sense of security there can be no effective compact among men based on conceptions of equality and fraternity. That entails, as a practical necessity, a constant recognition of the responsibilities as well as the rights of citizenship. There will be some who will be willing to exploit the Bill of Rights in order to destroy or mutilate the system which makes the Bill of Rights possible. But the defense against them is vigorous assertion by millions of Americans of their constitutional rights so as to preserve our basic freedoms, not to defile them. It is to be found in an alert and aroused citizenry intent on making the democratic processes function in any and all crises and resolved not to permit the forces of discord, fear, hesitation, or inaction to paralyze the operations of government.

Those who appreciate the human sacrifices which have made our free institutions possible know that rights are accompanied by responsibilities. They know that recognition of those responsibilities is the certain method of preserving and nurturing those rights. When rights and responsibilities go hand in hand, there is the strongest guaranty possible that liberty within the law is not mere temporary luxury but a permanent necessity for a free people. When the energies of the people are absorbed in that common endeavor the whisperers of hate and intolerance loom no more important than the occupants of psychiatric wards.

Whatever may be the specific ways and means, whatever the effort, the pole star will always be the ingredients of the democratic faith. These have recently been stated by an eminent American, Carl Becker, as follows:

To have faith in the dignity and worth of the individual man as an end in himself, to believe that it is better to be governed by persuasion than by coercion, to believe that fraternal good will is more worthy than a selfish and contentious spirit, to believe that in the long run all values are inseparable from the love of truth and the disinterested search for it, to believe that knowledge and the power it confers should be used to promote the welfare and happiness of all men rather than to serve the interests of those individuals and classes whom fortune and intelligence endow with temporary advantage—these are the values which are affirmed by the traditional democratic ideology.

In final analysis our individual and joint efforts must have as their end product the way of life which underwrites those eternal truths.

In 1775, when this nation was uniting against the tyranny of that age, a great patriot said, "We are not weak if we make a proper use of those means which the god of nature hath placed in our power."

Today those words ring as true as they did then.

The means which God has placed in our power embrace not only material resources but also great inner spiritual strength, an abiding sense of fair play, an abundance of common sense, a deep sense of fraternity, a great reserve of ingenuity, a desire for service. To evoke these qualities from all the people in times of peace as well as war will mean that our rich heritage of freedom will remain imperishable. Utilization of those tremendous reserves of strength will guarantee that this age is not a dream that is dying but one that is coming to glorious birth.

CHRISTMAS, 1940 [3]

and

ROCK AND FLOOD [3]

WILLIAM J. CAMERON [4]

W. J. Cameron delivered these addresses during the five or six minute intermission in the regular Sunday evening radio program of the Detroit Symphony Orchestra, under the sponsorship of the Ford Motor Company. "Christmas, 1940" was delivered on December 22, 1940, and "Rock and Flood" on May 4, 1941.

Mr. Cameron has been the intermission speaker on this Ford Sunday evening series since 1934. His skill as speaker and commentator has been unquestioned. Hundreds of thousands listen to him each week. Although born in Canada, Mr. Cameron has lived in Detroit since nine years of age. He was on the staff of the *Detroit News* from 1903 until 1918; since then has been with the Ford Company. He edited the Dearborn *Independent* (Ford's paper) until he became a radio spokesman. Although he is primarily a journalist, he is a homely philosopher of no mean ability, an oral essayist whose numerous short addresses have served as models in many a class in English composition and in speech, and a speaker whose calm, resonant, and persuasive tones suit the language and the ideas. Like Deems Taylor, Cameron blends with the mood of the program. He creates an effective synthesis of speaker, speech, audience, and occasion.

Is his performance merely "another form of sales plug?" When he began his talks seven years ago, he announced that "we will not use this famous orchestra to lure our friends within selling range. Our purpose is not to glorify industry. Our purpose is to make a contribution to our country's economic health." Candid listeners agree that he has not been a liability to the Ford Company's prestige and commercial campaigns. Some have even viewed with suspicion the tenor of his ideas as attempting to convert the American people not only to Ford cars but to a Ford economic philosophy of individual initiative and of the integration of industry under private management. But Cameron has used excellent technique in avoiding the customary sales appeals accompanying almost every popular radio "commercial." His repeated impressiveness in his didactic talks and his effective addresses before numerous visible audiences, usually business men's meetings, well entitle him to inclusion among those who have recently impressed American life through public address.

[3] By permission of Mr. Cameron. Text furnished through the courtesy of the speaker and of the Ford Motor Company.

[4] For biographical note see Appendix.

CHRISTMAS, 1940

The rulers of this world's darkness have contrived with terrible regularity to bring eclipse on every cherished Christian season. Now once again Christmas is beclouded, and again we are asking how shall we meet it? At any cost, let us meet it as *truthfully* as we can. The first Christmas Eve, as we are told, a glory shone in the sky; this year over western Europe the sky will be one glare of bursting shells. On the first Christmas Eve there was suddenly with the Messenger a multitude of the heavenly angels; this year the only wings men see will be those of bombers silvered by the searchlights. Immortal song floated from the skies on that first Christmas Eve; this year the only sound descending will be showers of shrapnel on roof and pavement.

"Oh," we say, "forget it! We want to celebrate Christmas!" If that means, "Let's not talk about it for the children's sake," of course we shall not talk about it. But if grownups think to put a black-out on the facts, they will soon discover not only that they *cannot,* but also that in *trying to* they take a beauty out of Christmas.

Night brings out the stars and Christmas has a special brightness for darkened times like these. For the Season points not only backward to a sacred Event; the Event itself is always pointing forward to a liberated future. It is history, yes, but not like that of a Caesar who is born, dies and then recedes with time; it is rather like the birth of a world, the release of a new force—a seminal beginning that grows and expands with time. What we comprehend under the name of Christmas is a new force invading the race, lifting it to a higher frequency of perception—a potency that will not cease until all that it portends shall be accomplished, nor even then, for *then* it will only have begun. Christmas is the guarantee that everything that darkens it now—everything!—is definitely *defeated*—judged, condemned and marked for expulsion from the world of men. And that is a great thing to celebrate.

Some find this hard to believe. But when we consider, first, how short a time the world has known the Christmas spirit; and second, how comparatively few persons in any generation have creatively embodied it; and third, how much it has accomplished in spite of that, for since it entered the world it alone has succeeded, and all things contrary, without exception, have miserably failed; when we consider these things, belief is not so difficult.

Perhaps we have not fairly understood the Christmas process. There is a world of difference between the natural law operative in these matters and the higher law that Christmas represents. On the natural plane *evil is in control of evil*. One evil curbs another. Injustice is restrained by the disorder it produces. Iniquitous ambition is cut down to size by equally iniquitous envy. Wicked nationalistic designs are tamed by the evil of war. One evil checks another *but neither is destroyed*—the root remains. This good natural order prevents any single evil from consuming the world, but does not of itself greatly reduce the sum of evil, it only holds it in precarious balance.

Christmas signifies a higher providence, a higher law. It is the science of a higher Force that denatures, absorbs, wholly overcomes evil, and transmutes it into good, leaving no root of it, leaving only good as the end result. Society is well-equipped with laws, police and military force to check its evils, but is ill-equipped to create the good and establish it. And society is growing tired of the necessity, generation after generation, of always using a lower force to check another lower force that will break out again; it is feeling the need of this higher science that overcomes recurring wrong by substituting a never-wavering and self-perpetuating Right. This greater power is the Christmas Power; it is less spectacular but more effective than any force we know, and Christmas is the prophecy that this Power holds the future.

Why hesitate, then, about celebrating Christmas?—the Good Will that creates social, economic and personal peace, which alone is the ground of international peace?   For all this is coming, and some of it is here.   Why not celebrate it?   *Chime* the bells and *deck* the trees and *spread* the feast; *carol* the Yuletide on the frosty air and *tell* the Christmas story round the fire—it is not make-believe! "Peace on earth to men of good will" and "Merry Christmas" are still valid; we still can make Christmas memorable for little children who are nearer its fulfilment than we are—it is not pantomime.   We are celebrating that which *was* and *is* and *is to come*.   Friends of the Sunday Evening Hour, this year we wish all of you this kind of "Merry Christmas."

ROCK AND FLOOD

In the face of absolute evidence that the present pattern of affairs is the oldest unchanged pattern in the world, the idea is diligently propagated that these are times of unintelligible change. Now, human reason never has recoiled from the fact of change, but has sought in change its changeless center. The central quest of art, philosophy and religion, and now of science, has been to find stability in the midst of flux. But the spirit of confusion wants no footing in the flood; it bids us fling ourselves away as driftwood smashed and splintered by the flood. "It's the break-up of everything," we are told; "overboard with your intellectual and spiritual treasures; a new Atlantis rises from the deep."

Well, let us see.   A time of change should exhibit some change.   Here are two quotations, one from a French victim of despotism 135 years ago. He said: "The continent of Europe is a vast prison house cut off from communication with England, that haven of thought and freedom, that sanctuary of the human spirit."   Even to the detail that the "prison house" of this quotation is not England cut off from Europe, but Europe cut off from England, need we alter one syllable to describe conditions at this very hour?   Then where is the change?   The second quotation is from Ralph Waldo Emerson concerning the Italy he knew 108 years ago: "Everyone," he says, "who was in Italy will remember the caution with which his host or guest in any house looked around him, if a political topic were broached." That is precisely what travelers say arriving last week. Where is the change?

A time of change should present some element of surprise; even the slight novelty of the unexpected is not afforded by present world conditions. For five years past it has not been necessary to read the newspapers to know what would occur,— so like is this period to others preceding it. When certain signs appeared, the course events would take was as clear to the observer of mankind as the course of measles or smallpox to the physician.

No new basic technique has been developed, not one new lie or one new trick since the despotic art was practiced in Babylon. Everything that was there is here. The *same* psychology of preparation; the *same* denials used as prelude to performance; the *same* inciting a people to trample the liberties of a race or a class, that, being themselves degraded, they might more easily be stripped of their own freedom and used as instruments of tyranny. The *same* doctrine that temporary surrender of liberty is necessary to perpetuation of liberty. The *same* dazzling lightning changes, for as Napoleon said, and every dictator knows, "We must give the people something new every three months." The *same* governing principle that everything must be done *for* the people and nothing *by* them. This has been the method for 3,000 years. Even the *same* fatality by which the aggressor makes one by one and in the *same order* the *same mistakes* that lead to the *same inevitable end,* in modern Europe as in ancient Assyria. As the French say, "The more it changes, the more it is the same." There is a sharper efficiency in the *role* of the villain, but there isn't a new line or a new character in the entire drama.

What, then, is the drama? Those who would have us lost and bewildered in the midst of something new and strange, are blind to the oldest moral continuity known in human life. It is the age-old struggle of innate despotism *against* innate liberty, of brains divorced from conscience *against* brains in league with freedom—a struggle needlessly prolonged for two reasons: first, indifference of the friends of Light and Progress until faced with a crisis; and second, with all that indifference, their inflexible resolution never to surrender their vision. And, so—

> Till the war drum throbs no longer and the
> battle-flags are furled
> In the Parliament of man, the Federation of
> the world—

till Angel prove stronger than demon, that struggle will *continue*. It is old, it is changeless, but it moves. The earth has its motion but always on its axis, and soars in ageless flight but always round the sun—and not in aimless repetition, for "the thoughts of men are widen'd with the process of the suns"; so does this struggle move, true to its center but always nearer its goal.

Now, that is the rock that gives us footing in the flood. The flood is a fact, and can be made a confusing fact, but a greater fact is the rock, for on it men may build. Creators of confusion would center our emotions in the flood—because *that* destroys *all* belief and action. Rather than be demoralized into mental jitterbugs danced around by every fear and uncertainty, most of us choose to believe in the rock of a continuous, intelligible and ongoing purpose. The only thing that can deceive us is our inability to see the obvious.

If we know these things, we shall rightly interpret the storm that rages now. There are storms that bring winter and *they have brought winter*; this storm heralds a springtime of order and amity for the nations.

> Well roars the storm to those that hear
> A deeper voice across the storm.

UNIVERSALITY OF MUSIC [5]

Deems Taylor [6]

Deems Taylor gave this intermission talk on the regular Sunday afternoon program of the New York Philharmonic-Symphony Orchestra, April 20, 1941, broadcast as a sustaining program over the Columbia Broadcasting System's network. John Barbirolli was conductor.

Since 1936 Mr. Taylor has talked during the orchestra's intermissions. Sometimes he has reviewed the composer's life and times; sometimes he has interpreted musical trends. His popularity, apparently with all classes of listeners, has been great and has steadily increased. His clear, well-controlled voice, excellent in quality, his informal, humorous, conversational mode, his skill in conveying to the millions of listeners his "radio personality," partly explain his success.

His picturesque career and activities are by no means a liability to him. Well known to all musical Americans is the fact that he has composed some fifty musical selections, including the "Through the Looking Glass" suite, "The King's Henchman," and "Peter Ibbetson;" that he was educated at the Ethical Culture School and at New York University; that he helped write an undergraduate musical comedy that found its way to Broadway; that he then began to study music seriously; that a short time later he won first prize in a symphonic contest; that he was on the editorial staff of various publications, including encyclopedias, the *New York Herald Tribune, Collier's Weekly,* the New York *World, Musical America;* that he was a foreign correspondent in France; that he paints ("for his own amazement"); that he continues to write music and to translate from several languages.

How does he prepare for his broadcast? His effective directness and seeming extemporaneousness are the product of long and painstaking preparation. First he does the necessary research on Bach, Wagner, or whatever his theme. Then, segregated in his study in New York City, he starts simultaneously talking and composing. He repeats a sentence forty times, if necessary, to be sure it sounds perfectly natural. He uses no secretary to help with such composition, but "pecks out by ear the final version." (*Newsweek,* 12:24, December 26, 1938) Other speakers, whether they are to speak over the radio or otherwise, may profitably use a similar method to secure the oral quality.

Mr. Taylor may spend five hours on a twelve-minute script. During that time he "practically lives with a dictionary," because, as he says, "the minute one slips over the radio, there are thousands who won't wait one minute to write in about it." At every turn he feels the pulse of his nation-wide audience, quotes them, replies to them

[5] Reprinted by permission of Deems Taylor. Text furnished by the speaker.
[6] For biographical note, see Appendix.

as if they were especially singled out as individuals for his attention; and he seems to adapt his voice and mood to the atmosphere of the symphonic program. His presentations are excellent demonstrations of the rhetorical virtue of artistic blending of speaker, speech, audience, and immediate occasion.

I had some letters, this week, about last Sunday's all-Wagner program. There weren't many of them, I'm happy to say, but there were enough to make me wonder just how many there were of you who thought the same thing but didn't take the trouble to write it. Generally speaking, these correspondents objected to playing Wagner's music on Easter Sunday. Easter, they said, was a time of peace and happiness, and Wagner represented a country whose philosophy of living is opposed to everything that, to us at least, makes life worth living. One woman wrote that all the time the music was being played she couldn't escape from the thought that it is the favorite music of Adolf Hitler.

Well, to comment on that last remark first, isn't it a little childish to take the stand that, since somebody holds certain opinions with which you violently disagree, you must be very careful to disagree with *all* his opinions? Now most of us, I believe, think that Mr. Hitler is very wrong about a great many things. That being so, isn't it rather encouraging to find that he's right about *something*? Besides, if you're going to reject everything that Mr. Hitler likes, just to show your disapproval of his policies, where are you going to stop?

He likes to hear the piano, for instance! Is that a good reason for not listening to Mr. Rudolf Serkin, next Sunday, play the Brahms piano concerto? Mr. Hitler probably likes bacon and eggs. Shall we cut out bacon and eggs? He never drinks anything but water, I understand. Shall we give up water, and all become chronic alcoholics, just to show that he can't dictate to us?

Besides, consider the case of Wagner, one of the greatest individualists that ever lived, and one of the greatest exponents of the essential nobility and freedom of man. Just how would

he get along in present-day Germany? Where would he be?
I'll tell you where he'd be. If he had any luck, he'd be here.
If he hadn't, he'd be in a concentration camp.

Two or three of those correspondents raised the point that
Mr. Hitler's entire political philosophy is based on Wagner's
Nibelungen trilogy. In the first place, that's not a new idea.
Today the whole world celebrates Mr. Hitler's birthday, each
after its own fashion. Well, quite a while ago, at a time when
Mr. Hitler was only nine years old, George Bernard Shaw published a little book in which he proved—to his own satisfaction
at least—that the Nibelungen trilogy was an allegory of the
struggle for social freedom.

Wotan represented the Church and the law, Alberich the
capitalists, who exploit the working classes, as represented by
the rest of the Nibelungs and the giants, and Siegfried—well,
more or less the Communist Party, come to free the workers of
their shackles. When he got to Gotterdammerung he rather
got stuck, because there, apparently, capitalism stabs communism
to death; so he side-stepped that by explaining that Gotterdammerung is only a conventional grand opera, anyhow, and
so doesn't count. Get the book some time, and read it. It's
called *The Perfect Wagnerite*. It may make you mad, but at
least it will hold your interest.

In the second place, if Mr. Hitler is really inspired by the
Ring trilogy, don't forget that Wagner didn't invent it. He put
it together, out of several legends, most of which belong, originally, not to German, but to Norse mythology. Wotan is nothing but the Norseman's Odin; Dionne is merely Thor under
another name. Siegfried is just another name for Sigurd. What
Wagner did contribute was a comment, an underlying philosophy
—a moral, if you like. And what is that moral? Now if you
read Siegfried, you will find something that looks very much
like a plea for a superior race of heroes, a Herrenvolk, who are
stronger than the gods, and are the natural masters of the inferior races of man.

But I would recommend to Mr. Hitler that he read *all* of the Ring. Read Rheingold and Gotterdammerung with particular care. What are the two points that Wagner makes in "Das Rheingold?" What are the two underlying causes of the entire tragedy? One is, that if a man abjures love, if he bases his career on hate, he can seize great power. The other is, that even a god dare not found his power on a lie; that if his pledged word is worthless, if no promise of his can be trusted, he will not endure. From the moment that Wotan breaks his word to the giants, he is doomed, betrayed by his own betrayal.

And what do we see in that terrible and magnificent closing scene of Gotterdammerung? We see Valhalla in flames. The gods are dead, because they did not keep the faith. Nagan, the dwarf who seized power at any cost, has reached for it once too often. He, too, is swept away. Dead, too, is the race of heroes, the master race. They all tried to rule the world, and they were not worthy. There remains only man, to face his destiny alone, to make or destroy a world, according to his strength or his weakness. If I were a dictator, it is not to Wagner that I would go for inspiration.

You see, we're living in a very perilous time, a time when many of us feel that the civilization we have acquired so slowly and so painfully, *our* ideal of civilization, is at stake, is undergoing its supreme test. But there's no use in supporting that civilization with our voices, if we're not going to support it in our hearts. It's not enough to say that we're civilized; we've got to *be* civilized. Let's not be Nazis. Let's not be a nation of witch-burners; let's not burn books, either literally or figuratively; let's not boycott artists, because of the race to which they belong.

We are fighting an idea, a concept; and the great danger, in fighting an idea is that, in the struggle to destroy it, you adopt it, unconsciously, as your own. We must keep our vision clear, we must keep our values. And what are those values? What are the things that last, that are of final importance?

Well, let me repeat something I said almost exactly a year ago. Those things are science, philosphy, religion, and art. Those are the things that distinguish life from mere existence, the things that man does not share with his brother animals. I may be biased, but I can't help thinking that of all the arts, music is the one most closely allied to the spirit, the most tangible, the most innocent. If music is closely related to all religions, that fact is significant.

People will tell you, even now, that some music is friendly, some is hostile, some is pure, some corrupt. You will be told that more and more loudly, I think, in the days to come. Don't believe that. Music has not politics, no race, no loyalties, no treasons. Every composer, living or dead, is your friend and brother. Remember that. Don't betray that friendship.

Brahms, whom we are to hear shortly, today, and Wagner, whom we heard last week, represent a Germany that—so her leaders say—exists no longer. I find it hard to believe that that Germany is dead, that the race that gave us that priceless treasure of music during the 18th and 19th centuries is gone forever. I can't help feeling that somewhere, however bound and gagged, she lives.

But if her leaders are right, if that Germany really *is* dead, then all those great men of the past, and the works of those men, are, literally, homeless. They are the most helpless of all the refugees, because they can no longer even ask for our help. And so, let us not imitate the man who drove them out. We have many living refugees with us, writers like Thomas Mann, and Emil Ludwig, composers like Kurt Weill, Jaromir Weinberger, Erich Korngold, Arnold Schönberg.

We welcomed them, and are glad to give them what their persecutor calls "Lebensraum," room to live. Have we then no room for Haydn, and Mozart, Beethoven, Weber, Mendelssohn, Schumann, Wagner, Brahms? Can we not be as hospitable to the dead as we have been to the living?

LABOR, FREEDOM, AND DEMOCRACY [7]

WILLIAM GREEN [8]

William Green, president of the American Federation of Labor, gave this Labor Day address before a crowd of more than 25,000 in the City Park, Denver, Colorado, on September 2, 1940. The speech was broadcast over the National Broadcasting Company network.

The speech was delivered just a year after the beginning of the World War II and echoed the problems that faced America, including labor, at the beginning of September. After the collapse of France and the entrance of Italy into the war, the United States moved with all haste to develop a vast defense program. A few days before Green talked at Denver, the Senate, by a vote of 58 to 31, had passed and sent to the House of Representatives the Burke-Wadsworth Selective Service Bill, calling for the conscription of all American manpower between the ages of twenty-one and thirty-five. To this piece of legislation was added the Overton-Russell Amendment which gave to President Roosevelt power to take over all industry which might be deemed necessary for the furtherance of the national defense program. Thus with the prospect of the enactment by Congress of these measures and the quick launching of stupendous industrial activity that would require the complete cooperation of American labor, the attitude and remarks of the leader of the A. F. of L. had more than routine significance.

Green's visible audience was composed of the members of the International Brotherhood of Teamsters, Chauffeurs, Stablemen, and Helpers of America, the largest affiliate of the American Federation of Labor. All important to the country was it that labor remain loyal; that strikes be reduced to a minimum; that the fifth column and subversive elements in labor unions be crushed through labor opinion; that a high degree of efficiency and morale be maintained so that the vast amounts of war materials could be produced.

Green's position was highly reassuring to the friends of Roosevelt's immediate policies. The labor leader in this speech (1) warned that the nations of the Western Hemisphere might be the next targets of the European dictators if England should fall (Lindbergh and his group would deny this assumption or conclusion); (2) urged that the United States extend all possible help short of war to Great Britain as good national defense policy (a position in accordance with American public

[7] By permission of William Green. Text supplied through the courtesy of the speaker.

[8] For biographical note see Appendix. Le Roy Cowperthwaite, a graduate student in speech at the State University of Iowa, summer of 1941, presented a report on Green to which the author is indebted.

opinion as shown by the Gallup poll); (3) pledged the services of American workers to the successful completion of the defense program (in contrast to the alleged attempts of certain local labor groups to block that accomplishment); (4) demanded that economic and social gains must be maintained (good Roosevelt New Deal philosophy, a program the President continued to affirm), and that the creation of war millionaires must be prevented (a policy the Government later attempted to carry out through huge taxes and other checks); (5) expressed opposition to the Burke-Wadsworth bill but declared that if the Government proved that conscription were necessary (in other words, if the bill were made law), "we are ready to approve it"; (6) assailed the Fifth Column activities and urged that the Communist Party and Nazi Bund be outlawed (in the subsequent activities of the A. F. of L. their record of opposition to such groups was consistent, at least to the time of this writing); (7) called for labor peace (but the strife between C.I.O. and A. F. of L. continued, even though John L. Lewis retired in November as president of C.I.O. and Green reminded his hearers that A. F. of L. was stronger than ever before); (8) said nothing about specific methods of preventing strikes.

What of Green's delivery? According to George Creel (*Collier's*, 98:14, July 11, 1936), Green is "somewhat ecclesiastical in dress, with a marked pulpit manner; his oration was almost religious in its emotional appeal." The same remark would apply to the Labor Day address. Green prepared to enter the ministry and in fact delivered a number of sermons as a Baptist preacher (*New Republic*, 94:71, February 3, 1936, "Shoot the Works," Heywood Broun). The *Literary Digest* (116:10, September 16, 1933) described him as "plodding and tenacious, conciliatory rather than explosive." Although he is no orator, he has plenty of physical animation in speaking; his voice is high pitched, his rate of delivery measured and inclined to be retarded; he measures each word; "his voice lacks resonance to stir deeply" (*Review of Reviews*, 88:21-3, November, 1933, "Labor's Chief: William Green," Raymond Clapper). His gestures are usually the same—either with fingers outstretched ("as if about to wrap themselves around the miner's pick-handle he once wielded in the sooty pits," *Literary Digest*, 121:10, June 6, 1936) or with clenched fists but "with loose-handed wave" (Clapper). He has plenty of force in delivery and "is inclined to be on the emotional side."

Since President Roosevelt on this Labor Day delivered two speeches dedicating Great Smoky National Park and Chickamauga Dam, the utterances of Green and other prominent Americans were somewhat obscured. Remarked the *Christian Science Monitor* (September 3, 1940, p. 16), "With the United States launching on a tremendous defense program, there are encouraging signs that Americans are gaining fresh appreciation of the necessity of mutual sacrifice. Labor Day statements by the President and heads of great labor organizations all reflected in some degree the understanding that work and more work is the prime requisite in effective defense measures."

Concerning Mr. Green's speech training and preparation of this particular speech he states, "My education afforded no particular training for public speaking, as it did not extend beyond high school. I have been compelled to do so much public speaking, however, that I have been interested in the use of voice and other techniques in delivery, and have read considerable on this subject. As to preparation of manuscript, I usually have some mental outline which I follow in dictation. My more important public addresses are always prepared in advance, and usually I adhere quite closely to the manuscript." [9]

On Labor Day we in America celebrate the economic freedom of American workers. It is a national holiday. Just as on July Fourth we commemorate the Declaration of Independence which gave America its political freedom, so on the first Monday of each September we pay fitting tribute to the progress of the organized labor movement which serves to emancipate the workers of our country from wage slavery.

The significance and importance of your Labor Day Celebration here in Denver is immeasurably increased through the attendance and participation of the representatives of 150,000 members of the International Brotherhood of Teamsters, Chauffeurs, Stablemen and Helpers of America. These workers are a part of the largest international union affiliated with the American Federation of Labor. The paid-up membership of this International Union is in excess of 400,000, and I predict that within a reasonable length of time it will be increased to 600,000. I welcome these sturdy, loyal, devoted members of the American Federation of Labor from the far-West. We are happy because they are with us. We ask them to join enthusiastically and wholeheartedly with us in this great Labor Day Celebration. We extend to them the hand of friendship, and the felicitations of five million of their fellow members affiliated with the American Federation of Labor.

Working people cherish freedom as a priceless possession. For this reason, they unite in opposing regimentation, governmental or otherwise. They will never surrender their personal liberty, freedom of action, freedom of speech, freedom of as-

[9] Letter to the editor of this volume, March 28, 1941.

semblage, and the exercise of the right to organize into free, democratic unions.

A new appreciation of the value of freedom and liberty has developed in the hearts and minds of American workers. This has been brought about because the World War has opened their eyes to the horrors of industrial regimentation of workers in totalitarian countries, where everyone is subject to governmental control, even in the ordinary and normal activities of social and economic life. Through contrast, American workers have learned a lesson which they could not gain from a purely academic source.

From the beginning the American Federation of Labor has condemned with equal and unqualified force the dictatorships of Stalin, Hitler and Mussolini. We saw at once, as all discerning Americans see today, that dictatorship in any form and under any label deprives the great mass of human beings of their basic and inalienable rights and liberties. We warned then, and we warn with even greater fervor now, that the hunger of the European dictators for more and more power can never be appeased and that their continued existence constitutes a menace to freedom and democracy in every part of the world, including our own beloved country.

Who could have imagined on Labor Day a year ago that within a few months practically all of Europe would be devastated by war? Who could have believed that the rights of the free and peace-loving peoples of Czechoslovakia, Poland, Norway, Denmark, Holland and Belgium would be crushed by a war machine that totally disregards human decency? Who would have thought that the great army of France would crumble so quickly in the face of the blitzkreig? Who could have predicted that the threat of invasion from across the seas would ever face America?

Yet these things have happened with breathless speed and today America is threatened—America and civilization. Today Great Britain, with her navy depleted, her air force weakened and her whole population with their backs to the wall, stands as the last obstacle between us and the onward march of the dictators.

This is Great Britain's hour of need and extremity. She needs help as never before. The American Federation of Labor believes that the United States should extend every help to her, short of entry into the war. We are convinced that in assisting Great Britain now we are strengthening our own national defense.

That is not an involved or far-fetched statement. Like all truths it is simple and compelling in its logic. If Great Britain succumbs, the United States and her sister republics in the Western Hemisphere may be the next targets of the European dictators. We may face immediate war. The war may be an economic one at first, but it will be bitter and costly. The Atlantic Ocean may no longer be an insuperable barrier to military invasion of this hemisphere.

On the other hand, if Great Britain triumphs and Hitler is overthrown the threat to America will be dispelled. As long as Great Britain and her navy bar the way, Hitler and his blitzkrieg can never come here.

Therefore, the American Federation of Labor believes that this nation should not only extend sympathy to Great Britain but we should give her all the help and assistance we can.

We hope and pray that Great Britain will be victorious in her present death struggle with Hitler. But we must be prepared for the worst. Therefore, the American Federation of Labor pledges its full and unreserved support to the gigantic national defense program undertaken by President Roosevelt. Let us build more ships and more planes. Let us expand and modernize our army. Let us broaden and increase our industrial production. Let us show those who would destroy our nation and our liberties that we are prepared to meet force with greater force in defense of our homeland.

Because I know the hearts and the minds of American working men and women, I can publicly pledge their services will be willingly and loyally devoted to the successful completion of our defense program. America's workers can be relied upon wholly and absolutely to do the job the nation requires and demands. Furthermore, as their spokesman, I pledge to our Government that the workers of America will respond whole heartedly to the call, if it ever is needed, to take up arms in the defense of our homeland, our freedom and our American way of life.

The great army of workers and the unions represented by the American Federation of Labor courageously face the fact that the preservation of America and democracy transcends all other considerations.

Truly observing the spirit of Labor Day, we stand here and publicly proclaim that we are ready to work, we are ready to sacrifice, we are ready to fight for America.

Our National Preparedness program must provide for the maintenance of our economic and social gains. They must neither be lowered nor wiped out. Profiteering and exploitation must be prohibited. The creation of war millionaires must be prevented and governmental guarantees must be given that no one called to serve the nation will be sent abroad to engage in a European conflict. We must prepare for defense but never for aggression.

I am gratified to report that the Government of the United States knows and appreciates the loyal spirit of America's workers and has made a solemn pledge to them. That pledge is the assurance that the great advances achieved by organized labor after more than a half-century of struggle will not be scuttled to satisfy the greed of war profiteers. The American standard of work and the American standard of living will not be discarded, but will be fully upheld, in the defense program. In other words the Government recognizes that industrial democracy must be preserved if we are to preserve our national democracy.

In order to strengthen our military forces, Congress is now considering a proposal to conscript an army of a million men for military training and service. This measure was sponsored by men who do not enjoy the full confidence of organized labor. It was not drafted by the Administration, but by men who have consistently opposed the Administration. The bill has been so widely amended from day to day that the American people have not been able to keep up with its manifold changes.

The American Federation of Labor opposes the Burke-Wadsworth bill. We have no more confidence in it than in its sponsors. We do not consider it well-drawn or well-planned. On a matter as vital as this to the nation's welfare, we feel that it is the duty of the President of the United States to send a message to Congress stating the manpower needs of the nation's military forces and recommending a definite program to fulfil these needs.

This is the first time in history when the American people have faced a proposal for peacetime conscription. We should not undertake such a step blindly or lightly. The American Federation of Labor will not oppose conscription if it can be proved that the traditional method of voluntary enlistment has failed. But there has been a great deal of misinformation spread on this subject. Present enlistment procedure calls for long-term service. We suggest that the Government offer a new kind of enlistment, say for a training period of one year or a year and a half, with the guarantee that recruits will not be called upon to serve in a European war. Let the Government offer these inducements, together with reasonable increase in soldiers' pay, and we predict that thousands who are now hesitant would flock to the colors. At any rate, the position of organized labor is that voluntary enlistment should and must be given a fair trial first in the traditional American way. Then, if this system fails, the nation will without hesitation agree to the final expedient of compulsory conscription. I have great confidence in the common-sense judgment of the American people.

I think their reluctance to accede to compulsory conscription in time of peace is sound and justified and patriotic. On this issue we say to our Government:—"We do not know what this is all about. We are not obstructionists, we are patriotic Americans. Give us the facts. Show us frankly why conscription is needed. If we actually need conscription, we are ready to approve it."

American labor already has demonstrated that it recognizes and is capable of assuming its responsibilities in the defense program. There have been few, if any, serious strikes since the inception of the defense drive. Organized labor, as represented by the American Federation of Labor, realizes that at a time like this industrial conflict would be stupid and dangerous. We urge workers and employers alike to be calm and patient. We appeal to them to be governed by fair play in human relations in industry. American labor, suffering from a ten-year plague of unemployment, does not want strikes. It wants work. Nor does American industry want strikes. It is now gearing itself for greater and greater production. Let both sides follow the peaceful and sensible policy of collective bargaining in the settlement of any disputes that may arise. That is our prayer and our purpose.

There is more to national defense than armament. The forces of communism, nazism and fascism have not conquered in Europe by armed might alone. They have organized subversive movements and undermined in advance the nations they planned to invade. They have used the Fifth Column as the first battering ram against the defense of their victims.

The Fifth Column has now moved across the Atlantic. The agents of Stalin, Hitler and Mussolini have penetrated every key country in the Western Hemisphere, including our own United States. They are here, operating secretly and behind many disguises.

The American Federation of Labor has resisted and defeated every attempt by Communists, Nazis or Fascists to bore from within and weaken the firm structure of loyalty upon which its organization rests. I am proud to repeat now the statement I have consistently made these many years that there is no room in the American Federation of Labor for nazism, communism or fascism. We regard these philosophies as hostile to Americanism. We regard Communists, Nazis and Fascists as traitors to America. We strongly urge that such traitorous organizations as the Communist Party and the Nazi Bund, be outlawed.

We deplore the fact that Communists have attained positions of influence and power in labor organizations not affiliated with the American Federation of Labor. And we are encouraged by increasing evidence that the loyal workers in the rebel movement are getting disgusted with Communist leadership and are fighting to get rid of it. That is good news not only for patriotic reasons but because the sooner Communist influence is eradicated from the dual movement, the sooner labor peace can be restored. From the beginning, the Communist Party has aided and abetted discord and strife and done its utmost to prevent unity in the labor movement.

Never before was it so important that American labor should be strong and united. Powerful forces are trying to move heaven and earth in an effort to whittle down labors' gains and destroy its standards. Organized labor will need to draw upon its full resources to resist such selfish attacks.

Why, then, is labor peace being delayed? Who is the obstructionist? Certainly it is not the American Federation of Labor. The President of the United States, himself, has attested to the fact that the American Federation of Labor has responded willingly to every call for negotiations to bring about a settlement. It is the leader of the dual movement who refused. It was this same individual who vetoed a peace agreement which had been drawn up and approved by committees representing both sides. He is the sole obstructionist.

Let me repeat once more the position of the American Federation of Labor so that there can be no misunderstandings or mistakes. The American Federation of Labor is willing to do anything in reason to promote peace. We are willing to let bye-gones be bye-gones. We want those who left us to come back home. We will welcome them without discrimination and without penalties of any kind.

The American Federation of Labor reiterates this standing offer not because it is weak, but because it is strong. At this moment, the membership of the American Federation of Labor is higher than at any previous time in its history. The prestige of the American Federation of Labor is at its peak. Its influence in national affairs has never been greater. The voices of America's workers speak to the nation through the American Federation of Labor.

In the interests of our national defense, this nation must do more than ever before to strengthen its national economy. Organized labor has made a great contribution in this direction by lifting the standards of work and living to a high level by collective bargaining and by legislation. But there is still one great, gaping hole in our economic armor. That is the chronic condition of unemployment from which we have suffered for the past ten years. We must overcome this economic handicap to attain our full strength as a nation. The latest estimates of the American Federation of Labor show there are still more than nine and a half million unemployed in this country. We are convinced that the Government is doing everything in its power to provide jobs for them and to alleviate their distress. We hope and expect that the national defense program will, for a time at least, provide vast new employment opportunities. But we feel it is incumbent on our Government to find a permanent cure and solution of this pressing problem.

The strength of the American Federation of Labor rests upon a solid foundation of democracy and loyalty. We have never sacrificed these principles for any reason whatsoever. We have never resorted to dictatorship. We have relied on the intelligence and good sense of the members of the American Federation of Labor unions to see to it that their unions are operated, legally, constitutionally and in accordance with the highest principles of trade unionism. Members of a union, just as citizens of our democracy, must be vigilant and active if they want good, clean government. This is a serious responsibility of every good trade unionist and every good citizen. It is a responsibility that cannot be shirked or passed on to someone else. That is the price of democracy. Your union and your government are what you yourselves make it. That is your right and your privilege as American workers. The American Federation of Labor stands as the immovable protector of those rights and privileges. It will never invade them or seize them in the manner of dictatorships.

It is eminently fitting that the President of the American Federation of Labor, the historic labor movement of America, should participate in the Labor Day Celebration this year here in Denver, a city located at the base of the Rocky Mountains; the center of the nation, and figuratively speaking the heart of America. Here, at an elevation one mile high, towering above the sea-level industrial cities of the East, we renew our vows of devotion to American democracy, freedom and liberty. We solemnly rededicate ourselves to the task of defending our homeland against invasion, and to the preservation of our form of government, our democratic institutions, our individual liberties and our free, democratic trade unions.

The great Rocky Mountains, which serve as an appropriate stage setting for this historic Labor Day Celebration, with all their challenging majesty, typify the set purpose of the officers and members of the American Federation of Labor to resist the efforts of subversive forces to penetrate into our economic, industrial, social and political life.

We who have faith in humanity, in justice and in a Divine Power refuse to believe in the triumph of evil. We who seek the light are not afraid of the dark. We know a new day is coming, we know that peace and progress will once again be restored to humankind. Until that day comes we are ready to fight to the last drop of blood to defend and preserve America and the American way of life.

THE CONTRIBUTION OF THE CHRISTIAN FAITH [10]

OSCAR F. BLACKWELDER [11]

Dr. Oscar F. Blackwelder delivered this sermon on Sunday afternoon, June 9, 1940, at 4 p.m., on the regular "Sunday Vespers" program sponsored by the Lutheran Laymen's Radio Committee. The address was a presentation of the National Broadcasting Company, and was distributed over the Blue Network.

Dr. Blackwelder was graduated from Roanoke College in 1917 and from the Southern Lutheran Seminary three years later. He served as pastor of the Virginia Heights Lutheran Church, Roanoke, 1920-25, Christ Church, Baltimore, 1925-33, and more recently has been pastor of the Church of the Reformation, Washington, D. C. He has held important offices in the Lutheran Church of America, was member of a National Preaching Mission in 1936-37 when he preached in numerous cities throughout the country, and in 1941 was president of the Washington, D. C., Federation of Churches. His audiences have been large and enthusiastic. His fame as an inspiring preacher has grown steadily. An important governmental official recently stated that "Dr. Blackwelder is one of the foremost living preachers of America." He has frequently appeared on the "Vespers Hour" and has gained a national reputation as a radio preacher.

Among Lutheran ministers of recent days, Dr. Blackwelder stands high in a group which includes Rev. Paul Sherer, Rev. Ross Stover, Rev. Carl Rasmussen, Rev. Arthur J. Pfohl, Rev. F. H. Knubel, Rev. H. W. A. Hanson, Rev. R. A. Wentz, Rev. G. W. Englar, Rev. C. P. Wiles, and Rev. R. E. Tulloss.

At least one of his sermons has been reprinted in the *Congressional Record* (See Extension of Remarks of Senator J. J. Davis of Pennsylvania, Tuesday, July 11, 1939.).

Dr. Blackwelder from his preparatory school days has been active in public speaking. He states that in sermon preparations he writes out a large part of his speeches and sermons; what is not written in full is mentally prepared almost word for word so that "I speak nearly verbatim, and I carry full notes in the pulpit or on the platform." He believes in "clear, clean-cut outlines." He explains that such organization helps the hearers "to get a total picture of the field of study or the presentation of a problem." [12] The sermon below has

---

[10] By permission of Dr. Blackwelder. Text furnished through the courtesy of the speaker.

[11] For biographical note see Appendix.

[12] Letter to the author, May 1, 1941.

the virtue of such organic structure; well-articulated thought; excellent vocabulary; clear grasp of a major problem facing American people; and a constructive Christian philosophy for dealing with these difficult times.

Dante begins his "Divine Comedy" with these words, "Midway upon the journey of our life, I came to myself in a dark wood, where the right way was lost. Ah, how hard a thing to tell what this wild and rough and difficult wood was, which in thought renews my fear." You and I can share Dante's anxiety in our day for we also face a wood and a world as dark as his. And ours is perhaps more complex. But Dante didn't stop with anxiety and neither can we. This was the theme of the hymns of Paul Gerhardt, who was like a lark singing in the heavens far above the red battlefields of the Thirty Years' War. The glint of the Eternal is in men like Dante and Paul Gerhardt. They dramatize that which is imperishable. They are custodians of those things which will not die. They symbolize "The Contribution of the Christian Faith to the Present Hour."

Let me begin with the observation that each of us may live in three areas or levels of life. There is one's own intimate inner world. And there is the ultimate world of nature and of God. In between the intimate personal world and the ultimate life of God is what we call the stage of history. When this stage of history is so violently upset as at the present time, the task of making personal religion and faith in God practical is exceedingly difficult for many people, but equally imperative. How can we teach the guidance of God to such a trembling, broken world? How can we believe in the moral determinism of history? How can we give men the sense of destiny and faith in Providence? How can we help men believe that something eternal may be getting done in the midst of this cruel and difficult day? What is the contribution of the Christian faith to the present hour?

First, the Christian faith must give a permanent background to the passing, tragic drama.

"Oh, where are kings and empires now of old that went and came? . . ." And they still are passing, but they pass in front of the eternal hills. "Social philosophies may wax and wane, civilizations may rise and fall, epochs may come and go because they all share in the frailty of mortal things." It is therefore the mission of the Christian faith to keep before men's minds as vividly as possible the permanent background in front of which the scenes of 1940 pass.

This is not alone the task of the historian. Certainly he must point to the lessons of the past and judge the future, but it is quite inadequate to regard the present events of the world simply as part of a process or alone in the grip of military might. We are related to the past and future as to a stream, but we are also related to that which is beyond history and from that relationship, which transcends all that now happens, we may gain wisdom, light and power by which to interpret, judge and guide the passing scene.

We have been hearing much about economic determinism. We will probably hear more from the better minds about the moral determinism of history. Men and nations are remarkably free to make their decisions and fling their armies, but if history has one lesson to teach, it is that beyond certain limits men and nations cannot go. Men either make or break themselves as they deal with the ultimate facts of the universe. Something more than human exhaustion or the victory of armed might seems to be present at hours of surrender and armistice. Scotland has her Bannockburn; England has her Yorktown; France has her Waterloo; Germany has her Verdun; America has her Gettysburg. It seems to me at those points something structural was reached—and the nature of the structure is moral. It is the permanent background before which the scene passes—the eternal hills beyond which men cannot go—that higher order, however we may conceive of it, in which God reigns beyond man's inhumanity to man and for which He has created us.

You and I watch the turbulent storm of history, bearing all of mens' hopes and fears, knowing that these events must and will end. In the meantime the Christian faith asserts that the providence and purposes of God work out through this world, that there is or can be a relation between the temporal and the eternal. The consciousness of God, working in history, comes not alone from the contemplation of events but by confidence in a central Person, Jesus Christ, who is in history but beyond it and who makes it possible for us to interpret these events. To see the eternities of God coming into human flesh and life through Jesus Christ is to be aware of that which is permanent behind the passing, tragic drama.

Second, it is the mission of the Christian faith to provide the way and method by which men may ally themselves with that which is permanent and which towers o'er the wrecks of time.

I have been watching references in recent months to the guidance and power of God as expressed by various national leaders. These modern words seem strangely reminiscent of Abraham Lincoln's classic concern that we should be on God's side. Men yearn for God's alliance. So someone has insisted that "in order to live triumphantly a man must feel that he is allied with that which will endure," with something greater and infinitely more permanent than the recurring squabbles and fights of nations. Men crave fellowship with the Divinity that shapes their ends. To fulfil this universal yearning is the purpose of prayer and worship.

The meaning of prayer is not to influence the purposes of God but to learn those purposes. Christian prayer is built upon the conviction that it is possible for men to share in the purposes of God, that men may know something of what God is doing in the world, for He does not call us servants who merely take orders, but friends who share His creative purposes. Likewise, worship is dedicated to the practical aim not of changing the will of God, but of cooperating with that will, not of bend-

ing the will of God down to us, but of lifting the will of man
to God and working together. What a difference such a point
of view makes! For example, a so-called modern thinker has
written, "Man is left more and more alone in a universe to
which he is completely alien." Another has affirmed that life
is cruel and futile, that we humans are trapped, driven almost
insane by our own frustrations, that "there is no reason to suppose that man's life has any more meaning than the life of the
humblest insect that crawls from one annihilation to another."
You can't even make men fight on that kind of thinking—let
life go to pot and be done with it.

The kind of faith in God and man which allies us with the
permanent beyond transient darkness is expressed most clearly
in the Cross of Christ. You see the Cross says that human
tragedy and divine faith belong together. Jesus cried on the
Cross, "My God, why hast Thou forsaken Me?" And that is
the cry of mankind today. But Jesus also prayed on that Cross,
"Father forgive them. . . . Father into Thy hands." Along-
side the fact of tragedy is the fact of faith. Faith does not
mean blind superstition, it does not mean simply believing
where you cannot prove. Faith means finding the eternal God
through the tragedies of life, it means finding Him intimately
in the things that make you uncertain. It means that the more
insecure a man feels financially, physically and socially, the more
he may become aware of that which economic security cannot
provide or the lack of it take away.

Thus the Christian faith, centering in the Cross, is not alone
something you hold or do not hold. It is also somethng—and
Someone—that holds you. It unites your life with the eternal
and the permanent. Such faith means alliance with the eternal
God. It means being added to God. Other relationships may
give us breadth—this gives us height and permanence.

What is the contribution of the Christian faith to the present hour? First, it must keep men aware of what is permanent
in a shifting civilization. Second, it must provide the way for

men to be allied with that which is permanent. Third, the Christian faith must do for men and women today what nothing else can do.

This Christian faith is the custodian, the guardian, the liberator of life's imperishable faiths and hopes. Something beyond military fighting is necessary to defend the things men hold dearest. The positive and constructive defense, for example, of our American way of life and of our liberties is ultimately in the hands not of armed might, but of our educational forces and the Christian faith. To illustrate exactly what I mean, the other World War did not make the way safe for democracy even with military victory, because the positive forces at that time failed. Will these constructive forces succeed now? It is my personal conviction that such forces will succeed only as this Christian faith is incarnated in living minds around the world. Clear, calm thinking and high faith must keep the torch of truth and liberty burning.

One of my friends in the Congress said to me last week that in his judgment the greatest tragedy of the hour is that many people will have their viewpoint of life so twisted and gnarled that as long as they live life will look like what it isn't. Who is going to keep alive the true meaning of life which is violated on so many fronts today? There is no social or political philosophy which can answer that question as can the Christian faith. What are these imperishable truths which men dare not forget?

Here's one: The God of our Fathers is our God. His authority lives on. He is able to keep His promise, "Lo, I am with you alway even unto the end of the world." He lives despite the wretched mismanagement of men in earth's affairs. His wisdom and strength operating through human life are able to transform the misery and loss of the present hour into something permanent. The Christian faith must show men how to pray to and trust Him above anything and everything their human rulers attempt to do or fail to do.

> Wide as the world is Thy command,
> Vast as eternity Thy love,
> Firm as a rock Thy truth must stand,
> When rolling years have ceased to move.

Still further, the Christian faith must keep men conscious that in Christ all men are brothers, no matter how impossible that may sound in many ears today. Wild men at the heads of governments who fling youth into bloody cauldrons will be forgotten, but the spirt of Christ is eternal. This spirit enables men to develop courage without malice, which is absolutely imperative for calm, clear thinking. If hate is required to build courage, then the cause itself is questionable. In the words of Douglas Horton, "The call today is for men and women whose souls are great enough to receive the gangrenous streams that are running through the hearts of men, to receive them and never let them issue forth again. To bear the brunt of selfishness, to feel the wash of hysteria, to admit them to our hearts and there to abolish them from life! Strange power of God, that Thou shouldst have given to us the power to administer eternal death to evil." In the midst of a day of hate, may the spirit of Christ in us devour hate.

And the Christian faith is the guardian of our liberties. It has been frequently asserted that America's most distinctive gift to the science of government is the guarantee of religious liberty. Our form of government rests not upon race or economics, but upon character and intelligence. These are spiritual possessions which depend upon the practice of religious liberty for their existence. Therefore, all who trust in God must come to a new consecration of themselves and what they possess, so that the will of God may be enthroned in our national life. We must translate "In God We Trust" from coins to character. So shall our liberties be preserved.

Finally, the Christian faith points to the ancient prayer of Jesus as the hope of the nations: "Thy kingdom come, Thy will be done on earth as it is in heaven." The kingdom of God on earth is the only intelligible way I see for the future of the human race. I wish I had the power both of thought and of expression to make you see and feel deeply this afternoon what Jesus and the kingdom of God could do for our broken and harassed world. Here is the greatest social conception that ever entered human history, by which the nations of the world may conserve their best traditions and cultures, but find a way and a spirit to transcend all that now divides and alienates them. Here is the loyalty strong enough, intelligent enough, moral enough, great enough to overcome racial bitterness, national narrowness and economic jealousies.

> For only Christ can set men free
> And give them vision new;
> Grant us our fairest dream to see,
> O land where dreams come true.

AMERICAN EDUCATION

MOBILIZING THE MIND [1]

Alan Valentine [2]

President Alan Valentine, of the University of Rochester, delivered this address at the opening session of the Tenth Annual Forum, under the auspices of the *New York Herald Tribune*, at the Waldorf-Astoria Hotel, New York City, on Tuesday afternoon, October 22, 1940.

Preceding Dr. Valentine during this three-hour session were Walter Lippmann and Eleanor Roosevelt.

Mrs. Ogden Reid, in introducing the speaker, said: "It is hard to introduce the last speaker. Although he occupies the dignified position of a university president, after being selected from a list of 100 possibilities, and has carried off many scholastic records as a Rhodes scholar at Oxford and a professor at Swarthmore and Yale, he is known as 'the wicked Valentine' for having introduced, for the first time on French soil, our native flying tackle in a rugby game, which he had also played so successfully in England that he was congratulated by the king.

"Summer holidays were varied by representing the Quakers in a European conference and working as a riveter in the wartime shipyards at Camden—a position I suspect he only achieved through breaking the child labor laws. Last May he inaugurated a clinic at Rochester University called 'New Frontiers in American Life,' at which industrialists joined in round-table discussions with students in order to help undergraduates to discover what they might best do for themselves after finishing a college course. Recently he was given a two months' leave of absence to serve as chairman of the Democrats for Willkie Committee in the present campaign.

"I have the honor of introducing to you one of the youngest and most dynamic of our college presidents, Dr. Alan Valentine."

Alan Valentine, by general educational and speaking experience, was unusually well equipped to round out a session featured by distinguished addresses. He was a college speaker of merit, member of Delta Sigma Rho, society for superior debaters, Rhodes scholar, student of English literature, teacher and writer in that field. In the present

---

[1] By permission of President Valentine and of the *New York Herald Tribune*. Text supplied through the courtesy of the speaker, and reprinted from *Dusty Answers,* 157-163, a selection from the addresses by Alan Valentine, printed for private distribution, Rochester, New York, 1941.

[2] For biographical note see Appendix.

address he reflects timeliness of theme, acuteness of analysis, directness in his development of it, obviousness of structure yet freedom from mechanism, simplicity, variety, and rhetorical vividness of sentence structure, accuracy and warmth in language usage. Note the forthrightness of the conclusion. The speech is in keeping with the speaker's warning against resort to "cheap emotions."

This speaker, like all others, is to be judged by the effectiveness with which he accomplishes the kind of address required by the occasion. This speech will bear study as the restrained and dignified utterance of an educator talking to an educated audience (and invisible radio listeners).

It has been said that Americans are lacking in discipline. As your twelfth speaker at the end of your third hour, and as I bring you approximately the same message as my eleven predecessors, I deny that statement, and marvel at your attention as I thank you for your courtesy.

In 1917 Woodrow Wilson called upon the American nation for force, force without stint or limit. In 1940 America is again mobilizing its force. This time we do so not to make war but to prevent it. But once again the need has arisen and we must face it. We must meet this latest challenge of modern barbarism with more than the physical force of a million men and machines. We must meet it with the constant daily service of every American. This is the threat of total war, and it demands total defense, covering as never before the whole area of American life and thought.

Mr. Lippmann has narrowed the Atlantic and Pacific and announced our dependence on the British fleet. Miss Clare Boothe has not left us too confident that many individual Americans can rise above fear to meet successfully the demands defense will make upon them. I am more optimistic than either, but only if as individuals we will prepare our minds.

The immediate weapons of our defense remain physical weapons—ships, airplanes, tanks and soldiers. Other speakers have dealt with these specific aspects of our defense. But the creation and direction of these physical defenses depends more than ever before upon human intelligence and the human spirit.

Mobilization for defense means the mobilization of the minds of the nation. Physical defenses are the products of physics, chemistry, mechanics, and organization, but they in turn are the products of men's brains. With the steel turrets of our battleships must stand the steel turrets of a nation's morale. Behind the discipline of regiments must be the harder discipline of trained minds. Beside the wings of air defense must fly the more precious wings of our creative imagination. These are the elements of victory, and they lie not in our hands but within our compass. For the strength of America lies not only in its factories, its farms and the muscles of its men; it lies also in the free loyalty of its free citizens, multiple-minded in their thoughts and convictions, but single-minded in their devotion to democracy. We now face the task of mobilizing in freedom this multiple-minded democracy, of achieving national unity in one thing through freedom in all other things. That is a work more difficult and more noble than the creation of armies and airplanes.

Free men must know for what cause and what ends they curb their freedom. For what purpose do we marshal force without stint or limit? To what end do we mobilize men and minds? Surely we do not forge swords that our children shall live by the sword. Surely we do not mobilize to make mobilization the permanent American order. Our fathers did not come to America for this; our experience and education did not lead us to this end. No, we are compelled by those who live by force to oppose their domination in the only terms they understand. We forge swords to defend ourselves from those who would rule by the sword. We mobilize so that we may be free not to mobilize again. To avoid the rule of force we are compelled to create it. As we do so, we must not forget our purpose—to preserve freedom and the ways of peace. We must not fall in love with force, and with giving or receiving commands. A nation so strong in arms that all the world fears it and does its bidding is not and must not be the ideal of American democracy.

A sense of power has betrayed many men and nations. As our power develops, we must see that it does not betray us, that we do not lose our way in a world of force. We must mobilize our minds not only to create force but to measure and control it. This is the great paradox of thoughtful Americans— that disliking force we must help to create it; that while creating force to resist others we must resist it ourselves; that in the interests of freedom we must welcome the ending of the very force we are creating. This is the only way to preserve our own integrity and our nation's freedom.

We are helped by the real meaning of the word mobilize, for it means not only to prepare for active service, but to bring into circulation and to render movable. The intellect of America is called into active service, and every American is summoned to keep the circulation of his mind vigorous and clear. But more than this, he must keep his mind movable by seeing that it is alert and flexible, ready to adapt itself to whatever service, whatever adjustments, may be required. A slave state may drug the minds of its citizens, but a democracy cannot defend itself by denying, even temporarily, the mobility, the flexibility of its ways of thought. The man who can turn off his mind is not likely to turn it on again; the man who will give up his freedom for the duration is not likely to win it back again.

Men are free in America because they are cooperative. Each grants others the right to their opinions, so that he may expect in return freedom to express his own. Individuals who differ widely cooperate to protect their right to differ. This is mutual respect, and upon it our democracy is based. It demands not the enforced and absolute unity of a dictatorship but the partial, shifting, imperfect unity of free men. That imperfect unity is the life blood of the American system. Even the demands of defense must not force that free, imperfect unity into the absolutism of perfection. Emergency may lead to temporary concessions of liberty to achieve unity, but such concessions must be freely given and vigorously regained.

This is one aspect of national defense through intellectual preparedness; there are many others. Men and women with special scientific talents will loan those talents to the immediate needs of national defense. We are told that there would be no London now but for three British scientists who through brilliant research found ways to cope with German bombers. American scientists can do as much. Many universities are making their greatest contribution to national defense through the loan of their best research men.

Some with different talents will be needed to explain to others the substance of American ideals. Still others must see that 130 million men, women and children understand the American defense program and their part in it. If all teaching is propaganda, then this is propaganda, and let us make the most of it! It is high time that American ideals were more clear to every American, high time that the easy appeals of simpler, barbaric forms of government are counteracted by a better understanding of the essence of democracy. The blessings of liberty are more clear when presented in contrast to the slavery of dictatorship. The challenge of barbarians is best answered by enlightenment at home. If men are cowards they are cowards through ignorance. Enlightenment can make them brave.

There are special talents, and the defense services of those talents are specific. But only a few of us have special aptitudes for making shells or bearing arms; most of us must mobilize our bodies and our minds in some less dramatic way. How are we ordinary citizens to do that?

Part of the answer lies in making our minds fit for active service. The young man from civilian life will begin his military training unable to march 15 miles with a pack on his back. He must have a period in which to harden his muscles, to develop himself for his new military career. We who are to mobilize our minds must put ourselves through a similar period of mental conditioning. The minds of most of us have grown soft on the pabulum of daily clichés, careless thinking and emotional decisions. The mobilized mind is one which can distinguish between fact and opinion, between what is true and what is merely said to be true. How rare is this ability, how consciously it must be developed!

Plato said that false opinion comes from a mixture of thought and sensation. The mobilized mind will avoid that mixture. It will search for truth amid the welter of half-truths. It will be its own master and not the tool of a mass hysteria. It will roam widely and ceaselessly over the national scene, slow to crystallize into fixed convictions and ready to modify conclusions in the pressure of new facts. Aware that mobilization means flexibility, the mobilized mind will keep its own intellectual stream in motion, so that ice will not form upon its surface. It will desire certain things mightily—truth, reason, freedom, peace—and from that strong desire will come the power to create them.

"But," says the average man, confused by these abstractions, "that sounds very well, but I am no scholar or intellectual. My mind is only average, and it has been rusty for years. What can I do to sharpen and mobilize it? I am not capable of mental acrobatics!"

That may be true, and certainly one cannot condition his mind without practice any more than without practice the soldier or athlete can condition his body or the pianist coordinate his hands and brain. Only slowly and with effort do soft muscles harden, new professions unfold, or careless minds become efficient. There is a manual of arms for the conditioning of the mind.

The first step is to reduce excess mental weight, to slough off the fatty tissues of the mind. Put to one side all the things you do not know from personal experience to be true. You will be surprised at how easy it is to cope with what is left. That is your mental foundation upon which to build anew. Every timber that you add must be sound and true. The world will lay material before you in the form of millions of words, thousands of judgments, hundreds of ideas. They will come to you from conversations, books, newspapers, speeches, pictures. From this chaos accept for your mind only what you know to be true; put the rest in a separate limbo for further consideration. Ask of every statement: "Is this a fact, or only a report?" Ask of every judgment: "Is this a logical deduction from ascertainable truth, or only an opinion perhaps based on misinformation?" Defer your judgments until you have the true facts, and all of them. Try to recognize in your own thinking what part emotion plays, and what part logic, and evaluate each for what it is worth.

This is the first step in the mental manual of arms; once learned the rest will follow. Instinctively you will be on your guard against careless statements, exaggerated headlines, the hyperbole of eloquence, the deceit of propaganda. You will be less likely to hate the other man because he does not agree with you—for aware of possible fallacies in your own judgments you will be sympathetic with his. Finding ever keener pleasure in the freedom of your own mind, you will value that freedom for others, and so avoid intolerance, hysteria, jingoism. And when you have reached that stage your mind will be mobilized and I, in my turn, shall come to you for the next step.

Your mental manual of arms will warn you against cheap emotions. A man does not become a good soldier by the single achievement of thrilling to a military band. His mind is not better fitted to serve his country simply because it is influenced by jingoism. This is no time to plunge into the hot bath of unintelligent emotionalism. That will not make the mind more competent, but only make it more primitive. We shall do our nation no service by pretending that war is anything but a brutal and distasteful business, to which necessity might compel us. I hope we shall hear little talk, now or later, about the glories of war, and the rough, rude currents of health and regeneration that war will send through the body politic! War is man's primitive effort to solve his problems, and itself creates new evils—economic depression, disruption of civil and domestic life, intolerance, savagery, hate.

Fate has put American democracy on trial. It has been on trial before, and by the courage and wisdom of our forefathers it has endured. Can we be equally courageous and wise? Can we think as well as fight our way to a finer American freedom, a more perfect union? This is not only a test of our political system, of our factories, of our power to organize. It is a test of our capacity to think truly, to understand, to retain old visions and create new ones. In that effort we think of our schools, our colleges and universities as the first line trenches. But we must not leave this task to them; they can be little more effective than the American society from which they derive. We must discover a common ground for all Americans of 1940— a true Americanism for which laborer and professor, ploughboy and banker can unitedly stand. We must set our minds resolutely to work to discover how to achieve the lasting peace that must ultimately come.

Before the jury of its own ideals, the mind of America stands on trial. The verdict will determine the future of our country.

ARE WE EDUCATING FOR
NATIONAL STRENGTH? [3]

JOEL H. HILDEBRAND [4]

Dr. Hildebrand delivered this address before the Commonwealth Club of California, San Francisco, on August 23, 1940. The address is here included both because Dean Hildebrand on that occasion as on other occasions was a highly popular and effective speaker and secondly because this address illustrates the attitude taken by wise college university administrators after 1940 toward the problem of national preparedness and its relation to education.

At the time Dr. Hildebrand spoke, the program of national defense was just getting into its stride. The American citizens were beginning to hear the new plans for the fortification of Alaska; Defense Commissioner W. S. Knudsen was doing his best to close army and navy contracts; the army's first parachuters were beginning to get their training; on the way through Congress were bills recommending over three billion dollars for the United States Navy; the 300,000 regular national guard and reserve soldiers were ending the army's greatest peacetime maneuvers in America's history; and the congressional debate in support of the President's plan for selective service was well under way.

Dr. Hildebrand here boldly put down as a premise to any program by which education can help national defense the necessary toughening of our national character through physical, mental, and moral strengthening.

He demands that we address ourselves more earnestly to the proposition that in school and college education should focus upon straight and creative thinking. To establish his point he resorts freely to his own observation and authority. He refers, for example, to the education of military and naval officers and cites incidents out of his own experience. He was in World War I, captain of the Officers Reserve Corps, major and later lieutenant colonel in the Chemical Warfare Service, and was director of the Chemical Warfare Station laboratory near Paris and later commanded Hanlon Field (Chaumont), which included an A.T.S.S. Defense School; and he was awarded the Distinguished Service Medal.

When he turns to discuss proper education for colleges and universities, he again speaks out of his long experience as teacher and administrator. He served as professor of chemistry at the University

[3] By permission of Dr. Joel H. Hildebrand. Text furnished through the courtesy of Dr. Hildebrand.

[4] For biographical note see Appendix.

of California from 1918 to 1939, and since 1935 he has been Dean of the College of Letters and Science. His attitude toward "idlers" is typical of his educational philosophy.

Again his examination of high school training, as illustrated in chemistry, is based upon his own "experience of teaching large freshman classes in chemistry in the University of California through a period of twenty-seven years."

His analysis of the causes for deficient preparation of the secondary school pupils is acute. Unlike other educators whose speeches are included in this volume, he views the problem from an administrative angle and becomes concrete in his criticism. Women teachers, "educational expert" administrators, a "social science" curriculum, and "newer" education to him explain the sterile results. Anecdotes, dialogues, and specific statements throughout illustrate how well this speaker adjusted his ideas to his audience.

Dean Hildebrand had some formal training in public speaking as an undergraduate at the University of Pennsylvania. His subsequent career included lecturing to large classes and the delivery of numerous public addresses.

He has no stereotyped method of speech preparation, but is likely to jot down, as they occur to him, thoughts pertinent to the subject to be discussed. These ideas are organized in logical arrangement and are later expanded "by putting flesh and blood onto the skeleton." The present address is well organized, and proper illustrative material is included under each section of the skeleton.

Dr. Hildebrand states that he prefers not to write an address word for word since he prefers "to be guided by the logical rather than by the verbal sequence." This practice enables him to take advantage of the inspiration of the moment, "which is often considerable under the stimulus of a live subject and a responsive audience, and also of incident or reaction on the part of the audience." In dealing with students he finds that it is "especially advantageous to exhibit quickness in seeing such advantages rather than to be bound to a rigidly prepared manuscript." If, however, the address is to be delivered upon some formal occasion or broadcast where time limits are imposed, he finds that it is "desirable if not essential" to read from the manuscript. He explains that the address which is included in this volume was broadcast over a California station and hence he followed the method of reading. He adds that the address was delivered exactly according to the text herein printed.

Dr. Hildebrand gives a few suggestions to young speakers: "(a) Begin ordinarily with something concrete; one has to lead his audience from something familiar to them; (b) stick to essential ideas even though you may give humorous applications or illustrations; (c) master the subject upon which you presume to speak. Avoid the error common to debaters to try to win an argument as if it were a game rather than to bring out the truth; (d) have some punch in your conclusion." [5]

[5] Letter to the author, March 25, 1941.

Interestingly enough this advice the Dean embodies to a complete degree in the specimen herein printed.

We have been accustomed in this country to regard "life, liberty and the pursuit of happiness" as rights so natural as to be almost automatically self-perpetuating. The majority of us, however, have now been shocked into realizing that our Bill of Rights is not alone sufficient to guarantee the maintenance of these privileges. We have seen enlightened, free nations engulfed one after another, by dictatorships that respect no rights standing in the way of their unbounded ambitions. Although this deluge of tyranny is still far enough from our own doors as to be invisible to the nearsighted, there are a good many who have come to see the folly of such assurances as that uttered not so long ago by a former chairman of our Senate Foreign Relations Committee, that we could easily keep out of war by minding our own business, like the Scandinavian countries. The subsequent fates of these nations have served to pry most people loose from any such naive faith. Although there is a noisy minority still telling us that it might not rain and we should not bother to fix the roof until the storm actually begins, there is hope that the more farsighted will drown out this council of inaction and that we may be able to mend the roof now, so as to be prepared for rain whenever it comes.

Our efforts to do this are, however, hampered by those who cry that the organization necessary to carry out the repairs might become permanent and so we had better run the risk of getting wet than of having to get up at the whistle some morning when we might prefer to lie abed.

It is a pitiful dilemma that is delaying effective action in Washington these days. Recent events have made it fairly clear, on the one hand, that a nation today cannot safely hope to defend itself by "a million men springing to arms over night." Hitler has never yet given to his intended victims enough advance notice to permit arming from scratch. On the other hand, some are crying that if we train and equip an army in advance we will lose our freedom to a hypothetical domestic dictator. It looks as if a democracy is simply destined to go out of business for inability to defend itself. One would think that Uncle Sam, the once hardy pioneer, born in battle, had grown so feeble as to think of nothing better than ducking under the bed clothes, holding his breath and hoping the burglar would not notice him. The dictators are chuckling over these exhibitions of doubt of the vitality of democracy on the part of its last defenders.

The paralysis of fear is the most threatening danger of all. We must have sufficient faith in our own freedom to make us bold in its defense. I have lived in Germany under Kaiser, Republic and briefly under Hitler, and have seen a good deal of other European countries. The United States of America is so far superior, despite great imperfections, in affording hope for better humanity, that any temporizing with its defense by all possible means would be one of the greatest tragedies in history. If the freedom to search for truth, whether in the press, the pulpit, the philosopher's study, or the scientist's laboratory is to survive here with us, in almost its last stronghold, we shall have to support it with all our resources, material, mental and moral. We must see as never before that an Athenian civilization can be long maintained only by citizens with Spartan qualities. Whenever a people become soft they become the prey of tougher barbarians.

Now there are various ways of being tough. Tough talk is usually a mere cloak for tender courage. Tough bodies, on the other hand, are an important asset in national strength. We might do better in this respect. Athletics for the majority is yelling in the grandstand. We take the elevator to ascend one floor and we jump into an automobile to go three blocks.

Of still greater importance is tough character, sustaining high ideals. There is still more room here for improvement. The grandstand attitude has affected character. For example, a baccalaureate preacher recently assured his audience that they need do nothing about the threat of Hitlerism but simply trust the Lord to make everything turn out all right. They should just sit in the grandstand, as it were, and cheer while the Lord gives Hitler the quietus. One would think that a preacher who has undoubtedly drawn texts from the record of the Children of Israel might have noted that they usually used their faith in Jehovah as a support rather than as a substitute for their own initiative. David prayed for help but then marched out to battle with Goliath of Gath.

But there is another element of national strength that has been far less stressed than most others and to which I invite your attention, namely, active intelligence, well fortified by knowledge. Faith may lead but to delusion and a stout heart but to stubbornness unless guided by intelligence. Tough moral fiber requires the support of a clear head. Integrity must extend to honest thinking and industry to hard mental effort. A soft head and a flabby character are partners. National strength requires not only strong muscles and sound characters but clear, vigorous minds. Education which produces these makes an essential contribution to national strength, one, fortunately, which is of value alike for peace or for war; alike for the welfare of the state and of the individual.

Working effectively with one's brain is not easy and there are several popular substitutes. One of these is sought in formulas derived in advance by someone else. You commit to memory just long enough to get by the emergency. A formula is like a sausage machine. You feed the data into it, turn the crank and, lo, out comes the answer. You need not be able to construct or even to understand it. The method is quite easy but suffers, unfortunately, from two serious disadvantages. First, there are so many problems that it is impossible to remember all the formulas. Second, a new kind of problem pops up now and then for which no formula has been derived. Perhaps it is an electron which does not obey the laws for a baseball, or it may be a new disease, or a new international situation. If we cannot solve the new problem, it may be very serious.

Another substitute for straight thinking is "intuition." Women sometimes credit themselves with special powers of intuition and some men appear to think they share the gift. However, the reliability of intuition in either sex was well expressed by the man who defined a woman's intuition as "that which tells her she is right even when she is wrong." Other substitutes for clear thinking such as prejudice, passion and slogans are equally misleading. No, if education is to be effective in equipping one to meet new situations it must afford a great deal of practice in the processes of solving problems by scientific analysis.

There is nothing mysterious about these methods. They are used in progressive business as in the research laboratory. They involve experiment, search for and selection of data, judgment, induction and deduction and particularly the unprejudiced testing of conclusions. They are not modern inventions but their conscious, large-scale application is distinctly modern and the command we have gained, at least over the material world, is a direct result. An individual must be trained to his utmost capacity if he is to be prepared for a life bristling with new problems.

Let us apply this touchstone to several stages of education. May I pause to say, since I have not come to pour weak tea today, that I assume sole responsibility for this speech. It has been neither censored nor approved by any official of my University. On the other hand, I am not in the position of a flier dealing with foreign affairs nor of a chemist discussing aviation; I have first-hand knowledge of all I shall discuss:

Let us begin, in view of the national emergency, with the education of military and naval officers, to whom war presents unsolved problems of the utmost urgency and seriousness. Here we immediately run afoul of another necessary element of military training—namely, discipline; not intellectual discipline but obedience to authority. This often conflicts with initiative and in that conflict discipline usually gains the upper hand. This is the way it works. An officer in a naval unit attached to a university was explaining to his class the tendency of a torpedo to deviate from a straight course. The explanation appeared to a senior student majoring in physics to reverse the actual facts and he questioned it. Now an instructor in physics would welcome such intellectual initiative on the part of a student, but not that officer. He let it be distinctly understood that a cadet should not question the word of an officer.

Again, an officer of the Chemical Warfare Service was standing during the last World War beside an American general who pointed to a distant wood, saying: "Look at the enemy advancing into that wood; I shelled that place with gas about eight hours ago." The other asked what kind of gas. The general replied, "What gas? Oh, just gas." Now a modicum of scientific insight would have revealed to a man properly trained the absurdity of confusing a true gas such as phosgene, which would drift away in the wind, with a so-called gas, such as mustard, which is scarcely more volatile than sewing machine oil and might remain for days. Ah, but you say, you can't expect a field officer to be a scientist. But this general had been a professor of military science and tactics. Surely, he should have been able to appreciate a few kindergarten facts about the materials he was using.

Again, a British chemist suggested the use of mustard gas, as early as 1915 but the army authority could not see it until, two years later, the Germans used it against them with terrible effect. Illustrations of this sort could be multiplied at length.

This slowness on the part of many military and naval men to invent or even appreciate novel ideas is no original discovery of mine but has been deplored by members of both services. Admiral Sims once stated: "That military men are conservative admits of no doubt. Whether they are more so than civilians is beside the question. The important point is that their conservatism may be so dangerous that it is highly important that they should so train their minds in logical thinking as to eliminate or at least minimize this danger." And again, in a minority report as a member of the Board of Visitors of the U. S. Naval Academy he said: ". . . it is an outstanding fact that the Navy has never initiated any one of the really fundamental reforms that were essential to bring it to its present efficiency. All of these reforms were forced upon the Navy from the outside; and in every case against determined opposition. And the Navy still resists perfectly legitimate criticism." You will recall that Admiral Sims was not cordially regarded by some of his brother admirals.

Such an attitude toward innovations is highly inappropriate in view of the long list of military successes that have been achieved by aid of new inventions. The war game cannot be counted upon to remain the mere maneuvering of troops on the field of battle, like the pieces on a chess board. Warfare may be expected to introduce new pieces that do not move in the orthodox ways adhered to by the historic pieces. To appreciate what I mean, try playing chess with the sudden addition, for example, of a piece that can move straight ahead, like a tank, capturing not one opposing piece at a time but several. There is nothing in a book to tell you how to adapt your game to the novelty. You have to figure it out for yourself. This kind of change happens frequently in war.

Consider the Assyrian chariot; the pitchers, torches and trumpets used by Gideon's small, highly selected army against the Midianites; recall the Greek phalanx; and the Roman legions designed to outmaneuver the phalanx; Hannibal's elephants, and then the Roman device of disposing of them; recall the boarding bridges used by the Roman against the Carthaginian fleet. Consider the English long bow, the Monitor, the tank, the submarine, the varieties of smoke and gas each with its appropriate tactics; the technique of the now famous ski troops of Finland. Consider, finally, the airplane, whose full possibilities in the hands of the Germans were not foreseen by either the French or the British. You see, the main uses of the airplane in 1919 were reconnoitering and artillery fire control. We may well ask whether our own Army and Navy fully realize even now the extent to which war has become engineering. Our preparations till recently furnish but little evidence that they do. A press item reports 350 fine riding horses at West Point but not a single tank. Why are bow and arrows overlooked, I wonder?

I am not airing this subject to attack individuals. I have had pleasant personal relations with and high regard for many officers in both services. What I am criticizing is a system of education which is not productive of scientific thinking. Warfare is becoming more and more a matter of science and engineering, waged by the entire nation rather than a professional class, and the nation must therefore be in a position to use its best brains and all of its technical and scientific knowledge. A successful military establishment is always tempted to rely on the methods it used in the last war. The French debacle shows how fatal this may be. The Germans, with no such handicap, invented and imposed a new game of their own.

Even in the World War most of the new ideas came from Germany rather than from the Allies. We were busy much of the time devising defensive measures against novel German offense. This may be attributed in part to a far closer connection between the German Government and leading scientific and technical men of the country than existed in any other nation, and in part to the familiarity of scientists with military affairs resulting from universal service. I am opposed for this reason to exempting scientific students from military training.

The training of officers for this kind of warfare cannot take place in institutions far removed from the creative and inquiring habit of mind. We hear now and then complaints that research distracts attention from teaching. This confuses real teaching with the mere retailing of facts or the entertainment of students too lazy or dull to masticate their own fodder.

There can be no great teaching by men who have too little curiosity to explore the frontiers of the fields they presume to teach. An investigator is produced by contact not chiefly with records of long past discoveries but with the actual processes of exploration. Experience with these methods is far more important than mere knowledge of the results. The scientific departments of our best universities and our leading engineering schools are turning out students who have got something of this divine spark which a mere trade school cannot give. Our national defense would be vastly strengthened if our military and naval academies became graduate professional schools for students recruited from the graduates of institutions of the type just referred to. The basic scientific and cultural training would be much sounder and the time necessary for the military training could be greatly shortened, permitting the larger output of officers which the present situation demands.

Let us next consider our colleges and universities. We may note, first, that while our faculties and student bodies, fortunately, include valuable souls who work from inner rather than outer compulsion, nevertheless, since life in a university can be very pleasant, there are others whose ideal is to "get by." I think we can no longer afford to tolerate these idlers. While we propose to be even more solicitous than formerly to adjust new students to the greater rigors of university standards of work, and to allow for ill-health or self support, we shall not permit other students to remain long if they fail to meet the C-average required for graduation. Most border-line students are able to meet higher standards if they must, and less attention on their part to the side shows and more to the main business should fit them better for life in the world just ahead. Training in the art of clear thinking can be had only by serious effort.

I believe we must make more distinctions in the treatment of students of different grades of ability. A student capable of rapid progress should be more fully released from what Stephen Leacock, in a wise recent book calls the "convoy system," wherein everybody adopts the speed of the slowest. Although the temptation is especially strong in a large institution to adopt uniform rules for everyone, this very size affords the possibility of greater variety of treatment, just as a city can cater to more differing tastes than a town. We can shift the emphasis from teaching to learning, from lectures to books and laboratories. There can be more effort to appeal to reason rather than memory; to ask questions which present problems.

There are many other ways of increasing the contribution of the university to national strength, but since my time is limited and since I am in a position to agitate from within I shall pass on to a closely related problem.

If the more advanced stages of education are to be successful they must receive well prepared material from below. This brings us to a consideration of the education offered in the schools. I shall begin by giving certain observations drawn from my own experience of teaching large freshman classes in chemistry in the University of California through a period of twenty-seven years. Frequent examination of the records of students by high schools has brought to light the fact that the preparation in different schools is very unequal. One large high school, for example, sent to the University in August, 1938, students so well prepared that 58 percent received grades of A and B while only 2 percent received unsatisfactory grades of D, E and F. Another high school in the same year provided only 20 per cent A's and B's and 32 per cent D, E, and F. The quality of instruction in the schools must bear the major responsibility for such enormous discrepancies. One may pertinently ask: Are the students from the latter school getting a square deal? Much is made in some schools now-a-days of developing personality, making pupils happy, teaching them to "sell themselves," and adjust themselves to life. But however well they may seem adjusted to the easy-going environment of the school, they often face serious readjustment when they learn that the standards set by the professions are far more severe than those required by the school.

These standards are neither unreasonable nor unattainable for a large proportion of high school students.

We have applied various tests of high school preparation and natural aptitude at the time of registration. Let us look at one of these tests. The first part was designed to bring out awareness of ordinary chemical environment. Accordingly the student was expected to know that burning wood yields carbon dioxide and not natural gas; that air is composed mainly of oxygen and nitrogen; that the core of a lead pencil is made of graphite, not lead. A student with any natural aptitude picks up such information merely by keeping his eyes and ears open.

In the second part of the test we gave a short paragraph describing the structure of an atom and asked the students to indicate, not even what the paragraph said, but merely the location therein of several of the main topics. It is one thing to read a story, another thing to read a scientific exposition and the student who has never learned to do the latter will have a hard time with any intellectual endeavor later on.

The third part of the test was made up of such easy questions as the sum of 2/5 plus 1/2; the placing of decimal points in easy long division; the square root of 64; the price of five eggs at thirty cents per dozen; the average speed of an automobile which traveled 70 miles in 1 hour and 45 minutes. These are all absurdly simple operations that anyone must be able to perform rapidly and accurately in order to cope with even elementary science in any of its branches but, what do we find? I have the paper of a graduate of a San Francisco high school who answered but two out of fifteen such questions. Another, credited with grades of B in plane geometry and two courses in algebra answered correctly but three. Such operations should have been thoroughly mastered long before matriculation in the university. High school courses that fail in this aim should be designated not arithmetic, algebra, or geometry, but with more honesty, Kindergarten 2, Uplift 1, Personality 4. Such training produces the kind of clerk I once encountered in a baker's shop.

I asked the price of some cup-cakes. She replied that it was three for ten cents. I said, "there are four of us at home tonight. I want four." She said in dismay, "Oh! I would not know how to sell you four!"

What are the reasons for such miserable results? In the first place, there are not enough male teachers in our schools. This has been said by many others, but apparently not yet loud enough. Students taught until the age of eighteen chiefly by women are not well prepared for life in the existing world. This is especially serious in mathematics and sciences, for our higher education bears witness, despite brilliant exceptions, to the superior flair of men for these subjects. Further disadvantages of this preponderance of women teachers follow from the more rapid turnover among women and hence relative inexperience in teaching and also greater expense to the state in maintaining the supply. The same money spent in making the profession more attractive to able men would promote both economy and efficiency.

In the second place, the emphasis in teacher training has been misplaced from subject matter to methodology and administration and many teachers are assigned to teach subjects in which they have had no preparation whatever. This is a comforting possibility for those unable to meet the intellectual standards of rigorous subjects and has even been elevated into a brazen doctrine of mediocrity. I quote from one of its exponents: "A teacher does not need ever to have studied economics in order to give a good course in the subject. All that is needed is a teacher who is alert to the problems of the day, who is open-minded, who can stimulate pupils to bring economic problems to class for discussion, who permits and encourages free and open discussion of all controversial subjects, who instills into the pupils a spirit of tolerance for all views and a respect for the opinions of others and who shows in all discussion that he or she has at heart the solution of the economic ills of the day in a way that will restore prosperity and happiness to the whole people." Such a claim is, of course, a mere deification of ignorance. My subject, chemistry, for example, is mere a-b-c in comparison with economics and yet a high school teacher proposes to show the way to "restore prosperity and happiness to the whole people" without having ever studied economics.

As a third factor in the situation I would name an overemphasis in these early stages of education on what is called social science. Mathematics, science and language have been under attack by the educational theorists and administrators during recent years and have been displaced to a great extent by such courses as "personal management," "social living," "citizenship," or something misnamed economics. The unacknowledged basis for this is in part the fact that anyone can talk glibly about them. Strain on students, teachers and parents is largely avoided. Even grades are dispensed with as being "undemocratic." Why force anybody to exert himself. Does not the state owe everyone a living?

The substitution of these subjects results also, in part, from the realization that our political, social and economic problems are terribly pressing. The fallacy, however, consists in assuming that they are to be solved by ignorant teachers and minor children dabbling in them in high schools. I would rather trust the teacher of arithmetic to protect us from "thirty dollars every Thursday" than the teacher of a so-called social science.

This shift of emphasis to social studies has resulted in large part also from a laudable desire to produce better citizens. It is time, however, to judge the change by its results. Has it produced higher ideals; greater loyalty; more self-reliance; a less self-centered outlook on life? I leave it to you to answer such questions.

This preoccupation with social studies in school has led to a weakening of study in the essential tool of language, both English and foreign. I recently heard from a student dismissed from the university for low scholarship at the end of his freshman year. He blames his failure in foreign languages to lack of instruction in English grammar in high school. One of my own sons told me while in junior high school that he liked Latin because it taught him something. He said, "You learn in Latin in a few days what an adverb is, but it takes a year in English." Now it seems to me that the distinction between an adverb and an adjective is essential to clear thought and expression but it appears to be rather hazy among our freshmen. I once quoted to such a student a remark I had heard made by another who said: "I thought I did pretty good in that exam and yet they flunked me." "What was wrong," I asked the first student, "with that sentence?" He considered for a moment and then said, "Well, 'did' was wrong, wasn't it?" It is easy to see why students thus educated in school have difficulty in wrestling with a paragraph on the structure of an atom.

We have been told by the theorists that foreign languages should be largely abandoned because few people have any use for them and no one really learns them. There is truth in both of these statements but the answer is not to abandon foreign languages but to teach them so that they can be used. Not only is the sense of language, necessary for effective use of English, strengthened by study of a foreign language, but we should read foreign languages for other reasons. It would have been very salutary if a large number of our citizens had been able to read Hitler's "Mein Kampf" in the original German. Command of the languages both of foreign friends and potential enemies is sound strategy. German, since 1918, should never have had to struggle for a place in school curricula. It would doubtless help us immensely in the coming years if large numbers of us could read and speak Spanish not to mention Russian and Japanese.

We should not forget that subjects differ greatly in value as intellectual training at the school stage. The results of reasoning in connection with a mathematical problem or a

chemical analysis can be put to objective test. The teacher
may even be corrected by the student. A youngster in elementary
school came home very late and his mother asked him where
he had been. He replied: "It took me all this time to prove
to the teacher that she was wrong." "Did you succeed?" his
mother asked. "Of course," replied the little fellow, not in a
boastful spirit but in the confidence engendered by sound
reasoning. It is to the credit of the teacher that she allowed
herself to be convinced. But that was arithmetic. What chance
would he have had if it had been economics? The teacher
might then have uttered the rankest nonsense without facing the
bar of juvenile justice.

A fourth factor in the weakness of much school preparation
is the domination of education by administrators and amateur
philosophers. It used to be that a high school principal would
have years of successful teaching experience, preceded by training in an old-fashioned college that insisted upon a good deal
of real scholarship. Now-a-days, however, there are back doors
to administrative positions. One may secure a special credential
to teach, say, physical education. Later on, if one is a good
fellow, he easily slips into a principalship without ever having
had any serious intellectual experience in his life. Or, he may
prepare directly for a principalship and skip the teaching by
devoting his attention largely to courses in school administration,
given by professors recruited from the ranks of school administrators rather than creative investigators. Now, in order to
attract professional attention there are several pseudo-scholarly
procedures that such a professor is tempted to adopt. He may
circulate questionnaires. Or, he may think up a new word
or slogan to serve as basis for a semi-evangelistic campaign
to make over society. Recent years have witnessed a succession
of words serving to stimulate volume in educational literature
just as new styles stimulate sales of clothing. Such words as
"integration," "motivation," "evaluation," "progressive," "core
curriculum" has each had its day. A ponderous jargon is much

used, reminding one of the excessively ornate wrapping often used to cover a cheap article. Let me give a few samples. Here is a definition of education: "It is the total procedure of reciprocating life-responses by which personality, institutional progress and civilization are achieved." I wonder what that would be expressed in plain English? Again, listen to this: "Society consists of Persons plus Psycho-Social Processes plus the Products of these Processes, plus the Patterns which result from them. And the whole system of relationships between these factors is what the sociologist calls Culture." If you can swallow that without choking, try this: "The Business of Education is to universalize the historico-scientific minded-ness. . . . The spreading of this historico-scientific minded-ness is the process of enriching the social soil." These choice morsels of wisdom were extracted from an official document published, at your expense, gentlemen, by our own State Board of Education!

The poor teachers have to put up with such nonsense, changing their methods to accord with the latest brain-storm of a principal or superintendent. One suffering teacher complains: "In my thirty-five years' teaching experience, I've seen district superintendents come and go, and each time we got a new superintendent we introduced new methods. The word spread that he's a bug on this, that, or the other thing, so we all placed red lines here, or we made a rush for the flash cards or we hastened to introduce the activity program. . . . If our supervisors will change their tactics and give the teaching staff a chance, we'd have better schools."

Again, a group of science teachers in Tulare and Kings Counties stated that, "Administrators in general, due likely to their disproportionate exposure to and contact with educational theory, procedure, management, fads, fancies, and experiments, are ever in danger of minimizing or losing the fuller perspective and greater significance of departmental subject matter, and the problems of the classroom teacher in adequately building the student appreciations and backgrounds essential to meaningful and worthy educational progress. Teachers are over-encouraged, if not required, to overload with courses in various and often theoretical or fanciful methodologies at the expense of confidence, and satisfaction in mastery, on the part of students. In this latter phase, and there only, is found worthy and lasting satisfaction in accomplishment for students and instructors alike."

Some of you doubtless, read in the *Saturday Evening Post* of March 16 a vigorous article by a high school teacher. Note her reaction to domination by uneducated superintendents: "My own superintendent's academic equipment is typical; it is only roughly that of a college freshman. The remainder of his 200 credit hours are courses in administration and theory. He is a Ph. D.; his doctoral thesis, an imposing piece of scholarship, examines into the Optimum Window Area for a Classroom of Twenty-five Pupils in the Junior High School. He knows nothing about English, the languages, the humanities, or sciences. But he can and does tell us teachers exactly what methods to use in teaching all these subjects.

"How many of us would employ a physician who had spent one year studying the diseases of the body and six more on How to Approach the Patient? How can my administrator, so trained, be expected to examine critically, to evaluate intelligently, the newest movements in education? He doesn't; he can't."

More than one thousand Colorado teachers believe that "the 'newer' education is cheapening the general quality of the education process"; that "education is being made too easy"; that "pupils do not have enough discipline in the school and the home," and that "the school is spending too much time in trying to educate the 'whole' child, mentally, physically, socially, and emotionally."

These teachers also asserted that "schools today are so over-crowded with extracurricular activities that it becomes necessary to shirk the formal subjects of the schools, resulting in a high degree of superficiality in reading and learning in general."

I have dealings with a good many high school teachers and I find among them a large proportion of well-prepared, earnest, competent teachers, but they feel themselves dominated and hampered in their work by such principals and superintendents. There is a remarkably fine teacher in a small school in this region who sends me annually only a few pupils but none of them fail and about half of them get A's and B's. This teacher came to my office one day and said: "Dr. Hildebrand, my principal told me to go to a certain model high school," which he named, "in order to learn the latest methods of instruction. Now, Dr. Hildebrand, do you think that I am all wrong and that I should change my methods?" I said to him: "My dear fellow, I advise you to go back to your principal, to stick your chest out and your chin up, and to say 'Mr. Principal, there isn't a single thing which that school can teach me about teaching chemistry.' "

These principals talk a great deal about democracy, but it does not seem to occur to them that the school staff might be a more democratic organization. The president of a university does not tell members of his faculty just what and how they should teach, and the principals, as a class, are even less qualified to do this to their teachers. I suggest, gentlemen, that as citizens and parents you call off the administrators and social theorists and give the teachers a chance! Don't be scared by the big words of the theorists; they don't mean anything. After all, administrative officers, like janitors, are necessary to keep the plant running but should be content to perform well their own duties without encroaching upon the business of the teachers. I should be allowed to say this without offense since I am a dean part of the time. I regard my professorship, how-over, as far more influential and important.

It is now time to realize that although turning the schools into kindergarten has been an amusing experiment in times of peace and plenty the serious outlook for our future demands a return to a more solid education. We should get back to work. Those who cannot work effectively with their brains should at least work with their hands. Overalls and aprons are as honorable as academic robes. Some of our girls now devoting themselves to glamor would be happier if they cut their finger-nails and learned at least to wash the dishes.

J. B. S. Haldane, a distinguished British biochemist of Cambridge University, discussing the lessons of the World War, wrote prophetically: "If then in future wars we are to avoid gross mismanagement in high places, and panic and stupidity among the masses, it is essential that everyone learn a little elementary science, that politicians and soldiers should not be proud of their ignorance of it. . . . If we persist in the belief that we can be saved by patriotism or social reforms, or by military preparation of the type which would have sufficed in former struggles, we shall go down before some nation of more realistic views.

"The Roman and Spanish Empires appear to have perished largely from intellectual torpor. Are we going to go the same way?"

Is the United States of America to go the same way? We have exhibited in recent years an appalling amount of self-delusion. We deliberately turned our backs upon collective security. We destroyed the foreign commerce that makes at least business friends. We have achieved an isolation once thought splendid but now appearing very lonely. We elect to office politicians who urge the upholding of the Monroe Doctrine one moment and oppose at another the means whereby Latin-American countries may be bound to us by practical ties. We commit our international policies to men who specialize in ignorance of foreign nations; men who preach that we may escape war merely by running away from it; men who tell the whole world that they do not intend to defend our land until an enemy has passed the three-mile limit. Such matters call for more hard thinking than they receive.

The remedy I am urging can furnish only part of the vitality the nation needs for survival, but it is an essential part. Planes and tanks alone will not save us. We must become stronger not only in materials and in character but also in trained intelligence. This must be fostered by all possible means from childhood to old age, in school and college, in industry, in business, in army and navy. If we are determined to survive we must educate for national strength.

EDUCATION WITHOUT CULTURE [6]

WALTER LIPPMANN [7]

Walter Lippmann delivered this address before the ninety-second meeting of the American Association for the Advancement of Science, at Philadelphia, on December 29, 1940. Three thousand leading scientists and educators were gathered there. Since the defense program loomed large, the unofficial keynote of the meeting was suggested by the "concern of many of the speakers and attending members concerning the evaluation of scientific and cultural activities." The question was, "Should theoretical study and experimentation continue in the face of the immediate crisis, or should all effort be directed towards the practical needs of the moment?"

Lippmann's address was the chief feature of a meeting of the United Chapters of Phi Beta Kappa. A considerable proportion of the members of the A.A.A.S. also belonged to Phi Beta Kappa. Six hundred and fifty heard Lippmann.

The speaker had been highly influential for twenty-five years in molding public opinion. His writings, books and daily editorials in a large syndicated list of newspapers, and his frequent addresses "reached an amazingly large public" (McFarland). He is one of the few journalists who also is a genuine philosopher. His first book, *A Preface to Politics*, printed when he was twenty-three, was described as "a keen, cultivated, deeply interested and amazingly interesting searching out of the workaday motives and spontaneous impulses that underlie human action and human enthusiasm in the political field." (*American Hebrew*. 125:83. June 7, 1929. "Walter Lippmann, Connoisseur of Public Affairs. Lionel Hill.)

Theodore Roosevelt was impressed by the Lippmann ideas. In the *Preface to Politics, Drift and Mastery, Preface to Morals*, and numerous other books, including his *Good Society*, may be found the essence of his philosophy, part of which suggests that men in the modern day have lost faith in the old gods and have found no new ones, though the people need a final authority "as never before." Lippmann suggests that we find truth and good in man himself (a humanistic approach, echoing Lippmann's Harvard days), and that we need to give man proper dignity by recognizing his manhood as revealed in his own works.

[6] By permission and through the courtesy of Walter Lippmann. Text furnished by the author. For material of this introduction the writer is partly indebted to Lewis McFarland, graduate student in speech, State University of Iowa, Summer Session, 1941.

[7] For biographical note see Appendix.

Walter Lippmann's Philadelphia speech should be read in the light of his twenty-five years of theorizing about man and education. The address is typical of its author in its technique of listing a series of theses for demonstration. His explanation of the origins of "western culture" is in line with his concept of our civilization as developed by those who were "rational and free," those who were capable of "comprehending the moral order of the universe and their place in this moral order." Freedom he regarded as a matter of "personal moral responsibility to perform their duties and to exercise their corresponding rights." This rational basis gave the conception of law; from the conception of law was derived the American concept of constitutional government and civil liberty. Lippmann's view of culture is somewhat like Arnold's—a compounding of reason and morality, "sweetness and light." His "democracy" is not far different from that implied (perhaps) in Plato's *Republic*. His solution to the problem of redressing the wrongs done by the modern educators is inconclusive. The speech is largely destructive, negative. "Progressive" educators would challenge many of these assumptions and propositions.

In this speech, the speaker is controlled by sanity, aloofness from "contemporary enthusiasms," freedom from emotionalism; the speech contains logical consistency and penetration, clearness in stating issues, intellectualism, a minimum of the customary arts of rhetoric (a "defect" of popular audience appeal that probably limits somewhat the extent of Lippmann's reading public). In this address, according to Mac-Farland, "Mr. Lippmann represented something of the aspect of melancholy Jacques weeping into the babbling brook," and finding little good in anything.

The mood of Lippmann in speaking is that of contemplation rather than of will to persuade an audience through the usual rhetorical devices. He is a little like his own detached "scholar in a troubled world." Drama is lacking in Lippmann's oral style. His consciousness of this "lack" perhaps prompted his statement that, "I do not think of myself as a public speaker."

Mr. Lippmann's method of speech preparation depends on the occasion. Sometimes he speaks "without making any notes"; on other occasions he uses a few notes, an outline, or a prepared text. In speaking over the radio he follows a written text invariably, but on other occasions he uses one as circumstances seem to dictate. With this speech he followed the text "almost exactly." [8]

This speaker has a well-modulated, pleasing voice, which expresses intelligence and cultural training. He avoids oratory or many gestures, but he is alive, responsive to his ideas and somehow leads his audience (an intellectual group) to think with him. Dr. F. R. Moulton, secretary of the A.A.A.S. reported that "he delivered a thoughtful and critical address on education." [9]

[8] Letter to the author, March 31, 1941.

[9] For further comment on Lippmann see *Representative American Speeches: 1937-1938*, p. 122.

It was once the custom in the great universities to propound a series of theses which, as Cotton Mather put it, the student had to "defend manfully." With your permission I should like to revive this custom by propounding a thesis about the state of education in this troubled age.

The thesis which I venture to submit to you is as follows:

That during the past forty or fifty years those who are responsible for education have progressively removed from the curriculum of studies the western culture which produced the modern democratic state;

That the schools and colleges have, therefore, been sending out into the world men who no longer understand the creative principle of the society in which they must live;

That, deprived of their cultural tradition, the newly educated western men no longer possess in the form and substance of their own minds and spirits, the ideas, the premises, the rationale, the logic, the method, the values, or the deposited wisdom which are the genius of the development of western civilization;

That the prevailing education is destined, if it continues, to destroy western civilization, and is in fact destroying it;

That our civilization cannot effectively be maintained where it still flourishes, or be restored where it has been crushed, without the revival of the central, continuous, and perennial culture of the western world;

And that, therefore, what is now required in the modern educational system is not the expansion of its facilities or the specific reform of its curriculum and administration, but a thorough reconsideration of its underlying assumptions and of its purposes.

I realize quite well that this thesis constitutes a sweeping indictment of modern education. But I believe that the indictment is justified, and that there is a *prima facie* case for entertaining this indictment.

Universal and compulsory modern education was established by the emancipated democracies during the nineteenth century.

"No other sure foundation can be devised," said Thomas Jefferson, "for the preservation of freedom and happiness." Yet as a matter of fact, during the twentieth century the generations trained in these schools have either abandoned their liberties or they have not known, until the last desperate moment, how to defend them. The schools were to make men free. They have been in operation for some sixty or seventy years, and what was expected of them, they have not done. The plain fact is that the graduates of the modern schools are the actors in the catastrophe which has befallen our civilization. Those who are responsible for modern education—for its controlling philosophy—are answerable for the results.

They have determined the formation of the mind and education of modern men. As the tragic events unfold, they cannot evade their responsibility by talking about the crimes and follies of politicians, business men, labor leaders, lawyers, editors and generals. They have conducted the schools and colleges and they have educated the politicians, business men, labor leaders, lawyers, editors and generals. What is more they have educated the educators.

They have had money, lots of it, fine buildings, big appropriations, great endowments, and the implicit faith of the people that the school was the foundation of democracy. If the results are bad, and undubitably they are, on what ground can any of us who are in any way responsible for education disclaim our responsibility, or decline to undertake a profound searching of our own consciences and a deep re-examination of our philosophy.

The institutions of the western world were formed by men who learned to regard themselves as inviolable persons because they were rational and free. They meant by rational that they were capable of comprehending the moral order of the universe and their place in this moral order. They meant when they regarded themselves as free, that within that order they had a personal, moral responsibility to perform their duties and to exercise their corresponding rights. From this conception of the unity of mankind in a rational order the western world has derived its conception of law, which is that all men and all communities of men and all authority among men are subject to law, and that the character of all particular laws is to be judged by whether they conform to or violate, approach to or depart from the rational order of the universe of man's nature. From this conception of law was derived the idea of constitutional government and of the consent of the governed and of civil liberty. Upon this conception of law our own institutions were founded.

This, in barest outline, is the specific outlook of western men. This, we may say, is the structure of the western spirit. This is the formation which distinguishes it. The studies and the disciplines which support and form this spiritual outlook and habit are the creative cultural tradition of Europe and the Americas. In this tradition our world was made. By this tradition it must live. Without this tradition our world, like a tree cut off from its roots in the soil, must die and be replaced by alien and barbarous things.

It is necessary today in a discussion of this sort to define and identify what we mean when we speak of western culture. This is in itself ominous evidence of what the official historian of Harvard University has called "the greatest educational crime of the century against American youth—depriving him of his classical heritage." For there will be many, the victims of this educational crime, who will deny that there is such a thing as western culture.

Yet the historic fact is that the institutions we cherish—and now know we must defend against the most determined and efficient attack ever organized against them—are the products of a culture which, as Gilson put it, "is essentially the culture of Greece, inherited from the Greeks by the Romans, transfused by the Fathers of the Church with the religious teachings of Christianity, and progressively enlarged by countless numbers of artists, writers, scientists and philosophers from the beginning of the Middle Ages up to the first third of the nineteenth century."

The men who wrote the American Constitution and the Bill of Rights were educated in schools and colleges in which the classic works of this culture were the substance of the curriculum. In these schools the transmission of this culture was held to be the end and aim of education.

Modern education, however, is based on a denial that it is necessary, or useful, or desirable for the schools and colleges to continue to transmit from generation to generation the religious and classical culture of the western world. It is, therefore, much easier to say what modern education rejects than to find out what modern education teaches. Modern education rejects and excludes from the curriculum of necessary studies the whole religious tradition of the West. It abandons and neglects as no longer necessary the study of the whole classical heritage of the great works of great men.

Thus there is an enormous vacuum where until a few decades ago there was the substance of education. And with what is that vacuum filled? It is filled with the elective, the eclectic, the specialized, the accidental and incidental improvisations and spontaneous curiosities of teachers and students. There is no common faith, no common body of principle, no common body of knowledge, no common moral and intellectual discipline. Yet the graduates of these modern schools are expected to form a civilized community. They are expected to govern themselves. They are expected to have a social conscience. They are expected to arrive by discussion at common purposes. When one realizes that they have no common culture is it astounding that they have no common purpose? That they worship false gods? That only in war do they unite? That in the fierce struggle for existence they are tearing western society to pieces? They are the graduates of an educational system in which, though attendance is compulsory, the choice of the subject matter of education is left to the imagination of college presidents, trustees and professors, or even to the whims of the pupils themselves. We have established a system of education in which we insist that while everyone must be educated, yet there is nothing in particular that an educated man must know.

For it is said that since the invention of the steam engine we live in a new era, an era so radically different from all preceding ages that the cultural tradition is no longer relevant, is in fact misleading. I submit to you that this is a rationalization, that this is a pretended reason for the educational void which we now call education. The real reason, I venture to suggest, is that we reject the religious and classical heritage, first, because to master it requires more effort than we are willing to compel ourselves to make, and, second, because it creates issues that are too deep and too contentious to be faced with equanimity. We have abolished the old curriculum because we are afraid of it, afraid to face any longer in a modern democratic society the severe discipline and the deep, disconcerting issues of the nature of the universe, and of man's place in it and of his destiny.

I recognize the practical difficulties and the political danger of raising these questions, and I shall not offer you a quick and easy remedy. For the present discussion all I am concerned with is that we should begin to recognize the situation as it is really is and that we should begin to search our hearts and consciences.

We must confess, I submit, that modern education has renounced the idea that the pupil must learn to understand himself, his fellow men and the world in which he is to live as bound together in an order which transcends his immediate needs and his present desires. As a result the modern school has become bound to conceive the world as a place where the child, when he grows up, must compete with other individuals in a struggle for existence. And so the education of his reason and of his will must be designed primarily to facilitate his career.

By separating education from the classical religious tradition the school cannot train the pupil to look upon himself as an inviolable person because he is made in the image of God. These very words, though they are the noblest words in our language, now sound archaic. The school cannot look upon society as a brotherhood arising out of a conviction that men are made in a common image. The teacher has no subject matter that even pretends to deal with the elementary and universal issues of human destiny. The graduate of the modern school knows only by accident and by hearsay whatever wisdom mankind has come to in regard to the nature of men and their destiny.

For the vital core of the civilized tradition of the west is by definition excluded from the curriculum of the modern, secular, democratic school. The school must sink, therefore, into being a mere training ground for personal careers. Its object must then be to equip individual careerists and not to form fully civilized men. The utility of the schools must then be measured by their success in equipping specialists for successful rivalry in the pursuit of their separate vocations. Their cultural ideal must then be to equip the individual to deal practically with immediate and discreet difficulties, to find by trial and error immediately workable and temporarily satisfactory expedients.

For if more than this were attempted, the democratic secular school would have to regard the pupil as having in him not merely an ambition but a transcendent relationship that must regulate his ambition. The schools would have to regard science as the progressive discovery of this order in the universe. They would have to cultivate the western tradition and transmit it to the young, proving to them that this tradition is no mere record of the obsolete fallacies of the dead, but that it is a deposit of living wisdom.

But the emancipated democracies have renounced the idea that the purpose of education is to transmit the western culture. Thus there is a cultural vacuum, and this cultural vacuum was bound to produce, in fact it has produced, progressive disorder. For the more men have become separated from the spiritual heritage which binds them together, the more has education become egoist, careerist, specialist and asocial.

In abandoning the classical religious culture of the west the schools have ceased to affirm the central principle of the western philosophy of life—that man's reason is the ruler of his appetites. They have reduced reason to the role of servant to man's appetites. The working philosophy of the emancipated democracies is, as a celebrated modern psychologist has put it, that "the instinctive impulses determine the *end* of all activities . . . and the most highly developed mind *is but* the instrument by which those impulses seek their satisfaction."

The logic of this conception of the human reason must lead progressively to a system of education which sharpens the acquisitive and domineering and possessive instincts. And in so far as the instincts, rather than reason, determine the ends of our activity, the end of all activity must become the accumulation of power over men in the pursuit of the possession of things. So when parents and taxpayers in a democracy ask whether education is useful for life, they tend by and large to mean by useful that which equips the pupil for a career which will bring him money and place and power.

The reduction of reason to an instrument of each man's personal career must mean also that education is emptied of its content. For what the careerist has to be taught are the data that he may need in order to succeed. Thus all subjects of study are in principle of equal value. There are no subjects which all men belonging to the same civilization need to study. In the realms of knowledge the student elects those subjects which will presumably equip him for success in his career; for the student there is then no such thing as a general order of knowledge which he is to possess in order that it may regulate his specialty.

And just as the personal ambition of the student, rather than social tradition, determines what the student shall learn, so the inquiry and the research of the scholar becomes more and more disconnected from any general and regulating body of knowledge.

It is this specialized and fundamentally disordered development of knowledge which has turned so much of man's science into the means of his own destruction. For as reason is regarded as no more than the instrument of men's desires, applied science inflates enormously the power of men's desires. Since reason is not the ruler of these desires, the power which science places in men's hands is ungoverned.

Quickly it becomes ungovernable. Science is the product of intelligence. But if the function of the intelligence is to be the instrument of the acquisitive, the possessive, and the domineering impulses, then these impulses, so strong by nature, must become infinitely stronger when they are equipped with all the resources of man's intelligence.

That is why men today are appalled by the discovery that when modern man fights he is the most destructive animal ever known on this planet; that when he is acquisitive he is the most cunning and efficient; that when he dominates the weak he has engines of oppression and of calculated cruelty and deception that no antique devil could have imagined.

And, at last, education founded on the secular image of man must destroy knowledge itself. For if its purpose is to train the intelligence of specialists in order that by trial and error they may find a satisfying solution of particular difficulties, then each situation and each problem has to be examined as a novelty. This is supposed to be "scientific." But, in fact, it is a denial of that very principle which has made possible the growth of science.

For what enables men to know more than their ancestors
is that they start with a knowledge of what their ancestors have
already learned. They are able to do advanced experiments
which increase knowledge because they do not have to repeat
the elementary experiments. It is tradition which brings them
to the point where advanced experimentation is possible. This
is the meaning of tradition. This is why a society can be
progressive only if it conserves its tradition.

The notion that every problem can be studied as such, with
an open and empty mind, without preconception, without
knowing what has already been learned about it, must condemn
men to a chronic childishness. For no man, and no generation
of men, is capable of inventing for itself the arts and sciences
of a high civilization. No one, and no one generation, is
capable of rediscovering all the truths men need, of developing
sufficient knowledge by applying a mere intelligence, no matter
how acute, to mere observation, no matter how accurate. The
men of any generation, as Bernard of Chartres put it, are like
dwarfs seated on the shoulders of giants. If we are to "see
more things than the ancients and things more distant" it is
"due neither to the sharpness of our sight nor the greatness
of our stature" but "simply because they have lent us their own."

For individuals do not have the time, the opportunity, or
the energy to make all the experiments and to discern all the
significance that have gone into the making of the whole
heritage of civilization. In developing knowledge men must
collaborate with their ancestors. Otherwise they must begin,
not where their ancestors arrived, but where their ancestors
began. If they exclude the tradition of the past from the
curricula of the schools, they make it necessary for each generation to repeat the errors, rather than to benefit by the successes,
of its predecessors.

BIOGRAPHICAL NOTES [1]

BLACKWELDER, OSCAR F. (1898-   ). Born in Newberry, South Carolina; graduate of Roanoke College, 1917, Southern Lutheran Seminary, 1920; D.D. degree, Susquehenna University, 1928; pastorates, Roanoke, Baltimore, and at present pastor of Church the Reformation, Washington, D. C.; member, Executive Committee, Board of Publication of the United Lutheran Church in America; co-author, *Epistle Messages,* and author of numerous educational and religious articles; various executive positions with religious and educational organizations. Popular radio preacher.

CAMERON, WILLIAM JOHN (1878-   ). Born in Hamilton, Ontario; lived in Detroit since 1887; editorial staff, *The Detroit News,* 1903-18; with the Ford Motor Company since 1918; LL.D., Alma (Michigan) and Washington and Jefferson colleges.

DANAHER, JOHN ANTHONY (1899-   ). Born in Meriden, Connecticut; A.B., Yale, 1920; Yale Law School, 1922; law clerk, New York City, 1921-22; practiced law, Hartford, Connecticut, since 1922; assistant United States Attorney, 1922-34; Secretary of State, Connecticut, 1933-35; United States Senator (Republican) since 1938.

DONOVAN, WILLIAM JOSEPH (1883-   ). Born in Buffalo, New York; A.B., Columbia University, 1905, LL.B., 1907; LL.D., Niagara and various other institutions; began law practice in Buffalo, 1907; United States District Attorney, 1922-24; assistant to United States Attorney General, 1925-29; attorney in numerous important civil cases; Colonel in World War; wounded three times; awarded Congressional Medal of Honor, Legion of Honor, D.S.C., D.S.M., Croix de Guerre, and other similar honors; in 1941 went to Europe on a confidential mission for the Roosevelt Administration.

[1] The chief source of these notes is *Who's Who in America.*

DOUGLAS, WILLIAM O. (1898-   ). Born at Maine,
Minnesota; A.B., Whitman College, 1920; LL.B., Columbia,
1925; honorary A.M., Yale, 1932; honorary LL.D., Whitman,
1938; with law firm in New York City, 1925-27; member of
faculty, Columbia Law School, 1925-28; Yale Law School,
1928-39; active as a member of various governmental agencies,
including Securities and Exchange Commission; appointed by
President Roosevelt to Supreme Court, 1939; author of various
works including *Cases and Materials on Business Units—
Management,* 1931 (with C. M. Shanks).

DURANTY, WALTER. Has been foreign correspondent for
The New York Times since 1921; returned to the United States,
1941, from fourteen years of reporting in Russia; author of *I
Write as I Please,* 1935, *One Life, One Kopeck,* 1937, *The Gold
Train,* 1938.

GOTTSCHALK, LOUIS (1899-   ). Born in Brooklyn, New
York; A.B., Cornell University, 1919, A.M., 1920, Ph.D.,
1921; teacher of history, Cornell, 1919, University of Illinois,
1921-23, University of Louisville, 1923-27, University of Chicago, 1927-37, chairman, department of history since 1937;
Guggenheim fellowship, 1928-29; United States Navy, 1918;
author of *Lafayette Comes to America,* 1935, and other books;
contributor to many magazines; one of the editors of *Journal
of Modern History.*

GREEN, WILLIAM (1873-   ). Born in Coshocton, Ohio;
educated in public schools; President, Ohio district, Mine
Workers Union, 1906-10; member Ohio senate, two terms;
secretary-treasurer, United Mine Workers of America, 1912-24;
President of American Federation of Labor since 1924; member
of first National Labor Board; member of numerous national
boards related to labor affairs; editor of *American Federationist;*
author of *Labor and Democracy.*

HARPER, SAMUEL NORTHRUP (1882-   ). Born in Morgan
Park, Illinois; A.B., University of Chicago, 1902; graduate student, Paris, 1905; associate in Russian, University of Chicago,

1905-09; assistant professor of Russian language and institutions, University of Chicago, 1915, now professor; author of *Russian Reader, The Government of the Soviet Union,* and other books dealing with Russia.

HILDEBRAND, JOEL HENRY (1881-   ). Born at Camden, New Jersey; B.S., University of Pennsylvania, 1903, Ph.D., 1906; later studied at University of Berlin; teaching at the University of California since 1913, serving in turn as assistant professor of chemistry, associate professor, and professor, dean of men, faculty research lecturer, and since 1939, dean of the Colleges of Letters and Science; served as officer in the World War, 1917-18; has held numerous important offices in professional societies; author of *Principles of Chemistry,* other books, and numerous research articles.

HOOVER, HERBERT CLARK (1874-   ). Born in West Branch, Iowa; A.B. in engineering, Stanford, 1895, honorary degrees from Brown University, Columbia, Johns Hopkins, Oxford, Prague, and other institutions here and abroad; United States Food Administrator, 1917-19; director of various relief organizations for the war-stricken nations of Europe; appointed Secretary of Commerce in 1921; President of the United States, 1929-33; author of *American Individualism,* 1922, *The Challenge to Liberty,* 1934, and numerous addresses on government.

HUTCHINS, ROBERT MAYNARD (1899-   ). Born in Brooklyn, New York; A.B., Yale, 1921, honorary A.M., 1922, LL.B., 1925; LL.D. from West Virginia University, Lafayette College, and other institutions; Dean of Yale Law School, 1928-29; President of the University of Chicago since 1929; author of numerous articles on American education.

KALTENBORN, HANS V. (1878-   ). Born in Milwaukee, Wisconsin; A.B., *cum laude,* Harvard, 1909; reporter, *Brooklyn Eagle,* 1902-05; *Brooklyn Eagle* (New York) 1910-30 as dramatic editor, editorial writer, assistant managing editor, associate editor; radio news analyst since 1922; news editor of the Columbia Broadcasting System; with the National Broad-

casting Company since 1939; radio reporter, Republican and
Democratic Conventions, summer, 1932, London Economic Conference, summer, 1933, League of Nations, Geneva, 1935; author
of *We Look at the World,* 1930, *I Broadcast the Crisis,* 1938.

LEWIS, JOHN LLEWELLYN (1880-   ). Born in Lucas,
Iowa; educated in public schools; official, United Mine Workers
of America, 1909-11; officer, American Federation of Labor,
1911-17; President of United Mine Workers of America since
1920; President of Congress of Industrial Organizations,
1935-40.

LINDBERGH, CHARLES AUGUSTUS (1902-   ). Born in
Detroit, Michigan, son of the late Charles A. Lindbergh, a
member of Congress from Minnesota; graduate of high school,
Little Falls, Minnesota; enrolled in University of Wisconsin;
left in 1920 to enter flying school; awarded LL.D. at North-
western and other universities; notable achievements as an
airplane pilot, including non-stop flight from Roosevelt Field,
New York, to Paris, May 10, 1927; various honors and awards;
returned with family to the United States early in 1939, after
living in England; in 1940 began a series of public speeches in
opposition to aid Great Britain.

LIPPMANN, WALTER (1889-   ). Born in New York
City; A.B., Harvard, 1910 (degree taken, 1909); formerly
associate editor of *The New Republic;* editor of New York
World until 1931; now special writer for New York *Herald
Tribune* and other newspapers; author of *Public Opinion,* 1922,
A Preface to Morals, 1929, *The New Imperative,* 1935, *The
Good Society,* 1937, and other books; contributor to many
magazines.

MOULTON, HAROLD G. (1883-   ). Born in LeRoy,
Michigan; Ph.B., University of Chicago, 1907, Ph.D., 1914;
LL.D., Washington University, New York University, and other
universities; assistant professor, University of Chicago, 1914-18,
associate professor, 1918-22, professor, 1922-28; Director, Institute of Economics, Washington, D. C., 1922-28; President,

Brookings Institution, Washington, D. C., since 1928; author of numerous books including *Principles of Money and Banking, Financial Organization of Society,* and joint author of other books including *America and the Balance Sheet of Europe, Germany's Capacity to Pay.*

MURROW, EDWARD R. (1904-). Born in Greensboro, North Carolina; graduate of Washington State College, 1930; student at Stanford University and University of Washington; President of National Student Federation, 1930-32; assistant director of Institute of International Education, 1932-35; with Columbia Broadcasting System since 1935; chief of European service since 1937; author of *This Is London,* 1941, and other books.

PEPPER, CLAUDE DENSON, (1900-). Born in Dudley-ville, Alabama; A.B., University of Alabama, 1921; LL.B., Harvard, 1924; practiced law in Florida after 1925; numerous offices, elective and appointive, in Florida; United States Senator from Florida (Democrat) since 1936.

ROOSEVELT, FRANKLIN DELANO (1882-). Born in Hyde Park, New York; A.B., Harvard, 1904; attended Columbia University Law School, 1904-07; honorary degrees from Rutgers, Yale, Notre Dame, and other institutions; began practicing law in New York, 1907; Assistant Secretary of the Navy, 1913-20; Governor of New York, 1929-33; has been President of the United States since 1933; author of *Whither Bound,* 1926, *Looking Forward,* 1933, *Political Papers,* 1938, and other books; recognized as one of the foremost speakers in America.

SPELLMAN, FRANCIS JOSEPH (1889-). Born in Whit-man, Massachusetts; A.B., Fordham, 1911; S.T.D., American College in Rome, 1916; LL.D., Notre Dame, Fordham, 1935; assistant All Saints' Parish, Roxbury, Massachusetts, 1916-18; director of Catholic literature, Archdiocese of Boston, 1918-22, vice chancellor, 1922-23; editorial writer *Boston Pilot* (religious weekly), 1924; attaché Office of Secretary of State and translator of Papal broadcasts and encyclicals, Vatican, Rome, 1925-32; auxiliary bishop of Boston, 1932-39; archbishop of New York since 1939; translator of *The Word of God, In the Footsteps of the Master*.

SWING, RAYMOND (GRAM) (1887-   ). Born in Cortland, New York; educated at Oberlin College and Conservatory of Music; was in newspaper work after 1906, in Cleveland, Orrville, Ohio, Indianapolis, Chicago; Berlin correspondent, New York *Herald*, 1919-22; director of foreign service, *Wall Street Journal*, 1922-24; London correspondent of various American newspapers, 1924-34; news commentator on American affairs, British Broadcasting Corporation since 1935; American School of the Air, Columbia Broadcasting System, 1935-36; commentator on foreign affairs, Mutual Broadcasting System since 1936; author of *Forerunners of American Fascism*, 1935, *How War Came*, 1940; frequent speaker on commencement and occasions other than those of broadcasting.

TAYLOR, (JOSEPH) DEEMS (1885-   ). Born in New York City; graduate of Ethical Culture School, 1902, A.B., New York University, 1906, Mus.D., *honoris causa*, 1927; honorary degrees from Dartmouth and other institutions; studied music with Oscar Coon, New York, 1908-11; editorial work since 1906; with *New York Herald Tribune*, 1916-19, correspondent in France, 1917-19; music critic, New York *Herald*, 1921-25; with *New York American*, 1931-32; consultant on music, Columbia Broadcasting System since 1936; composer of *The Highway* (cantata), *Through the Looking Glass* (suite for orchestra), *The King's Henchman* (opera), *Peter Ibbetson* (opera), and many other musical compositions; author of *Of Men and Music*, 1937.

THOMPSON, DOROTHY (Mrs. Sinclair Lewis) (1894-   ). Born in Lancaster, New York; A.B., Syracuse University, 1914; graduate study in the University of Vienna; speaker in up-state New York Woman Suffrage Campaign, 1915-17; foreign correspondent for Philadelphia *Public Ledger* and *New York*

Evening Post, 1920-28; chief of Central European Service, 1924-28; member of American Academy of Political and Social Science; author of *The New Russia* and *I Saw Hitler;* columnist and radio commentator; contributor to American and British reviews.

VALENTINE, ALAN (1901-   ). Born in Glen Cove, New York; B.A., Swarthmore, 1921; M.A., University of Pennsylvania, 1922; honorary B.A., Oxford University, 1925, M.A., 1928; honorary degrees from Syracuse, Amherst, Union, Swarthmore, and various other institutions; with Oxford University Press, 1925-28; assistant professor of English and dean of men, Swarthmore, 1928-32; master of Pierson College, Yale, 1932-35; President of University of Rochester since 1935; author of *The English Novel,* 1927, *Biography,* 1927, *Dusty Answers,* 1941.

WILLKIE, WENDELL LEWIS (1892-   ). Born in Elwood, Indiana; A.B., Indiana University, 1913, LL.B., 1916; practiced law in Indiana and New York since 1916; President of Commonwealth and Southern Corporation since January, 1933; candidate for the Presidency of the United States on Republican ticket, 1940; although defeated polled over 22,000,000 votes; visited England in 1940 after the election; in 1941 strongly supported Roosevelt's foreign policy.

INDEX

CUMULATIVE AUTHOR INDEX

An author index to the volumes of *Representative American Speeches,* for the years 1937-1938, 1938-1939, 1939-1940, and 1940-1941. The date following the title of each speech indicates the volume in which it appears.

UNIVERSITY DEBATERS' ANNUALS

E. M. PHELPS, ED. *Cloth. Price* $2.25

Series of year books, each a collection of representative intercollegiate debates on important questions of the day. Constructive and rebuttal speeches for both sides. Each debate is accompanied by selected bibliography and briefs.

Vol. XXVII. 1940-1941.
Industry Can Solve the Employment Problem; Conscription of Capital for Defense; Preservation of Democracy Through Decreased Government Control; Interstate Trade Barriers; Japanese Aggression; Union of United States and British Commonwealth of Nations; Regulation of the American Press; Compulsory Military Training; Strikes in Defense Industries; Western Hemisphere Defense.

Vol. XXVI. 1939-1940.
The Basis of a Lasting Peace; Shall the United States Enter the War?; Government Ownership and Operation of Railroads; Neutrality of the United States; Extension of Reciprocal Trade Agreements; The Third Term for President; Should the Roosevelt Administration Be Approved?; The Dies Committee; Civil Liberties; Labor; Foreign Affairs; Government and Business.

Vol. XXV. 1938-1939.
The Increase in the National Debt; The Anglo-American Alliance; Government Ownership and Operation of the Railroads; Alliance of United States, France and Great Britain Against Fascism; Have the Achievements of Science Brought Progress?; American Solidarity; The Problem of Unemployment; The American Newspaper; "Pump-priming" Should Cease; Government and Health.

Vol. XXIV. 1937-1938.
Democracy and Economic Prosperity; American Isolation from European Affairs; Protection of United States Citizens on Foreign Soil; Academic Freedom; Grades and Final Tests Subversive of the Aims of Higher Education; American League of Nations; Anglo-American Mutual Assistance Pact; N.L.R.A. and Arbitration of Industrial Disputes; Unicameral Legislatures; Uniform Marriage Laws; Regulation of Advertising.

Vol. XXIII. 1936-1937.
The Constitution a Menace; Government Ownership of Electric Utilities; Subsidizing College Athletes; Teachers' Oaths; Unicameral Legislatures; Economic Internationalism; Minimum Wages and Maximum Hours (two debates); Consumers' Cooperatives; The Present-day Family as a Social Institution; The Sit-down Strike.

Vol. XXII. 1935-1936.
A Written Constitution a Hindrance to Social Progress; State Medicine; Compulsory Military Training; Legalization of Sweepstakes; Admission of Negroes to State Universities; The Neutrality Policy of the United States; The Parole System; Admission of Hawaii as a State; Limitation of the Power of the Supreme Court (two debates).

Vol. XXI. 1934-1935.
Equalizing Educational Opportunity; An Evaluation of the New Deal; Social Services and Unemployment Relief; International Traffic in Arms and Munitions; Democratic Collectivism; The Agricultural Adjustment Administration; Collective Bargaining; Government Ownership and Operation of Public Utilities; Pacifism the Highest Form of Patriotism; Japan and Naval Parity.

Vol. XX. 1933-1934.
British System of Radio Control and Operations; Armed Intervention; Japanese Policy in the Far East; A Department of the Consumer in the President's Cabinet; University of Chicago Plan of Education; Economic Reconstruction; Increasing the Powers of the President; Socialized Medicine; Freer Trade; Problem of State Liquor Control.

Vol. XIX. 1932-1933.
Limitation by Law of Gifts, Incomes and Inheritance; Property Taxation for State and Local Revenue; British System of Radio Control; Safety-Responsibility Plan of Automobile Insurance; Voluntary Domestic Allotment Plan; Federal Regulation of Electric Power Utilities; Dictatorship Versus Democracy; Capitalism Has Broken Down; Peace Is Impossible Under Capitalism; Stimson Doctrine of Non-recognition of Territory Acquired Through Violation of Treaties.

Vol. XVIII. 1931-1932.
Russian and American Civilizations; Control of Production and Distribution in Major Basic Industries; Wage Cutting and Business Recovery; Capitalism on Trial; Intervention in the Caribbean; Industrialism vs. Agrarianism for the South; Recognition of Russia; Centralized Control of Industry; Cancellation of International War Debts (two debates).